PALESTINIAN CINEMA

PALESTINIAN CINEMA
Landscape, Trauma, and Memory

Nurith Gertz and George Khleifi

INDIANA UNIVERSITY PRESS
Bloomington and Indianapolis

This book is a publication of

Indiana University Press
601 North Morton Street
Bloomington, Indiana 47404-3797 USA

http://iupress.indiana.edu

Telephone orders 800-842-6796
Fax orders   812-855-7931
Orders by e-mail iuporder@indiana.edu

This book was first published (as *Landscape in Mist: Space and Memory in Palestinian Cinema*) in Hebrew in 2005 by Am Oved and the Open University, Tel Aviv.

Originally published in English by Edinburgh University Press

The paper used in this publication meets the minimum requirements of American National Standard for Information Sciences–Permanence of Paper for Printed Library Materials, ANSI Z39.48-1984.

Manufactured in Great Britain

Cataloging information is available from the Library of Congress.

ISBN 978-0-253-35195-1 (cl.)
ISBN 978-0-253-22007-3 (pa.)

1 2 3 4 5 13 12 11 10 09 08

CONTENTS

To our children, Tyme, Bakr, Shlomzion and Rona

The research that this book was based upon was supported by the Israel Science Foundation (ISF) (grant number 786/03) and by the Israeli-Palestinian Science Organization (IPSO).

The authors thank Meital Alon-Oleinik who did the scientific editing.

INTRODUCTION

"History has forgotten our people," writes Yazid Sayigh (1998) about the Palestinians, while Emile Habibi, in his book *The Six Day Sextet* (1968a), presents the opposite position: "We are the people who have overlooked history." Today, with the establishment of Palestinian nationality and its historical narrative in writings, art, and literature, both positions seem inaccurate.[1] Yet, the notion that the post-1948 Palestinian historical narrative has thus far not been told in its entirety or, at least, that it has yet to find its full artistic expression, is still prevalent among writers and scholars. According to Anton Shammas, we can certainly find parts of this story in individual literary works such as *The Pessoptimist* (Habibi, 1974), *Arabesque* (Shammas, 1986), *Returning to Haifa* (Kanafani, 2000), and "Why Have You Abandoned the Horse?"[2] What is missing, however, is the overall story: "the experience of being uprooted, the banishment and the crime, the absence" (Khouri, 1998).

Researchers tend to cite various causes that have led to this predicament. Some remark that "chunks of the Palestinian memory have been subjected to colonization by other types of discourse" (Nassar, 2002: 27-8) and have been silenced by the Israeli narrative (Manaa, 1999b; Said, 2000). Consequently, Palestinian history has been told from the viewpoint of the winning side. As Manaa would argue:

> The Europeans followed by the Zionists – the powerful and triumphant side in the national conflict over the Holy Land . . . generally ignored even the mere existence of the indigenous people of the land and their right

over the country . . . The Palestinians have been described as nomads, as peasants, or as miscellaneous groups and sections lacking any national consciousness. (Manaa, 1999b: 9–10)

Yet, according to scholars, the Palestinians did not suggest a counter-narrative, either because "they had not realized the power historical accounts have to activate people," or because the connection between the people and the various quarters of the homeland had been an organic and intimate one and "they therefore did not see the significance of history as an argument for their national rights" (ibid.).

Several scholars and writers have referred to the difficulty of coping with the 1948 defeat as one of the reasons for the absence of such a national story. Anton Shammas, for instance, claims that guilt and shame over that devastating blow partially explain the lack of a Palestinian historical story (Khouri, 1998), and Rashid al Khalidi (2001) maintains that it is the consequence of Palestinian resistance to confronting the numerous reasons for that national failure.

Many writers attribute the absence of a Palestinian historical narrative to the exilic condition manifested in life behind shut-off borders, on the road, in a state of temporality. Elias Sanbar (1997) questions the possibility of organizing time when space is barred off. Edward Said ([2001] 2002), for his part, wonders how one might arrange time when "every progress is a regression," when "there is no direct line connecting the home to the place of birth, school and adulthood, when all events are accidental." Muhammad Hamza Ghanayem (2000) mentions that Palestinians have replaced a comprehensive historical approach with the ideology of refugees, which sanctions the "idea of temporality" and does not lend itself to structuring history.

For many years the refugee ideology dominated Palestinian culture. In other words, the idea of the temporal prevailed: while drifting about and fighting, the refugee always remains temporary, and in a transient condition there is no room for memory, except as the passing moment. (Ghanayem, 2000: 17)

Or, as Sanbar phrases it, "the strong consciousness of a transient state and of complete mobility gave [the Palestinians] a feeling that the only permanency is the one of the anticipation for the return to the homeland and with it re-immersion in the individual and collective time" (Sanbar, 1997: 24).

The difficulty in constructing a historical sequence is clearly revealed in the Palestinian tendency to "ignore the present by trading it for a past, which is static, a past ruled by images and rituals"[3] (Harkabi, 1975) and to fix the historical narrative along three veins: the memory of a paradise lost, the lament for the present, and the description of the intended return (Tamari, 1999a).[4] In this tendency, Palestinian history resembles other histories of exile and displacement, in which everyday existence is experienced through the mediation of nostalgia for the lost nature-and-nation unity, and for the utopian homeland that remains untainted by contemporary affairs (Jameson, 1986; Naficy, 2001: 153). These are histories of trauma, or in the words of Bresheeth (2002b), histories that can be understood in terms of melancholy.[5]

Trauma is such a severely horrific event that it remains unregistered by the consciousness, resisting the immersion into a sequential and causal story – whether a personal or a collective one. Trauma is indescribable in familiar terms derived from a known repertoire and, therefore, is unconnected to prior knowledge and does not become an integral link in a chain of events leading to the future. Ostensibly, it does not leave a trace.[6] Yet, it still exists as a repressed memory, and as Freud has suggested, after a period of latency the repressed surfaces disturb and damage the possibility of experiencing the present, or of integrating it into a causal sequence. Eventually, the trauma remains as a living event, enduring and unchanging, as if fully present rather than merely represented in memory.[7] Trauma, as such, cannot be placed in a historical past that might have led into and shaped the present. The reappearance of the traumatic event is not, at any rate, a return to what actually occurred, but a reliance on substitutes for it, a coming back to the actual, traumatic moment of loss, and also to what has been lost and is so difficult to let go of and so impossible to separate from (Freud, [1953] 1974b). Thus, since the lost object lives in the consciousness as if it still exists and because past events emerge in the present as if they perpetually reoccur, time stops. The past replaces the present and the future is perceived as a return to the past. That is why it is impossible to tell "history as a narrative, as a chronology of events, as rational cause and effect, as a directing of action" (Caruth, 1996). The more problematic the present is and the more violence repeats itself, striking against those who still have not forgotten the initial trauma, the more difficult it is to break free of this vicious cycle. The theory of trauma, therefore, indicates another way of comprehending Palestinian history, which incessantly revives both the idyllic past and its disintegration.

Palestinian cinema, in its attempt to invent, document, and crystallize Palestinian history, confronts the trauma. On the one hand, it attempts to construct a historical continuity, leading from the past to the present and the future, presenting traumatic past events and what preceded them as something that is both absent and present, as Elsaesser (forthcoming) puts it. Thus what it offers is a depiction of a forgotten past that does not replace the image of the present but is, rather, seen through it.[8] On the other hand, Palestinian cinema freezes history either in a utopian, idyllic past, or in the events of exile and deportation that disrupted it and are revived as if they were part of the present.[9] In Palestinian cinema, historical processes dictate to a large extent to which side of the equation the historical memory will turn.

The documentary cinema created during the late 1960s and 1970s in refugee camps (henceforth called third period cinema) was produced under the patronage of the Palestinian organizations and documented events of the period, constructing, for the first time, a cinematic representation of the Palestinian traumatic history. This was achieved through a plot outline which documented present occurrences, yet revived through them, in a very abstract and symbolic manner, the story of the past. Thus, life in the refugee camps, in the days prior to the bombings, the destruction of people's homes, and the massacre, was associated through various means with peaceful life in the homeland, while violent contemporary events were linked to the initial 1948 trauma.

This "traumatic structure" evoked a vision of the past in the present, but also had an additional role, serving as a national unifying factor. It allowed the spinning of the national narrative through what Anderson calls "erasure" (Anderson, 2000). Third period Palestinian cinema was created in a diverse society comprised of various diasporas, classes, generations, and religious groups. The narrative of trauma functioned as a unifying adhesive that enabled cinema to overcome controversies and differences, and to ignore the split, thus creating one history revolving around a single memory and shared by all. While this cinema blurred differences between genders, social strata, geographical areas, and generations within Palestinian society, it retained patriarchal stances that identified the homeland with masculinity. As Ghassan Kanafani's protagonist declares, in *Men in the Sun*: "The homeland has been lost and with it so has masculinity" ([1963] 1998). Palestinian cinema strove toward the crystallization of a national, homogeneous unity and created collective symbols that replaced the reality, heterogeneity, and diversity of Palestinian society.

In its insistence on a harmonious image of the past and in its attempt to unify and solidify Palestinian society, third period cinema relinquished the option to analyze and critique the era that preceded colonialism in Palestinian society (Said, 1991). It has ignored the fact that "the 48 society was one of industrious peasants, unconnected to other cultures" (private interview with Hani Abu-Assad, Jerusalem, 2003) and dwelled on it only through nostalgia generally directed toward the age of childhood innocence or natural life predating culture. Thus Palestinian cinema assimilated the historical event into universal, general longing for an era that never existed.[10] Later films also featured the aforementioned characteristics.

In the 1980s (henceforth called the fourth period) a shift occurred in Palestinian cinema, when several filmmakers attempted to extract the Palestinian narrative from the story of the actual land, the real place and the life being played out there, rather than evoking it out of the traumatic, abstract, perpetually repetitive revival of its destruction. This shift, which reflected the increasing importance of land as a symbol of Palestinian identity and nationality, was initially manifested in the works of directors who lived in Israel and could film there – mainly in the films of Michel Khleifi. Even though Khleifi, too, endeavored to reflect the past in the present and to recreate the lost unity of the national identity and the landscape, the diversity of present existence as expressed in his films locates the old structure next to, and within, a new structure, fracturing the total association of the present with the past and allowing each period its own separate existence. Since it occurs in a concrete, specific place that expresses the numerous national, familial, clan, class, rural, and urban identities in Palestinian society,[11] the varied present-day way of life unfolding in Khleifi's films deconstructs Palestinian society's image of unity and homogeneity, evoked by the idyllic perception of the past. Through the fusion of the two structures – the traumatic and the everyday – the films sustain different levels of reality at the same time: the reality of the distant past, that of the present, and that of the past existing submerged within the present, both overtly and covertly. Consequently, they both reflect the trauma and work through it, in an attempt to overcome it. To use Bresheeth's words, "They fortify the foundation of homeland by telling the story of 'heim and heimat'."[12]

Michel Khleifi was born and raised in Nazareth and has spent most of his life in Belgium. The freedom of movement he has enjoyed between countries and cultures, between his native home and his adopted home, has fed the ambivalence in his films, which utilize Eastern as well as Western models of home and exile.[13] While expressing the Palestinian people's longing for the return to Palestine, they both construct the nation's unity and deconstruct it, portraying an image of a utopian past and at the same time contradicting it. They shape what Edward Soja (1996) has called "a third space" where different cultures, positions, and identities coexist.[14] Other directors, living in different cultures, catering to diverse audiences, and using various financial resources, also created a similar space. Among those directors are Elia Suleiman, Nizar Hassan, Ali Nassar, Hani Abu-Assad, and others. In many instances, such a space is expressed in the works of directors who grew up within the boundaries of the state of Israel, among the landscapes of the Palestinian past, and at crossroads of cultural contradictions. But it can also be found in the *œuvre* of directors who were born in the West Bank and Gaza and in films that concentrate mainly on the lives of Palestinians in the camps, such as some by Michel Khleifi and Rashid Masharawi.

The 1990s were marked by the effects of the First *Intifada* and the economic recession that succeeded it, the wake of the Gulf War, and the continuing closure that was enforced on Palestinian residents, as also by the Second *Intifada* and the Israeli invasion of West Bank cities. From that decade on, the more the social, political, and economic situation deteriorated, and the chaos and destruction increased, the more Palestinian cinema was recruited in favor of the national struggle that called for unity. As a result, Palestinian filmmakers found it complicated to maintain the heterogeneous "third" space and the complex historical time that both expresses the trauma and copes with it.

This difficulty intensified in the face of the problematic dialogue with the political establishments, as well as with the cinematic (mainly critical) ones and with film audiences that required their cinema to "close ranks" during this difficult phase of the national struggle and expected a portrait of unity. Directors, who depended on the Arab audiences, criticism, and establishment, stepped up to the mark and met these expectations.[15]

On the one hand, the films created during these years attempted to shape a history coherently beginning in the past and progressing toward the future. They even succeeded in carving history out of authentic, personal memories. But, on the other hand, they perpetually held on to mythic images that revive the past and its loss in the present. While attempting to observe the heterogeneous nature of Palestinian society and to describe the classes, genders, and regions comprising it, they also strove to unite them all and to create shared national symbols, leading to a collective struggle. As the threat to Palestinian existence and land increased, this cinema reaffirmed anything that might reiterate and stabilize them. It relied on a mythical past and the homogeneous national story – on symbols that arrest time and ignore the changes it brought with it, reviving the past in the present and reducing the diversity of Palestinian society to a homogeneous representation.[16] Nevertheless, within the history that imposes unity of goals and memory, one finds individual testimonies and personal diversity that defy this unity. And in spite of the historical circumstances, several directors – most prominent among whom is Elia Suleiman – create a new kind of cinema and with it new means of coping with the past as with the hardships of the present. In Suleiman's first film, *Chronicle of a Disappearance*, there is no past to return to and no dreamed-about land in which one can arrive. Still, within this total void, the film searches for signs of a nonexistent presence. It bestows meaning upon the failure of memory, and turns that meaning into the core of the work.[17]

Like the historical time of the Palestinian nation, Palestinian geography, too, has oscillated between the abstract, mythical idyll and the concrete reality. In films produced in the 1970s, actual geography was not shown. In fact, the real events captured in these films were delineated in abstract time and space that symbolically represented the Palestinian space of 1948 or earlier. Michel Khleifi, alongside other directors, was the first to draw a composed, organized map of the real Palestinian expanses, whose borders are on the horizon and whose core is the home.[18] Other directors, mostly those following Khleifi, could no longer have depicted such a map. Over the years, the borders of the Palestinian space, uncertain to begin with, have become increasingly blurred and threatened, violated by the Israeli settlements and army, and replaced by roadblocks, controlled checkpoints, and closures which bisected Palestinian space and identity, severing and deconstructing them.

Many films have reacted to this threat of division and violation of the space by committing themselves to restoring it. Such self-recruitment is in line with the tendency of this cinema to freeze time and preserve a united, militant, homogeneous nationality. Against the divided space, lacking clear-cut borders, these films offer symbols representing a complete and harmonious space, revived from the past, frozen in the present, and preserved for the future. In the face of an unsecured identity and confined by uncertain geographic borders, these films form a homogeneous, unified identity and present distinct borders. However, just as the fixation of time is broken in some films, so too is that of geography. Various films that parody the fantasies of the expanses and symbols of space have at the same time enabled their reexamination, deconstruction, and renewal. The historical trauma and the ways of approaching it are, therefore, linked to the geographical trauma, and together they determine the history of Palestinian cinema.

The history of Palestinian film is closely connected to the history of Israeli film and to the Israeli historical narrative. It is the history of the endeavor to recount the Palestinian story, against the setting of the Israeli account that had previously silenced it. Thus, the Israeli narrative is confronted and parodied in various Palestinian films, some of which, especially later ones, attempt to replace the Israeli narrative with a separate, independent Palestinian one.[19] Even when these films do not directly allude to, examine, or represent the Israeli story, they manage to delay its advancement toward realizing its aims, since, in the course of relating the Palestinian story, they expose what that Israeli version had concealed.

The connection between the histories of the two nations is further expressed by the direct reference of Palestinian cinema to Israeli society. Generally, films indicating the heterogeneous nature of Palestinian society also recognize, to an extent, the heterogeneous nature of Israeli society. In other films, the idyllic harmonic image of Palestinian society is paralleled by a depiction of a homogeneous Israeli society, in which soldiers and settlers represent the entire nation. Thus, differences and variations in Israeli society are obscured, and even those groups fighting against the occupation alongside the Palestinians are ignored. Among all of the documentary films created recently, very few depict Israeli demonstrations against the occupation or mention the suicide attacks while referring to the vicious blood cycle of retaliation and counter-retaliation.

Palestinian cinema that reduces Israeli society merely to soldiers and settlers, while disregarding all other Israelis, contributes to a kind of a "cinematic" battle[20] against those who have obliterated the Palestinians from history and geography. Such films express the difficulty of the occupied, struggling for existence, in observing and paying tribute to the occupiers' positive sides. This tendency is strengthened by the reality in which those under occupation, in fact, always encounter the representatives of the occupation, namely soldiers and settlers, rather than other segments of the Israeli population, with which some of the directors have never come into contact. Another explanation for this inclination in Palestinian cinema is the urgency of a society that is not allowed to define its own borders, to erect cinematic borders that would define a clear, homogeneous identity, against a homogeneous external other. This need was well expressed by the critics and audience in their reaction to films that presented a different face of the Israeli side, such as those by Michel Khleifi and Elia Suleiman.[21]

Several Palestinian directors have referred to the over-simplification that has resulted in such a presentation of the two societies, Palestinian and Israeli.

> Palestinian cinema should reflect the heterogeneous nature of the Palestinian society [said director Hani Abu-Assad (private interview, Ramallah, 2003)], and while doing so, it should also deepen the familiarity with the democratic Israeli section. In fact, the Israeli presence in our lives is one-dimensional. We see soldiers, settlers, and bulldozers. Regretfully, we do not see democratically prone poets and artists, and it is a pity, because history, since '67, proves that there have been Israeli–Palestinian attempts to associate. It is a shame because in cinema there is something fundamental and that is vision – the look beyond the obstacles of the present, an expression of the hope that Israelis will not remain only settlers and builders of roadblocks.

Since the 1980s, Palestinian cinema has been striving to maintain a heterogeneous and open nature, despite a political situation that nurtures unity and isolation. These films have been produced in an era of distress, when the fate of occupation and repression is shared by an entire nation struggling to crystallize its oneness in the face of the outside Other. That state of urgency preserves the initial trauma of 1948 and rekindles the longing for the idyllic past preceding it. It also advocates the homogeneous portrayal in Palestinian films of both Israeli and Palestinian societies. However, simultaneously, Palestinian cinema also attempts repeatedly, in every possible way, to break down this image, to take it apart and to reassemble it, drawing from a mosaic of classes, generations, genders, regions, and nations.

During two years of collaboration, we have attempted to decipher this image and its diverse facets, in long work sessions, in film viewing, through countless arguments and over many meals of *hamin, borscht, maklouba* and Arab salads. Throughout, we were guided by the clear conviction that Palestinian cinema is one of the important manifestations of Palestinian society and that the profound bond between the two of us, co-writers of this book, which was formed while interpreting these films, can set an example for a possible connection between the two cultures established while viewing Palestinian cinema.

NOTES

1. See Said ([2001] 2002).
2. Referring to the title of a Mahmud Darwish poem.
3. For a discussion of the reconstruction of the past in Palestinian culture, see Litvak (1994).
4. See Kimmerling and Migdal (1993), Al-Hout (1998), Abu Amr (1990), Ashrawi (1990), Harkabi (1975), Jayyusi (1999), al Khalidi (1997), and Siddiq (1984).
5. The term melancholy provides, in the words of Bresheeth (2002b), "new insight into the state of stasis, where resistance is temporarily disabled, delaying the process of mourning and healing." The healing process, according to Bresheeth, "seems to be bound up with storytelling . . . In order to have some space to live in, to bring an end to personal and political melancholia, one must employ fiction and imagination, one must tell stories, even stories of disappearance" (Bresheeth, 2002b).
6. See Freud ([1953] 1974b) and Caruth (1991). Michal Friedman drew our attention to a selection of articles on the subject of trauma.
7. As "acting out." See LaCapra (1997).
8. Elsaesser (forthcoming) uses the term parapraxis for the purpose of describing the trauma and, following Freud ([1901] 1951), defines it as "a displacement in terms of time and place . . . doing the right thing at the wrong place, or the wrong thing at the right place." Originally, this term referred to what we call "a Freudian slip." Elsaesser expands its meaning to define any situation in which the absent (what is forgotten, distanced, hidden) appears as present, but is only fully present in the wrong place and at the wrong time. Like Freud, he associates this phenomenon with a kind of work of mourning: an attempt to evoke what is gone, lost, to reconstruct it again and again in different variations in the present, to revive it and thus work through it. The parapraxis, according to Elsaesser, allows the construction of a history conscious of the fact that one cannot overcome forgetting, that you cannot represent what has been repressed. It presents the picture of the forgotten past beyond the representation of the present, without canceling either of them. Thus it allows reference to the identity and history of each of these images. We will use this term to describe only one stage in the working through of trauma – the stage in which the past ceases to replace the present and exists, even if only as an absent present, beyond it.
9. In the framework of the stages of coping with trauma, according to Freud, this is the repetition stage – in which the traumatic memory is activated again and again in the present.
10. See LaCapra (1997), who speaks of the identification of the historical trauma with an existential one: that is, a trauma which is the inevitable result of a detachment from childhood. The nostalgia for "a past that never was" characterizes folklore, according to Gabriel (1989b), dealing with essential relationships of people to the land and the community, unifying oppositions and creating a balance between nature and humanity. In historical terms, that is nostalgia for a society that never actually existed, a society of abundant idyllic villages and an authentic community and life, a folkloristic life, related to the true values that were distorted by imperialism or technology. That is the Africa of the imagination, as Hall (1990) describes the preservation of the African myth in exile. Said (2000) explains the Palestinian leaning toward a general utopian past before 1948 by the fact that the Israelis erased the Palestinians altogether from the story of the distant past.

11. Most Palestinian historians discuss the many identities within Palestinian society. See, for example, al Khalidi (1997), who considers the balance between tendencies of separation versus solidarity, and Manaa (1999b), Rabinovitz and Abu Bakr (2002: 53), and Kimmerling and Migdal (1993: 261). For elaboration of this theme, see subsequent chapters.

12. Haim Bresheeth asks: "How can one make a film about people and places that are disappearing, about the fragility of this subconscious process? Memory is not enough. It proves nothing. The foundation of homeland must be fortified by one's own story and storytelling" (Bresheeth, 2002b).

13. His films refer to two cultures. Naficy (1993: 86) calls such cinema an in-between cinema that "subvert[s], alter[s] and even adopt[s] components of each of the cultures it interacts with."

14. Concerning this term, see Bhabha (1990), Soja (1996: 169), and Ferguson et al. (1990). Soja (1996) defines "third space" as a space in which subjectivity and objectivity, the abstract and the concrete, the real and the imagined, the known and the unknown, the repeated and the different coincide. See Zanger (forthcoming) for an elaboration of these terms. Bresheeth (2002b) applies the term to Palestinian cinema "Palestinian cinema therefore exists on a series of exilic interstices – between fact and fiction, between narrative and narration, between the story and its telling, between *documentary* and *fiction*."

15. For the matter of Arab criticism, see Chapter 1, "A Chronicle of Palestinian Cinema."

16. These symbols are national fetishes, as Naficy (2001) defines them, replacements of national existences that were lost, grew distant, or disappeared. They construct what Jameson (1986) calls a national allegory, a term that will serve us loosely. In contrast with his definitions of the third world allegory as polysemic, heterogeneous, multidimensional, and ever-changing, in his specific analyses Jameson reveals a simple one-dimensional relationship between the literary or cinematic sign and the meaning it represents, a significance which in the third world is always of a national nature (see Ahmad [1992]). We will distinguish here between a simple allegory of this sort, in which the private existence represents the nation, and a multidimensional allegory, which is a crossroads of national, class, gender, and universal meanings that build on actual, concrete details without replacing them or substituting for them. The term symbol will serve us in the same way.

17. In this respect, Suleiman creates the parapraxis that Elsaesser (forthcoming) discusses in a different manner to that employed by Khleifi and other directors.

18. Here and throughout the book, we will refer to geography as a given and to the map as a graphic representation of that geography, a representation that is, of course, culturally dependent.

19. See Shenhav and Hever (2002), who speak of the possibility of recounting a separate narrative, which is not subjugated to the hegemonic history.

20. A discursive struggle, in the words of Naficy (2001).

21. See Chapter 3, "About Place and Time: The Films of Michel Khleifi," and Chapter 7, "Between Exile and Homeland: The Films of Elia Suleiman."

1. A CHRONICLE OF PALESTINIAN CINEMA

In 1935, Ibrahim Hassan Sirhan filmed a 20 minute-long movie that documents the visit of Prince Saud to Jerusalem and Jaffa. The Saudi Prince was escorted on this occasion by the Mufti of Palestine, Haj Amin al-Husseini. This event constitutes the starting point of Palestinian cinema, whose history is divided into four periods echoing the various stages of the national Palestinian struggle, the topic on which Palestinian cinematic creation has fed and focused. Since the periods tend to stretch and overlap, the years marking their beginning and end are merely suggestions and by no means indicate clear-cut boundaries.

The first period is bracketed between 1935 and 1948, the year of the war that has been referred to as the *Naqba* ("disaster"), following which most Palestinians were compelled to leave their homeland. Information concerning this period has mostly been gathered from the testimonies of people who, according to their own claims, either initiated or participated in the cinematic undertaking of the era. Notices that were placed in contemporary newspapers and the registration documents of production institutions are additional sources of information. Other than these, no trace of the films produced has remained. Historians who have investigated the cinema of this period have relied exclusively on these pieces of evidence, and so shall we.

The second period, between 1948 and 1967, when almost no Palestinian films were produced, is dubbed the "Epoch of Silence." As in the case of the first period, we shall learn about this solely from documents, press announcements, and personal reminiscences.

The beginning of the third period, between 1968 and 1982, is marked by the

1967 Israeli occupation of the West Bank and Gaza Strip and the strengthening status of the Palestine Liberation Organization (PLO) and other Palestinian institutions. Palestinian cinema at that time was created in exile, mostly in Beirut, Lebanon, where filmmakers found refuge with the departure of PLO members from Jordan in 1970.[1] This period ended in 1982, when PLO members left Beirut following the Israeli invasion of Lebanon. During these years, the principal film production bodies, the Film Institute and the Division of Palestinian Films' halted their operations, as did the production institution of the Democratic Front. Only a few groups continued to function, including the PLO's Department of Culture, which produced some of the more mature movies of the period.[2] The films that were created during this era are grouped together and referred to, in the terminology of researchers and historians, as the "Cinema of the Palestinian Revolution" (Abu Gh'nima, 1981; Mdanat, 1990; Ibrahim, 2000) or the "Cinema of the Palestinian Organizations."

The fourth period, starting in 1980 and continuing to the present day, is characterized by cinema that is the product of several artists' individual initiatives. In the course of this term, the Palestinian struggle has intensified and two waves of popular uprisings, the First and Second *Intifadas*, have determined the agenda of Palestinian society and of the Palestinian Authority that was established as a consequence of the Oslo Accords. Palestinian film directors, whether in exile or in the homeland, have once again been compelled to find their own funding. As a result of the absence of any institutional support, however, they have also enjoyed creative freedom. Hence, despite pressing demands on this cinema to align itself with the aims of the national struggle, diverse, independent, groundbreaking, and internationally recognized and esteemed films have been created during this time. The main part of this book will be devoted to this fourth period, when one generation has given way to another, changes in modes of expression have occurred, and ideological stances, as well as means of production, have evolved.

While during the first and second periods, filmmakers had had creative independence and cinema functioned for them as a sort of a personal adventure, in the course of the third period they operated under the auspices of the Palestinian establishment: the PLO and its various divisions and organizations. Yet, due to the fact that this establishment was mostly occupied with the battle for its own existence and for its right to fight, it hardly found sufficient time, resources, and especially interest to devote to plotting the cultural, political, and artistic path of cinema. Thus, the fourth period is also defined by the adventurous enterprises of individual filmmakers.

THE FIRST PERIOD: THE BEGINNING, 1935–48

Up to the late 1970s, it appeared that Palestinian cinema had originated with movies that were created with the support and influence of the PLO and the

Palestinian organizations. Thus was the assumption of scholars until the Iraqi director, Kassam Hawal,[3] met Ibrahim Hassan Sirhan, a Palestinian refugee living in the Shatila refugee camp near Beirut, who attested to the existence of cinema in Palestine even prior to 1948. Hawal published Sirhan's reminiscences in the *Al-Balagh* Beirut newspaper and in a 1978 book called *The Palestinian Cinema*. Like precursory Palestinian film scholars, we too have relied on this and other testimonies.[4]

For 50 liras, in Tel Aviv, Ibrahim Hassan Sirhan bought the manual camera with which he documented King Saud's 1935 tour of the country. He read books on filming, lenses, developing, and editing, and learned how to operate the necessary equipment. Adnan Mdanat (1990), filmmaker, critic, and a scholar of film, reports that Sirhan assembled his editing table himself.

In order to shoot the movie delineating King Saud's visit, Sirhan followed the King around "from Lod to Jaffa and from Jaffa to Tel Aviv," presumably with the knowledge and encouragement of the Mufti, Haj Amin al-Hussaini. The latter "gave me [Sirhan] hints as to the important events which were to be filmed, [such as] meals, tours and meetings with people," relates Sirhan (Abu Gh'nima, 1981: 238–45). The result was a silent movie that was presented at the Nabi Rubin festivals.[5] While the film was screened, Sirhan played a record of music in the background, so that "nobody noticed that the movie was a silent one." Sirhan was joined by Jamal al-Asphar, the film's cinematographer, and together these men are considered the founders of pre-1948 Palestinian cinema.

Following the documentary, the two produced a 45-minute film called *Realized Dreams*, aiming to "promote the orphans' cause" and to prove that Palestinians "are capable of making movies, because people back then didn't believe [that Palestinians could make movies] like today they cannot fathom a Palestinian sending a satellite to outer space" (Abu Gh'nima, 1981). Sirhan and al-Asphar's next film was a documentary about one of the members of the Arab Supreme Council. According to Sirhan, he was paid 300 Palestinian liras for the film by the said official.

In 1945, Sirhan announced in the Jaffa press the foundation of a production studio called Studio Palestine. In the notice, he asked for donations to help him complete his project. Ahmad Hilmi al-Kilani, who had formerly studied film in Cairo and returned to his homeland in 1945, answered Sirhan's call. Together they established the Arab Film Company production studio. The company launched the feature film *Holiday Eve*, which was immediately followed by preparations for the next film, *A Storm at Home*, starring Ahmad Sam'aan and Hyat Fawzi. As to the fate of *Holiday Eve*, opinions vary. Al-Kilani claims that it was never completed (Abu Gh'nima, 1981), while Sirhan argues that there were indeed disputes as to the ending of the movie, but that it was completed and even screened at the home of Abd-er-Rahman, Sirhan's brother.

Furthermore, Sirhan produced an emblematic sequence in which the Mufti appeared with the Palestinian flag as backdrop.[6] This footage was shown in cinemas before each screening. It was also at this time that Sirhan established an advertising firm in collaboration with Zoheir as-Saka, a Jaffa journalist.

Undoubtedly, al-Asphar, Sirhan, and al-Kilani's attempts were not isolated efforts. Omeir Da'ana, a news-stand vendor at the Damascus Gate in Jerusalem, testifies that, as early as 1946, he answered an advertisement for extras for a feature film, and was even accepted and participated in the shoot for several days. The movie, starring Fuad Salam and the actress Shahnaz, was produced by the Al Jazira production studios, owned by Abd-er-Razak Alja'uni. According to Da'ana, although the movie was not shown in Jerusalem, he was told that it had been screened in other cities (private interview with Da'ana, Jerusalem, 2003).

Another figure with a part to play in pre-1948 cinematic undertakings is Muhammad Saleh Kayali, the owner of a photographic studio. Kayali traveled to Italy to study film and, upon his return, began to produce a movie about the Palestinian problem, which had been commissioned by the representatives of the Arab League in Palestine. The movie was not completed due to the outbreak of the 1948 war. Consequently, Kayali left for Cairo, where he produced a number of films about the Palestinian issue (Mdanat, 1990).

In the final years of his life, Sirhan worked as a plumber in the Shatila refugee camp near Beirut. His partner, al-Asphar, settled in Kuwait and was located in the 1990s by Hassan Abu Gh'nima, who invited him to be a guest on a Jordanian television program. Abu Gh'nima also managed to locate Kayali and to hear his story as well. The three give similar versions of events, though these are inconsistencies as to the role each one of them played in producing, directing, and shooting the film.

The films themselves have been lost and therefore cannot be studied. Sirhan and his friends fled Jaffa after it was bombed by the National Military Organization and the Freedom Fighters of Israel, and, as far as we know, left all of their filmed materials behind (Abu Gh'nima, 1981). The movies were possibly handed over to some anonymous clerk, who in turn passed them on to an archive, where they might still be lying, untouched, their whereabouts unknown.

Palestine, the Holy Land, had attracted cinematic attention as early as 1896, when the French Lumière brothers shot the first movie there. On their trail came other foreign film crews from Poland, Germany, France, and Austria. Among the foreigners who documented the country with their cameras were German pilgrims from the Templar Order, recording their itinerary in Jesus Christ's footsteps. Still others filmed dramatic adaptations of the New Testament stories. The films produced during this period all share a religious nature and a Christian target audience (Tzimerman, 2001).

The cinema produced in Palestine after the Lumière brothers in the early years of the twentieth century was predominantly documentary, leading the audience to believe that what they saw on screen was a true reflection of reality. That reality included the landscapes of the country and the Christian holy sites. The Palestinian population was treated by the filmmakers as an integral part of the landscape itself. The inhabitants and their living conditions were depicted on film, but no interviews with either Palestinian dignitaries or ordinary Palestinians were conducted, and therefore no one voice articulated their thoughts or presented their opinions.[7] In many newsreels and documentary films, Palestinians were portrayed as a backward, poverty-stricken population, while the Jewish settlements were credited as responsible for bringing culture to the desolate land.

Palestinians, like most Arab communities, were introduced to cinema in the 1920s. In the 1930s, movie houses were set up in all the major Palestinian cities. In 1929, a special Mandatory Law was passed, called The Moving Pictures Act, which bestowed the Mandatory Government with the authority to censor movies and plays for reasons of immorality or the corruption of the public (Mdanat, 1990). Despite all this, there was no reference to cinema in the Palestinian media.[8] As an example, Mdanat (1990) mentions the highly esteemed fortnightly publication, *Al-Carmel*, published in the Haifa area, which was the flagship of Arab nationalism and resistance to the Zionist enterprise.[9] The newspaper dedicated many of its issues in the 1920s to new inventions in the field of media (radio and music recordings, for instance) and followed the visits of writers, poets, and singers from Egypt and other Arab countries, but utterly ignored cinema and contemporary movies.

One of the obstacles that stood in the way of cinema being embraced by Palestinian society was the fact that the latter consisted predominantly of a peasant population. Only very gradually, mainly after the Great Arab Rebellion,[10] was Palestine transformed from a basically rural, homogeneous, and autarkic society to one which is aware of world politics and markets (Kimmerling and Migdal, 1993: 93). During the same period, in the middle of the 1930s, the political development of Palestinian nationality was accelerated as a result of increased Jewish immigration to the country, as well as the transfer of Palestinians from the country to the city (ibid.: 97).

Another possible reason behind Palestinian disregard for cinema is embedded in that society's perception of cinema as "a Western invention which corrupts morals" (Mdanat, 1990). But in that case, how can we explain the fact that Palestinians embraced the theater, also a Western invention, as a cultural, educational element which contributes to the strengthening of moral principles? The most obvious reason is that the medium of film was relatively new, did not enjoy canonical status, and was not considered a legitimate "cultural" element. However, there are many more explanations.

Theaters were first introduced into Palestine at the turn of the twentieth century in a small number of schools, but they soon spread to all the schools in the cities and villages (al Batrawi, 2002). The fact that theater's first steps were taken in an educational-cultural context, under supervision and after plays were adapted according to accepted norms, eased its reception by Palestinian society. Nasri al-Juzi, director and actor in pre-1948 Palestinian theater, remembers his teacher, Khalil Baidas, pioneer of the School Theater, who used to select plays for the students of the Anglican School in Jerusalem to perform "while casting, out the subjects that weren't appropriate for the Arab-Palestinian environment" (Oun, 2000). Jamil al Bahri, playwright, translator, and theater director, also used to shape both his original plays and his adaptations of Western works to suit the conventions and customs of the society of his day, taking into account, among other things, the fact that women were not allowed to perform on stage. He wrote close to a dozen plays, which were amongst the few to be printed and circulated as early as 1919 (al Batrawi, 2002).

Al Batrawi explains that, when adapting the Western play, *Prisoner of the Castle*, based on a romance, he introduced changes:

> that eradicated any reason to object to the morality of the play . . . I also exchanged the roles of the women and the lovers with roles that match them emotionally, but differ from them in terms of plot and the events, in order to shape [the play] into what people wanted . . . Love stories, as noble and respectable as can be, are not fit to be shown in schools, not to mention that it was very difficult to find young boys who would be willing to play feminine roles, even if these roles were not of lovers. ('Oun, 2000: 186)

For that reason, says al Batrawi, al Bahri removed from each play that he wrote or adapted "all the female roles, be them as they may, and kept only the historical events and the basic outline of each act" ('Oun, 2000: 187).

The title of the play, *Women's Greed*, staged by the Islamic Sports Club in 1929, bears witness to its content – preaching morality to women. Ironically, not one woman was among the actors or in the audience (ibid.). Nevertheless, women were not altogether absent from the theater and even prior to 1929 they made it to the boards. Dramas were put on in all-girl schools as well, and there the female students played male parts. In 1924, these types of play were performed in the all-girls Bir-Zeit College, later to become Bir-Zeit University, where the profession of the theater was introduced into the curriculum (ibid.).

How then, did theater succeed where cinema failed? The people who engaged in theater[11] had the insight to penetrate Palestinian society without resistance by engaging with two urgent issues on the Palestinian agenda. The first was Arab nationalism, which emerged out of the struggle against Ottoman rule;

later on the second topic Palestinian nationalism, evolved as a result of confrontation with the Zionist movement and with the policies of the British mandate.

Many plays presented figures and values from the Arab history. The characters of Omer Ben al Khattab, Salah A-Ddin (Saladin), Tarek Ben Ziad[12] and others appeared in plays by Jamil al Bahri, Nasri al-Juzi, and others. The reputation of these plays reached neighboring Arab countries and some were even performed there. The repertoire included works that dealt with the Palestinian past as well. A young Haifa stage actor and playwright by the name of Aziz Domat wrote a play called *The Governor of Acre*,[13] "whose reputation reached Germany, where the play was performed in the city of Stralsund" (ibid.).

Another topic investigated by Palestinian theater, despite the strict censorship regulations imposed by the Mandatory Government, was the conflict with the Zionist movement. Nasri al-Juzi's play, *The Ghosts of the Freedom Knights*, deals with the issue of selling land to the Zionists. The play recounts the story of a landowner who, falling into financial difficulties, decides to sell a plot of land to Zionist settlers. The landowner's son, a student at the University of Beirut, hears of his father's intentions and returns from Beirut in order to prevent the sale. To the son's aid come the ghosts of three of the most important figures in Arab history: Omer Ben al Khattab, the second Caliph to conquer Jerusalem, Khaled Ben al Walid, a hero and military genius from the first Islamic period, and Salah A-Ddin, who reconquered Jerusalem, then in the hands of the Crusaders. The three appeal to the father's heart, reminding him of the sacrifices that his forefathers made in order to erect a "magnificent and powerful Arab kingdom," and eventually he is convinced, backing down from his original intentions ('Oun, 200).

Due to the self-recruitment of Palestinian theater in favor of national causes and its embracing of social restrictions in schools, Palestinian society, whose daily existence was increasingly affected by the struggle with the Zionist movement and its causes, opened its doors to the medium. The first to accept the theater were the Christian religious institutions. Khalil a-Sakakini, a famous Christian Palestinian educator from Jerusalem, reported that the members of the Christian Greek Orthodox community decided as early as 1908 to set up a cultural society which would include a theater (Al Mallah, 2002). The trend soon spread to the Muslim community as well, and drama companies were established within the Islamic Sports Club, the Islamic Charity Society, the Young Muslims' Association in Haifa and Jaffa, and the Young Muslims' Club in Jerusalem and Jaffa. Similar drama companies were founded in Nazareth, Jenin, and Gaza. Yet theaters also mushroomed beyond educational and social institutions. In 1936, al-Juzi established an independent theater company whose members consisted of his two brothers and his sister (al Batrawi, 2002), and in Jerusalem actors set up their own company and association. Al Batrawi

(2002) counts no fewer than forty-three cultural groups that had drama companies, and no less than seventy plays that were performed between 1929 and 1948, not including those performed in schools. Thematically, pre-1948 Palestinian theater was simple, didactic, rhetorical, and melodramatic, deriving its inspiration from the Egyptian theater of the time. Technically, it did not use lighting and almost never had proper stage design (al Batrawi, 2002). Nevertheless, theater took an active role in Palestinian cultural and national undertakings.

Cinema, however, did not follow suit. Being a medium of new and expensive technology, it could not initiate activity in schools and the educational system. It was therefore prevented from traveling the same route as the theater – from the bottom upwards, from schools to the heart of the volunteer cultural groups of society, thus becoming a pivotal part of the Palestinian cultural scene. Cinema is an industry, and industries need financial resources, skills, strategic goals, and planning at a national level. But the contemporary Palestinian leadership, itself anachronistic and failing in its analysis of reality, knew neither how to manage the battle being fought by the society it led, nor how to choose the right tools and utilize them appropriately in order to achieve the national goals. It did not even determine what these national goals were in reality.

Another hurdle that stood in the way of cinema from the onset was the manner in which it was introduced into Palestinian society. Arabic movie theaters had existed since the late 1920s, initially in the big cities.[14] Movie repertoires were targeted at the Arabic audience and included mostly Egyptian films, yet these were mainly musical comedies and superficial melodramas about love, a topic to which conservative society objected. Mdanat (1990) claims that conservative and religious elements, not merely in Palestine but in Syria and Egypt as well, frequently used to appeal to the authorities to ban, or at least censor, movies dealing with love.

Furthermore, even if nationally motivated filmmakers had attempted to utilize cinema for the purposes of propaganda or as a tool for the construction of ideology, as Zionist cinema had done, the Mandatory Government's approach would not have allowed them to succeed. In addition to the Moving Pictures Act (1929) and the Newspaper Act (1933), which gave the censors powers of restriction, including the authority to shut cinemas down for reasons of immorality or the corruption of society, a new law was passed in 1935. This was the Public Amusement Act that defined the proper manner in which movies were permitted to be projected to the public. In addition to this constraint, from time to time new emergency regulations were passed which took the restrictions to extremes, especially during periods of increased Palestinian resistance.[15] In 1939, Regulation Number 57 added a special clause pertaining to the big screen, which obligated cinema owners to hand in the movie schedule to a police lieutenant in advance of screening, and forbade any alterations, including changes in screening times, without the lieutenant's consent. Mandatory Laws concerning the production of movies also became much stricter. Mdanat (1990) quotes a censor's decree from 1939 which forbade "printing, publishing, exhibiting or selling any paintings, photographs, films or any other pictures that include violent scenes, victims of violence, figures carrying arms or suspicious of carrying arms against the government, or pictures depicting military activity."[16]

THE SECOND PERIOD: THE EPOCH OF SILENCE 1948–67

After 1948, when the Arab Palestinian community ceased to exist as a social and political entity, utter silence fell. Urban life in the coastal cities disappeared almost completely, more than 350 villages and city neighborhoods were wiped out, and about half of the Arab Palestinian inhabitants were uprooted from their homes and became refugees. The experience of exile, being both a personal and a national tragedy, would overshadow everything else in the eyes of the generation living through this disaster: the *Naqba* generation (Kimerling and Migdal, 1993). For years, Palestinians attempted to come to terms with their new situation. This applies to refugees in the camps, as well as to the Arab population of Galilee, the "Triangle" (an area of Arab villages in central Israel), and the Negev in the south, where Arabs now found themselves in the unique position of a minority in their native land. This also relates to those who preferred exile, managing to integrate as an educated and skilled workforce into "host" societies in Egypt, Syria, and particularly the Gulf States.

The first to break the silence were the intellectuals, the writers and poets (Kimmerling and Migdal, 1993), including such authors as Abed al-Karim al Karmi, Ghassan Kanafani, Ez-Eddin al-Manasra, and Mo'in Bseiso in exile, and Hanna Abu Hanna, Mahmud Darwish, Tawfik Zayiad, and Samih al-Kassem in the homeland. Only at a later stage did secret political organizations begin to form. The initial kernel of the Fatah organization apparently crystallized in 1958, in Kuwait. The members of the group belonged to the new generation that turned its back on those who were in power up to the year of the *Naqba*. Although Fatah members had great personal respect for the old leaders, they felt no commitment to their legacy, since they held the leaders of the previous generation responsible, to a great extent, for the national disaster. The *Naqba*, they believed, was a consequence of the former leaders' failure to disassociate themselves from the Arab regimes, which were partly corrupt[17] and partly served as British protégés. In addition, the previous regime was criticized for holding secret negotiations with Zionist institutions.[18]

Cinematic endeavors, requiring infrastructure, professional crews, and finance, nearly ceased to exist for two decades, though not altogether. There are indications that the Palestinian producer, Ibrahim Hassan Sirhan, directed, filmed, or participated in a movie production in Jordan in 1957, but no definite proof of this can be found. *The Struggle in Jarash* (1957) was an adventure movie that did not relate to the Palestinian issue. The Jordanian authorities prohibited its release, because they believed that it gave a bad name to the city of Jarash, an important Jordanian tourist resort. After negotiations with the authorities, the movie was at last allowed to be released with revisions, thus becoming the first Jordanian feature film (Abu Gh'nima, 1981).

A Palestinian filmmaker was also involved in the production of the second Jordanian feature film. In 1964, the Palestinian director, Abdallah Ka'wash, made a movie called *My Homeland, My Love*, which played in Amman and other cities.

THE THIRD PERIOD: CINEMA IN EXILE, 1968–82

The third period began with the Arab defeat in the 1967 War (the *Naksa*), one of the most traumatic events in the modern history of the Arab people, which, for a time, resulted in the arrest of all the Arab countries' activities against Israel. The Palestinians, led by Yasser Arafat, who infiltrated the West Bank and tried to organize the resistance movement there, were the first to recover from this paralysis. The complications of operating within the West Bank steered Arafat towards Jordan, where he succeeded in establishing, along with several Palestinian organizations, a military infrastructure. In light of the continuing stagnation of the Arab regimes, the Palestinian forces were perceived as the only hope in the eyes of both the Arab population in general and the Palestinian masses in particular. In 1968, Fatah, headed by Arafat, took control of the PLO, a parent organization of the various Palestinian bodies, including, among others, certain cultural institutions.

A small photography unit, founded in 1967 by Sulafa Jadallah Mirsal, a young Palestinian who had studied photography in Cairo, illuminates, from its very beginning, the nature of the cinema which developed under these conditions. Mirsal's laboratory for developing photographs was set up in a kitchen, and her equipment was primitive. She toiled mostly over commemorative still photographs of Palestinian casualties, the *shahids* (Abu Gh'nima, 1981).

Later, her work was transferred to the Amman apartment in which the Fatah offices were located, and in 1968 the Department of Photography was established; within its framework came the first initiatives toward a Palestinian cinema. Fatah's leaders were doubtful of the need to extend the department's activities into the field of cinema. One of them decided on the department's objectives: documenting events, justifying Palestinian causes, and supplying services to the press (Abu Gh'nima, 1981, from interviews with Hani Johariya). As for cinema, it was decided that it was too early to discuss it. Nevertheless, Mustafa Abu-Ali and Hani Johariya, both Palestinians who had studied cinema and lived in Jordan, joined Sulafa Jadallah Mirsal. They found ways to integrate cinematic filming into the regular activities of the department. Both worked for Jordanian television, from which they borrowed cameras and film, and documented all that they could – demonstrations, public gatherings, and other cultural and political activities (private interview with Mustafa Abu-Ali, Ramallah, 2003).

Despite the early sparks of cinematic activity within the framework of the Department of Photography, still images, captured by Mirsal's elementary equipment, continued to be considered of greater significance. In 1968, following the battle in al-Karama,[19] the group presented an exhibition of photographs from the fighting in the al Wahdat refugee camp in Amman. The exhibition was a great success, which convinced the leaders of Fatah to supply the department with modern equipment, albeit solely for still photography. Abu-Ali, Johariya, and others continued to shoot films using equipment they borrowed from Jordanian television, as they had before.

The Early Movies

In October 1969, the American Secretary of State, William Rogers, presented the Russians and the rival sides in the Middle East with a peace plan. Made public in December, the scheme proposed a near-complete withdrawal of the Israelis on the Egyptian and Jordanian fronts and a comprehensive right of return for the refugees. The Palestinians opposed the plan,[20] as they believed that it ignored the PLO and the Palestinian people, and took to the streets of Jordan and other countries to demonstrate against it. The Department of Photography documented the demonstrations using a 16mm camera, and even recorded interviews with the objectors with synchronous sound equipment. Finally, the members of the film crew decided that they had gathered enough material to create a film. Thus the 20 minute film called *Say No to the Peaceful Solution* (1968), a collaboration between Mustafa Abu-Ali, Hani Johariya, and Salah Abu Hannoud, became the first movie of the third period. Lack of technology compelled the filmmakers to send the movie for editing to the Baalbeck region in Lebanon, where it was completed in their absence.

The plans of the pioneers of the third period went haywire in 1970, when the PLO was obliged to leave Jordan for Lebanon after the events of "Black September."[21] Abu-Ali's film group[22] also transferred to Lebanon, and in 1971 the department, led by Abu-Ali, produced a second documentary, *With Blood and Spirit*, which depicted the "Black September" incidents and was shot during the battles. Due to the comprehensive ban which the Jordanian authorities imposed on exporting filmed materials from the kingdom, Yasser Arafat delivered the footage to Cairo himself (Hennebelle and Khayati, 1977). Parts of it were screened during the Arab Summit, which assembled in Cairo to discuss the "Black September" events.

During this period, more than sixty Palestinian documentary films were made. The only dramatic movie to be produced in the course of that time was *The Return to Haifa* (1982), an adaptation of a short novel by Ghassan Kanafani[23] made by a director of Iraqi origin, Kassem Hawal. The movie was produced in 1982, at the close of the third period, by a group connected to the PFLP. The link to a particular political segment is characteristic of the third period. In addition to the central production body, the PLO's Department of Photography, whose name was later changed to the Film Foundation/ Palestinian Film Unit, each of the main political organizations established its own production unit. The Democratic Front for the Liberation of Palestine (DFLP) founded the Art Committee; the Popular Front established the Artistic Committee, and later the production studio Al Ard (The Land). Even the Popular Front – Ahmad Jibril's general headquarters – and the pro-Syrian As-Sa'ika, both minor groups, formed film departments and produced films.

'Movies of the Revolution' or Revolutionary Movies?

This vibrant political background could be considered a good starting point. At that time, the Palestinian organizations reiterated their belief in cinema as a significant tool for the advancement of their cause. They even specified clear goals for it: cinema was to document their struggle. It was intended to justify the Palestinian position, record the reality of people's everyday lives, harness the masses to the new enterprise, and advocate the new Palestinian image (the fighter to replace the refugee). Third period cinema was the offspring of the resistance movement, which was itself in its infancy. Palestinian cinema had associated itself with the national movement and, in doing so, entrusted its fate to the national movement. This is where both its strengths and its weaknesses lay. On the one hand, film production owed its existence to the national movement, which financed crews, offices, routine shooting sessions, and productions. On the other hand, everything ran according to the priorities of the organizations. Historians who have researched Palestinian cinema claim that, in retrospect, cinema did not rank very high on the resistance movement's scale of priorities.

Palestinian cinema was referred to as "the cinema of the Palestinian revolution." It embraced its causes and adopted its ideas, which were in fact those of the PLO and the other militant organizations affiliated to it. The Palestinian struggle was perceived as a "popular war" and was inspired by models of popular revolutions prevalent in those days in Vietnam, Cuba, Angola, Mozambique, and elsewhere. In accordance with the Marxist-Leninist outlook, great importance was attached to cinema as a revolutionary device, and the Palestinian movement claimed to share this point of view. The influence of the foreign revolutionary movements was so profound that even Fatah, the principal fighting organization, often expressed itself in Marxist terminology, in spite of being an a-Marxist organization.[24]

The "Cinematic Movement," to use the common terminology of the period, viewed itself as an integral part of the revolution, which was conducted in the form of a popular war. A statement submitted by the Palestinian delegation to the Round Table of the Afro-Asian Film Conference, held within the framework of the Tashkent Film Festival in 1973, contained the following:

> The people's war is what granted the revolutionary Palestinian cinema its characteristics and its mode of operation . . . the light weapon is the primary weapon of the people's war, and similarly, the light 16-mm camera is the most appropriate weapon for the cinema of the people. A film's success is measured by the same criteria used to measure the success of a military operation. [The film and the military operation] both aspire to realize a political cause . . . the desire to fight is the most important element in the people's war, and thus it is also the most important component of the cinematic effort . . . the revolutionary film is dedicated to tactical objectives of the revolution and to its strategic objectives as well. A militant film, therefore, must become an essential commodity for the masses, just like a loaf of bread. (Farid, no date: 249)

An additional element affecting the nature of Palestinian cinema of the time was the connection with revolutionary Western directors. During this period, a common tendency among Western filmmakers was to rebel against mainstream cinema, which was molded mostly according to Hollywoodian formulas, and which served – so they argued – the capitalist and colonialist interests of the dominant classes. Revolutionary groups in the West, and particularly in Europe, searched for a new cinematic language to purge films of the encumbering Hollywoodian style. The most renowned of these groups was dubbed the French New Wave. Godard, one of its most prominent figures, arrived in Jordan in 1968, toured the Palestinian bases, met Abu-Ali, Hani Johariya, and their friends, and filmed material in the refugee camps and around the *feday-een* bases. He used these materials in the film *Ici et ailleurs* (*Here and in Other Places*, 1970). Contacts of a similar nature[25] with revolutionary directors from the West, the East, and the developing world influenced the Palestinian discourse and encouraged a dialogue concerning the essence of Palestinian cinema.[26]

Theoretically, the condition of cinema seemed to improve, but in reality this was not the case. As previously mentioned, each political organization, including the most minor of them, zealously cultivated its own cinematic efforts, establishing separate film departments and committees. The fragmentation and squandering of resources weakened the organizations' commitment to cinema.

Mdanat (1990) emphasizes that Abu-Ali, Mirsal, and Johariya's Department of Photography, the most important cinematic body of the era, was established as a result of the three's personal initiative, rather than as a consequence of Fatah's efforts. The other film units were also not conceived by their respective organizations as such, but were the product of individual enterprises of certain filmmakers, who despite poor conditions began to produce films, backed by the organizations.

The organizations were undoubtedly aware of the propaganda potential of the media in general and of cinema in particular. Mdanat (1990) writes:

> The leaders of the revolution were not unconscious of the vibrant cinematic activity around them. Indeed, they enthusiastically agreed to appear in filmed interviews for filmmakers and foreign television crews, without (even) bothering to ensure that the image that they ultimately presented would actually reflect reality accurately. (851).

Mdanat's words prove that the main interest of the Palestinian leadership in cinema was its explanatory facet, and even more so its ability to influence public opinion in the West. Politically, the communist East and developing countries were considered guaranteed allies, since they shared obvious interests with the Palestinian national movement. Thus efforts to influence them were not deemed necessary.

Although the Palestinian leadership realized that, without a genuine transformation in the policies of the West, the task of the Palestinian national movement would be immensely difficult, and despite understanding that, in that case, the situation called for significant propaganda efforts to influence Western public opinion, cinema was still not utilized effectively as a change-inducing tool. One of the possible reasons for this might be Palestinian cinema's immaturity and its many weaknesses: lack of experience, as well as technical and artistic incompetence of the crews at all levels.[27] Another reason is the emphasis placed by the establishment on fighting for its life, enlisting most of its resources in support of that goal. The slogan coined by the organizations, "the voice of the gun should be louder than any other," summarizes this attitude, which leaves cinema, or any other expensive cultural activity,[28] a relatively slim chance.

Yet another explanation might in fact be found in the interest that Western directors and television crews took in the Palestinian issue. The Palestinian leadership understood that their case was being made by others, and did not feel the need to invest significant resources themselves.[29]

In his book, Mdanat (1990) suggests that "history repeats itself. The pre-1948 Palestinian leadership had not ascribed any importance to cinema . . . the leadership [in the seventies] also had no interest in it whatsoever." This statement is perhaps too extreme, for the Palestinian leadership did not refrain from investing in cinema altogether; however, those minor investments were directed toward documentary films. The leaders were satisfied with the propaganda benefits that cinema offered and did not bother to nurture cinema as an essential cultural need of the Palestinian people. Thus film crews were asked to document almost everything: daily life in the refugee camps, cultural events, political conventions, mass gatherings, and leaders' tours, as well as air raids, invasions of the Israeli forces, and the events of the civil war in Lebanon. Hours and hours of this documented raw material have accumulated during the course of the years, comprising the core of the Palestinian archive.

The filmmakers themselves never stopped fighting for the status of cinema and making movies, despite the scarcity of resources, the shortage of competent crews and professional equipment, and the relatively minor interest expressed by the organization's leaders. In order to produce a film, the directors needed to press the leaders day and night, until they succeeded in convincing them to release meager sums of money, which would suffice for some basic shooting. To complete the films, they used materials from the archives. In 1975, following the civil war in Lebanon,[30] laboratories no longer functioned and filmed material was sent for development to laboratories outside of Lebanon. Then "one had to wait for months to receive the material back, after which it needed to be edited and sent out of Lebanon again for copies to be printed, and all this merely in order to end up with a 15 or 20-minute long film" (Mdanat, 1990).

Ghaleb Sha'ath, one of the leading directors of the period, headed the film department of the Samed institution.[31] He convinced the body's leaders, among them Ahmad Krei', also known as Abu Ala', to set up a film laboratory in Beirut. The lab commenced operations in 1980, but was destroyed in 1982 during Israel's invasion of Beirut and the departure of the PLO (private interview with Ghaleb Sha'ath, Jerusalem, 1995).

Despite all the difficulties, attempts to make movies never stopped. Claiming that the fragmentation of the Cinematic Movement was at the heart of the problem, a number of filmmakers, including Mustafa Abu-Ali, established an independent film association called the Palestinian Film Group in 1972. Abu-Ali (private interview, Ramallah, 2003) remembers that the main purpose of the group was to unite the efforts of filmmakers from the different groups, and to give cinema an independent status within the PLO, with its own budgets and resources. The group hoped that independent status for cinema would pacify the organizations, which feared that such a union would lead to their assimilation within the bigger, stronger bodies. The group survived only one year, during which time it produced a sole film, *Scenes from the Occupation in Gaza* (1973), directed by Mustafa Abu-Ali.

The Films and their Themes

Obstacles notwithstanding, more than sixty movies were made before 1982, all but one documentary films. These films were screened at different festivals, including the Leipzig Festival in East Germany, the Baghdad Festival for Palestinian Movies, and the Carthage Festival in Tunisia. They were also presented at dozens of special events for Palestinian cinema in the West, and were shown regularly by the diplomatic delegations of the PLO, and by friendship or solidarity societies with Palestinians around the world.

Nevertheless, their audience mainly consisted of the Palestinians themselves. The first film, *Say No to the Peaceful Solution* (1968), was screened in Amman to an audience of the top Fatah people. The viewing was held in a basement and, "due to a lack of chairs, the leaders watched it standing up, on a dirt floor" (Abu Gh'nima, 1981). Mustafa Abu-Ali confesses pre-screening to the political leaders in order to seek their opinion before releasing the movies to the general public: "I'm not a political man, it was therefore important for me to know that the political messages were approved of" (private interview with Mustafa Abu-Ali, Ramallah, 2003). In addition, each cinematic body had screening units, including mobile ones. Khadija Abu-Ali operated one such unit in the PLO's Film Institute. She reminisces (private interview, Ramallah, 2003) about the period when committees from the refugee camps were invited to watch the movies during their editing stages. After the film's release, it was screened, by way of the mobile unit, in the refugee camps and to the fighters. Following the screenings, discussions were held with the audience.

A film industry that defines itself as "an inseparable part of the revolution" is bound to focus on the struggle of the movement to which it belongs as its primary theme. This is even truer when cinema engages mostly in documentary films. Examination of the films produced reveals several shared characteristics; many of them sport a newsreel style spiced with political analysis. They include footage of battles, bombings, destruction, and casualties, packed with militant narration and interviews with fighters and civilian eyewitnesses, as well as with political and military leaders. Even though the films occasionally make interesting use of the soundtrack (music), scenic long shots, and artistic *mise-en-scène*, their cinematic language is generally rather plain, rendered through simple narrative editing. Exceptions to this rule are the works of Mustafa Abu-Ali, Kaise à-Zubeidi, Adnan Mdanat, and Ghaleb Sha'ath, who, in many cases, used a much richer and more complex cinematic language.

The newsreel feel of the films as particularly prominent during the early part of the period. *Say No to the Peaceful Solution* (1968) documents and explains the Palestinian position with regard to the Rogers Plan; *With Blood and Spirit* (1971) delineates the events of "Black September"; *Zionist Aggression* (1973) deals with the destruction and loss of life caused by the Israeli Air Force bombardment of one of the refugee camps in Lebanon; *Kafr Shuba* (1975) and *United Guns* (1974) describe the war against Israeli operations in southern Lebanon in 1973; *War in Lebanon* (1977), Samir Nimer's feature film, is concerned with the civil war in Lebanon; and a number of films investigate the events occurring in Tel A-Za'tar camp near Beirut[32] – *A Report from Tel a-Za'tar* (1976), *Tel a-Za'tar* (1977), *Because Roots Don't Die* (1977) and more.

Some of the films are occupied with events that took place in the West Bank, in the Gaza Strip, or within the Israeli borders, the most famous of which are *Earth Day* (1978), *Scenes from the Occupation in Gaza* (1973), *Siege Diary* (1978), and *Barbed-Wire Homeland* (1982). European crews shot *Earth Day* and *Barbed-Wire Homeland* in Israel and the West Bank respectively, since their directors were not allowed to enter the shooting locations.

There were films that confronted the Palestinian issue in other ways. For example, *al-Bared River* (1971), *Our Small Houses* (1974), and *The Key* (1976) document the everyday reality in the An-Nahar Al-Bared refugee camp in northern Lebanon. *The Key* contemplates the living conditions of the Palestinian refugees, in view of the development of the Jewish settlements founded on land owned by refugees. Isma'il Shammut, a famous Palestinian artist, produced films that were based on his paintings. *Memories and Fire* (1973) is the most noted of these. Adnan Mdanat's *Palestinian Visions* (1977) recounts the refugees' tale through the story and art of one refugee, a painter and poet who lived in South Lebanon. And finally, Kaise a-Zubeidi's film, *A Voice from Jerusalem* (1977), tells the story of Mustafa-al-Kurd, a famous Jerusalemite protest singer.

Other films documented international events in which the Palestinians participated. Kassem Hawal's *Why We Plant Flowers, Why We Carry Weapons* (1974) chronicles the Palestinian delegation's participation in the international youth festival held in East Berlin in 1973. Jean Sham'oun produced a similar movie named *The Song of Freedom* (1980), which records the youth festival in Cuba.

Palestinians produced films about other Arab revolutionary movements as well. Samir Nimer, for instance, made the film, *The Winds of Liberation* (1974), about a left-wing rebellion against the Sultan of Oman, and *The New Yemen* (1974), concerned with the left-wing regime of South Yemen.

In 1982, Israeli military forces invaded Lebanon with the cooperation of the Christian Maronite forces. Israel's main objective was to destroy the foundation of the quasi-state which the PLO established in Lebanon. In August, Israeli forces surrounded western Beirut and the PLO evacuated its forces to Tunisia, Yemen, and Algeria. A new headquarters was established in Tunisia (Kimmerling and Migdal, 1993). The Film Institute and the various organizations' other cinematic units ceased to function. The PLO's Department of Culture continued to produce movies from its new domicile in Tunisia, among them some of the PLO's best films. Two of the films were directed by Kaise a-Zubeidi: *Barbed-Wire Homeland* (1982) and *Palestine: the Chronicle of a People* (1984). The first, which describes the expansion of the settlements at the expense of Palestinian lands, was the earliest Palestinian production to consider the settlers, "with the intention of presenting the racist aspect of their religious-patriotic beliefs" (private interview with Kaise a-Zubeidi, West Berlin, 1985). *Palestine: the Chronicle of a People* presents the Palestinian problem from the First Zionist Congress in Basel until 1948. The movie is based on archival footage, which was collected, sorted, and interwoven to form a cinematic whole. The film includes in-depth interviews with Palestinians who participated in the events described in it. A third film produced by the PLO, *The Dream* (1987), was directed by the Syrian, Muhammad Malas, one of the best contemporary Arab directors.

The Archive

The organizations' film departments had accumulated hour upon hour of raw footage documenting the lives of the Palestinian people and stored it in their separate archives. The largest and most important of these was the PLO's Film Foundation/Palestinian Film Unit. The footage it contained at the time was stored in boxes, on which the type of material filmed and the date of shooting were marked. The constant use directors made of the archive evoked the need to organize the material in a more efficient manner. Khadija Abu-Ali, who was in charge of the screening unit, was trained to respond to that need; in 1975 the archive was set up in a hall in the Film Institute in the al-Fakihani quarter of West Beirut.[33] The history of the Palestinian archive in Lebanon, which has been related to us by Khadija Abu-Ali herself (private interview, Ramallah, 2003), is well known.

Abu-Ali and her staff invested considerable time and effort, eventually managing to sort out the thousands of meters of celluloid. "It was time-consuming labor that took years," she recalls. "The footage in each box was classified and marked both on the box itself and on special index cards. There were no computers at the time. Finally, the place resembled a film archive."

The archive offered unremitting documentation of battles, bombings, political, cultural and social events, and interviews with politicians, military leaders, and notables from the cultural and intellectual circles of the time, many of whom have now passed away. In addition, it contained interviews with guests, documentation of delegations and receptions, a record of life in the refugee and guerrilla camps, and day-by-day documentation of the events of the civil war.

The archive also offered originals and copies of all the movies made by the Film Institute, as well as close to one hundred films donated by friendly countries[34] and by Western directors. Raw footage filmed before 1948 and purchased from foreign movie and television agencies, especially from the British Vis News, was stored there too, as was footage shot by foreign agencies in the West Bank and Gaza Strip.

Film Institute officials feared for the future of the accumulated footage, which included rare and valuable material, and so they examined the possibility of printing additional copies, which would be transferred to a safe haven outside of Lebanon. The cost of the project was estimated at a quarter of a million dollars. The PLO leadership considered the cost too high and the proposal was rejected.

Between 1980 and 1981, the war between Israel with its Lebanese allies, on one side, and the Palestinians with their allies, on the other, escalated. Aerial attacks on the PLO offices in the al-Fakihani quarter became more and more frequent. Therefore, Film Institute management decided to transfer the archive to a more secure area. They rented the basement of a building in the distant Sadat neighborhood, installed air-conditioning, and moved the archive there.

Khadija Abu-Ali claims that she personally approached Yasser Arafat and Khalil el-Wazir, also known as Abu Jihad, and told them that she was entrusting the fate of the archive to their hands. Abu Iad also expressed interest in the fate of the archive, and promised to do everything in his power to take it with him. Yet, a few days before the PLO left Lebanon, Abu Jihad had informed her that it would not be possible to take the archive out of Beirut for the time being; however, he had managed to obtain the French embassy's consent to secure the archive until its removal was possible. Meanwhile, the PLO paid two years' rent in advance to the owner of the basement. A cinematographer by the name of Omar a-Rashidi, who worked in the Film Institute, and two clerks from the institute's staff (all three possessing the right to Lebanese residency) were asked to guard the archive.

The PLO's departure did not end the Lebanese War. On the contrary, after a while, a severe dispute broke out between the Palestinians in the refugee camps and one of their main allies in Lebanon, the Shiite organization Amal. The strife led to the imposing of a blockade on the refugee camps in Beirut. A-Rashidi was compelled to leave Lebanon. The two clerks who were left behind to preserve the archive were apprehensive about possible harm to it, and turned to the Palestinian Red Crescent for help. The archive was consequently moved to the Red Crescenty's Akka (Acre) hospital and there it was stored "without a doubt, under conditions unfit for the storage of film," according to Abu-Ali (private interview, Ramallah, 2003). Later, the archive was obliged to migrate from the Akka hospital as well, and its whereabouts today remain unknown.

Only rumors have reached Khadija Abu-Ali's ears. One of these suggests that the Abu Musa faction, a pro-Syrian group that disassociated itself from the PLO after the Lebanese War, seized the archive. According to another source, a major Shiite figure has the archive in his keeping, in the hands of the

Hizballah. Yet another report suggests that the employees of the Akka hospital, fearing for the hospital's fate, buried it in a Palestinian graveyard.

Wherever it is, after over twenty years of wandering and inappropriate storage conditions, Khadija Abu-Ali is not optimistic as to the fate of her life's work. She fears that the memories of a whole generation have been lost without a trace.[35]

THE FOURTH PERIOD: THE RETURN HOME, FROM 1980 TO THE PRESENT

The continuing state of occupation has left its mark on both the Palestinian and the Israeli populations. As international initiatives to end it failed, the Palestinians, including the new generation raised or even born under the shadow of the occupation, began to abandon the principles of passive resistance and demand active opposition to Israeli rule (Kimmerling and Migdal, 1993: 225–6).

The economic crisis and the increasing unemployment rate that had left their mark on Israel in the late 1970s affected Israeli Arabs and, at the beginning of the 1980s, badly hurt the inhabitants of the Occupied Territories. Palestinians were the first to be made redundant. The difficult financial situation, along with the accelerated growth of new Jewish settlements in the occupied land, created a convenient foundation for a national awakening (Kimerling and Migdal, 1993: 230). This awakening reached its peak in the uprising against the Israeli occupation, the *Intifada* ("shaking off"), that broke out on 9 December 1987, in the Jabalya refugee camp in the Gaza Strip. The mass demonstrations that began in the refugee camps swiftly spread across the Gaza Strip and the West Bank. The intensity with which events erupted surprised both the Palestinians and the Israelis. It was an all-encompassing popular uprising (Kimerling and Migdal, 1993). Men, women, and children swarmed into the streets, attempting to evict Israeli soldiers from the city center.

Kimmerling and Migdal (1993) claim in their book that "*de facto* the *Intifada* had created a state of stalemate, in which each side felt defeated, even though neither side would admit it even to itself, and certainly not to the other side" (236). The Palestinians' support of the Iraqi ruler, Saddam Hussein, in the early stages of the Gulf Crisis in 1990, during the attacks of the Coalition Forces on Iraq and Iraq's Scud missile attacks on Israel in January 1991, reflected a desperate Palestinian hope of achieving in this way what the *Intifada* could not. However, rather than improving their situation, the economic crisis that followed the Gulf War and stagnation of the Israeli economy severely harmed the Palestinians. Their financial situation further deteriorated with the Arab countries' cessation of financial support for the PLO, which was designated in part for the aid of the inhabitants of the Occupied Territories.

Nevertheless, the *Intifada* was not perceived as a Palestinian failure. The events of the *Intifada* directly led to an accord signed six years later in

Oslo – the first official, written agreement between the Government of Israel and the PLO, designed to put an end to the conflict and drafted after a two-year period of secret negotiations. The agreement, known as the First Oslo Accord, granted the Palestinians a certain degree of autonomy. Following this pact, the National Palestinian Authority was established in 1993, an independent governmental body headed by Yasser Arafat, who was handed the authority over the operative government in the Gaza and Jericho vicinities. The Palestinian Authority appointed ministers to govern the up-coming nation-state, and responsibility for cinematic affairs was placed in the hands of the Minister of Culture, Yasser Abed Rabbu.

Thus the *Intifada* led to the signing of a peace treaty and to a period of relative calm in the Palestinian struggle. However, while the PLO was busy establishing the Palestinian Authority and founding the Palestinian Government, the Islamic resistance movement strengthened, and suicide attacks and armed operations against civilians in Israel continued with growing intensity. Such attacks and the continuous closures with which Israel responded led to an endless cycle that worsened the financial situation of the Occupied Territories' population. They also prompted the emergence of more *shaheed*, and resulted in another uprising, the Second *Intifada*, ignited in September 2000 by the visit of the head of the Israeli opposition at that time, Ariel Sharon, to Al Aqsa Mosque (Temple Mount). The Second *Intifada*, which in the beginning included an uprising of Arabs of Israeli citizenship, aggravated the condition of the Palestinians living in the Occupied Territories and increased the fissures within Palestinian society, as well as highlighting the militant voices of those in Israeli society and politics who opposed any peace agreement with the Palestinians. Yet, the on-going cycle of bloodshed, distress, and closures has resulted in fatigue in both societies and eventually in renewed negotiation efforts that exceed the scope of this book.

The 1980s and 1990s, thus, were particularly tumultuous years in the history of the Palestinian people. This was a period of both failures and achievements, a time when the fight for independence reached a peak. As in every other era in the history of the Palestinian people, cinema was pushed to the margins of the agenda of the national struggle. With the absence of any support systems for cinema and television within the Palestinian Authority, external financial bodies – mostly television networks and production companies from Europe, the USA, and even Israel – stepped in. After over thirty years of occupation, the Palestinian Authority has severe problems to attend to, such as shaky infrastructures, poverty, and unemployment. Thus, a change in its priorities in the near future does not seem likely.

The Palestinian filmmakers of our time have been burdened with a double role: both to continue their creative endeavor and to try to bring down the walls of apathy surrounding the international institutions that might be able to help fund the Palestinian cinematic effort. Despite these objective difficulties, directors have continued making movies, often with the assistance of foreign financial sources. The most important directors within Palestinian cinema have been working hard during recent years, and are gaining international recognition and prestige.

The fourth period began at the end of March 1980, when Michel Khleifi returned from Brussels in Belgium, where he had been living for a decade, to the city of Nazareth in Galilee, where he was born and raised. His purpose was to shoot his first documentary film. His brother, George Khleifi, a co-author of this book, who was to handle all aspects of production and to function as his assistant director, accompanied Michel. The film was intended to tell the tale of two women, one of whom is Khleifi's maternal aunt, a country woman in her fifties who was compelled to work as an employee in an Israeli textile factory after her land was expropriated. Khleifi had known his aunt his whole life and was very much inspired by her story. The other character was the writer Sahar Khalifa, who had published two novels up until that point in time, and whom Khleifi had gotten to know through her writing. He met with her on one of his visits to the homeland a few months earlier, and received her agreement in principle to participate in the film.

The technical crew joined Khleifi and his brother ten days later. The team consisted of three members in all: two cinematographers and a sound man. One of the cameramen drove most of the way from Belgium to Nazareth in a minivan; from Brussels he traveled to Athens, Greece, where he boarded a ship on its way to the port of Haifa. The same minivan was used as the production vehicle and was sold when the production was over. The movie's budget did not allow for a rented car.

The film was financed from three sources: the German television channel ZDF, and two television networks from Holland, NOVIB and IKON. The complete budget was equal to half that required for the production of a similar movie in Europe. For the production, Khleifi set up a company called Marisa Films, to be registered in Belgium.

Although Khleifi wished to shoot a documentary, it was his desire to use the techniques of a fictional film. He wanted to make an intimate movie, which would follow the daily lives of its characters. That goal required shooting at the rate of actual everyday occurrences, waiting for things to happen and filming them in real time. The shoot went on for forty-five days, and the crew lived in rented apartments in order to cut down on hotel expenses.

That was how the first film of the fourth period came into being, made by a director who became a symbol of the renaissance of Palestinian cinema. The conditions under which the movie was filmed foreshadow the conditions of those that came after. Other films would also be the result of the initiative of a single individual, who in most cases is scriptwriter, producer, and director – all rolled into one. The budget would be relatively low, generally supplied by European television networks and foreign support organizations. The production crew would be Palestinian, but the technical team would be foreign, mostly made up of Europeans.

Production and Financial Sources

During the 1980s, Khleifi was the most prominent name in the new Palestinian cinema. Soon, others began practicing the craft and started making movies, among them some of the major directors of Palestinian cinema to this day – Rashid Masharawi, Elia Suleiman, Nizar Hassan, Hani Abu-Assad. The cinema that they have created is referred to by various titles: "Independent Cinema,"[36] "Palestinian Cinema from the Occupied Lands" (Farid, no date; Mdanat, 1990), "Post-Revolution Cinema," or "Individualistic Cinema" (Shafik, 2001). All of these names refer to the nature of the films, which originated, developed, and gained international acclaim as a result of initiatives on the part of individual filmmakers, who operated without the support of either Palestinian public institutions or private Palestinian production companies.

Palestinian directors have been trained in their craft in a variety of institutions around the world (when they enjoyed such training at all). Michel Khleifi studied theater and television in Belgium; May Masri studied cinematography in the University of San Francisco Film Department; Subhi a-Zubeidi, Hana Elias, and Najwa Najar studied film or directing in the United States, George Khleifi and Omar al Quattan in Belgium; Azza al-Hassan studied documentary cinema in Scotland, Nazim Shraidi, Ali Nassar in Eastern Europe and Tawfik Abu Wa'el in Tel Aviv University. Elia Suleiman, Rashid Masharawi, Hani Abu-Assad, Nizar Hassan, and Abed a-Salam Shehada have not studied cinema formally at all; Hanna Misleh came to it from the field of anthropology; Muhammad Bakri, Juliano Mer and Salim Daw moved over from acting.

The filmmaker's work cycle spans many years – a long time passes from the initial stage of crystallizing the ideas, through development of the script, up to the stage of securing financial resources and finalizing production. Thus, in the entire period of 1980–2003 only twelve full-length films were produced, along with a few dozen documentaries, practically all of them made on very small budgets.

These directors have been working in a society in which the basic conditions for the existence of cinema are lacking; they are in need of national institutions for the advancement of cinema, production companies, companies for supplying equipment, film laboratories, skilled crew members, and institutions to train them. As an industry, Palestinian cinema does not exist. A Palestinian filmmaker who wishes to produce a movie is compelled to use foreign crews, or to make do with unqualified local teams. The post-production stage can only be executed in other countries, even in the case of a video production. Today the development of digital technology allows a number of directors, including some of the more prominent ones, to produce exceptional movies on very low budgets (up to $20,000 dollars), using small cameras and local technical crews, and occasionally with the directors themselves acting as cinematographers. Sometimes this is the only option available to directors at the beginning of their careers.[37]

A variety of financial sources have assisted the more prominent directors in producing their films. Some have received international funding, mostly from European countries. Michel Khleifi's films were financed from Belgian, Dutch, French, and German sources;[38] Rashid Masharawi[39] and Hani Abu-Assad[40] received contributions mainly from Holland; Elia Suleiman had American, British, and French sponsors;[41] and Nizar Hassan was aided by Swedish, Finnish, and American sources.[42] There were also those who were assisted by Israeli financial funds, including Masharawi,[43] Suleiman,[44] Nassar,[45] and Hassan,[46] and were severely criticized for it in Arab countries. Very few films enjoyed Palestinian funding,[47] and only one Palestinian movie received almost entirely Arab financial aid – Hani Abu-Assad's film, *Rana's Wedding* (2003), which was produced by the Palestinian Ministry of Culture using funds secured from the Gulf States.[48]

Subhi a-Zubeidi and Azza al-Hassan, two important directors who began their careers close to the end of the twentieth century, have made movies on minuscule budgets. Some of the films were produced at the request of Palestinian bodies or international social institutions which operate among of Palestinians. A-Zubeidi's film, *Light at the End of the Tunnel* (2000), which deals with Palestinian prisoners, was commissioned by a representative of the International Red Cross. The Red Cross imposed upon the director restrictions that form part of the organization's policies, and forbade a political approach to the subject. A-Zubeidi insisted on emphasizing the political aspect of the problem, and reached an agreement with the representatives of the Red Cross. He produced two different versions of the movie, one compatible with the criteria of the organization that commissioned it, the other more personal and political. Azza al-Hassan's film, *She, the Sindibad* (1999), endured the same fate.

The Cinema and its Audience

Another obstacle that Palestinian cinema has faced is the difficulty in reaching its audience, the Palestinian public. From the late 1970s, movie theaters in the Palestinian territories of the West Bank and Gaza Strip were shutting down one after the other. The main causes were television programs, broadcast by either

Arab countries or Israel, which replaced cinema, and the security situation, which began to deteriorate at around that same time.

Yet, even if movie houses had not been shut down, Israeli censorship and the military government would probably have deliberately put obstacles in the way of screening Palestinian movies in the West Bank and Gaza Strip. Cultural and artistic events that expressed Palestinian nationalism were perceived by the Israeli military government as acts of incitement. For every fine art exhibition, or poetry and theatrical event, special permission from the Israeli government was required. Usually, these requests were denied. Painters, singers, and people affiliated with the theater were arrested, imprisoned, and even expelled from the country. Jerusalemite protest singer, poet, and composer, Mustafa-al-Kurd, for instance, was asked to choose between one of two options: either he served a prison sentence or agreed to be "willingly" expelled from the country. Al-Kurd is known for singing patriotic songs, such as the one that first brought him fame, which calls for resistance to practice of selling land: "Bring the plough and the sickle/And you will never ever dare leave your land." Another of his protest songs, written in the 1970s, follows the death of a young woman from Jenin, by the name of Muntaha, during a confrontation with the Israeli army. One of the most famous songs of dissent which al-Kurd performed was written by Samih al-Kassem, and embodies the self-sacrifice of the Palestinian fighter:

> Welcome
> We waited for you for a long time
> We waited for you when one of our dead held the hand of another
> Welcome
> Did you eat, drink, and rest a little?
> O, my blood, my blood, my precious heritage
> So dear to me, I can't see you being squandered so
> But ooze, ooze
> Saturate me with new, unconquerable blood.

Al-Kurd chose "willful exile" and moved to Beirut in the late 1970s, where he told his life story in Kaise a-Zubeidi's film, *A Voice from Jerusalem* (1977). From Beirut he relocated to Berlin, after which the Israeli authorities eventually allowed him to return to Jerusalem in 1984. Another artist who suffered from the censor's heavy hand was Suleiman Mansur, whose art exhibition in Gallery 79 in Ramallah was closed down in 1980 by the military government, only six hours after it had opened. The pretext for its shutdown was the use of the colors of the Palestinian flag: red, black, green, and white. The military governor of Ramallah and a police lieutenant warned Mansur that if he made use of those colors again he would be accused of incitement (private interview with Mansur, Jerusalem, 2003).

Furthermore, even if commercial movie theaters had existed, they would probably not have been the proper venue for showing Palestinian movies because of their experimental nature.

Palestinian films encountered similar difficulties in Arab countries. Arab institutions treated Palestinian movies with the same mistrust as the Israeli institutions did and were not quick to allow screenings to the broad public. It seems that they were afraid of the nationalistic content and the messages of incitement, and perhaps even of the unconventional style of some of the films. In the instances when Palestinian films were allowed to be shown in Arab countries, screenings were held in closed forums intended for a specific and limited audience, such as festivals and cultural events. Commercial screenings of Michel Khleifi's film, *Wedding in Galilee* (1987), were permitted in only one Arab country, Tunisia. Another film of his, *Tale of the Three Jewels* (1994), was released commercially in Tunisia and Jordan. As far as we know, no other Palestinian films ever circulated commercially in Arab countries.[49]

As a consequence of all these limitations, an absurd situation evolved in which Palestinian movies stirred up a lot of interest at international festivals and were shown commercially around the world, but had difficulty in reaching their "target audience" in the West Bank, the Gaza Strip, and Israel proper, as well as their natural national audience in the Arab countries.

Attempts to acquaint the Palestinian audience with its cinema began in the early 1990s. In 1992, the Jerusalem Film Institute in East Jerusalem organized the first festival dedicated to Palestinian movies. Thirty-two films that had been produced since 1980 participated. The festival hosted ten artists, some of whom had their first meeting with the Palestinian audience on that occasion. The movies were screened simultaneously in East Jerusalem and in Nazareth, and some were even shown in Nablus and Gaza. A year later, in 1993, the festival was held for a second time, presenting additional films and dedicated by the Jerusalem Film Institute to alternative Arab cinema. Additional Palestinian movies were shown in the festival. After the Palestinian Authority was established following the Oslo Accords, in 1994, and until the Second *Intifada* broke out in October 2000, similar festivals were held in the West Bank and the Gaza Strip.

At that time, attempts were also made to establish mobile cinema units with the intention of bringing films to the villages and refugee camps. The first unit was initiated by the Jerusalem Film Institute and existed between 1992 and 1995. A second unit was established by the Cinematic Production Center in Ramallah, headed by Rashid Masharawi, and functioned from 1997 until 2000. The unit was closed down with the outbreak of the Second *Intifada*.

As a result of the Oslo Accords, cinemas were reopened in the cities of the West Bank and Gaza Strip, though they were temporarily closed down again with the eruption of the Second *Intifada*. In Gaza, fundamentalist Muslims set the local theater on fire and it has not reopened since. In Ramallah, two movie halls have been erected and play movies on a daily basis; these are mainly commercial films, but some are Palestinian as well. The better-known of the halls is the Kasaba. In Nazareth, a cinematheque was founded and operates to this day.

In recent years, Arab satellite television channels have begun to show more interest in screening Palestinian films and broadcast Khleifi and Masharawi's films from time to time. The satellite broadcasting network, Orbit, owned by Saudi Arabian media tycoons, even participated in the funding of Muhammad Bakri's film *Jenin, Jenin* (2002). Elia Suleiman's *Divine Intervention* (2002) is usually not broadcast to the general public on Arab television yet has appeared in the pay-per-view film list of the home cinema network in the Gulf area.

Directors and their Works

The individualistic nature of the films created by directors of the fourth period was directly influenced by the experiences that shaped each filmmaker's childhood, by the director's personal confrontations with the various Israeli governmental institutions, and by his or her desperate attempts to create films against all odds. In this section, we will explore these life-forming experiences, those childhood memories projected by the directors on to the screen, thus earning their creators local and sometimes international recognition.

Michel Khleifi

Michel Khleifi was born in Nazareth in November 1950. In the mid-1960s, he cultivated an interest in theater, like many other youngsters who perceived it as a means for national cultural activity. Never thinking of cinema as an option, he dreamt of studying theater and television abroad. The date of his flight was set for September 1970, the month that became known as "Black September," when, coincidentally, the Egyptian president, Nasser, died. Anticipating his departure, Khleifi visited Jerusalem and purchased portraits of the adored president. Such portraits were sold on every street corner in East Jerusalem. On his way back to Nazareth, he changed buses in Afula, and there he was stopped and searched by a police officer. The officer found Nasser's portrait, ripped it apart, and beat Khleifi severely, to the encouraging cheers of young Jewish boys of Khleifi's age. The bruise marks and the taste left by the blatant insult followed him when, a few days later, he flew to Belgium to commence his theater and television studies. By 1978, he was already accompanied by a Belgium television crew when shooting a filmed report in the Occupied Territories entitled *The West Bank: the Palestinians' Hope*. Khleifi only shot three reports, including one on Lebanon, before directing his first full-length documentary film, *Fertile Memories* (1980).

Fertile Memories was first screened in the 1980 Carthage film festival for Arab and African films held in Tunisia, where it provoked an overwhelming reaction. It was considered innovative not only by Palestinian standards but also for Arab documentary film in general. It won the prize for the first film (Prix de premiere œuvre) at the Carthage festival, from where it traveled to dozens of other festivals and events, including the Critics' Week of the 1981 Cannes Festival, where it was two votes away from receiving the grand prize, the Golden Camera. Yet, when Khleifi presented his film within the framework of the Solidarity Week with the People of Palestine and Lebanon, held in Cairo during the siege of Beirut in 1982, those attending expressed bewilderment at the fact that Khleifi, who had lived in Brussels since 1970, still held an Israeli passport in addition to his Belgian one.

The Palestinian and Arab audience in Israel had the opportunity to see *Fertile Memories* during special screenings at Bir-Zeit University, in the municipal cultural center in Nazareth, in a number of universities in Israel,[50] and in a few cultural clubs.

His fictional film, *Wedding in Galilee* (1987), was received in a similar ambivalent manner. On the one hand, after winning the PLO film award (Hani Johariya award), it was deemed legitimate by Palestinians; on the other, when it was awarded the Golden Prize at the 1988 Carthage festival, a Tunisian youth in the audience called Khleifi a "Zionist" (Farid, no date: 15). Similar accusations could be heard the following day during a discussion of the film, held in the Iben Khaldon cultural center, in Tunisia's capital.

The ardent debate over whether Palestinian cinema should be recruited in favor of the cause of national unity began with Khleifi's earliest works. In December 1987, the critic Khayria al-Bashalwi in *al-Hasnaa* wrote of *Fertile Memories*:

> This director makes us feel as if the occupation of the Palestinians by the Israelis is a given situation which worries no one. The director frequently compares the person carrying an Israeli passport to the Palestinian whose land has been stolen. He links the two in a rational cold, or lukewarm context, which makes us doubt his ability to take a neutral stand, as the whip of the oppressor rises and falls on his back, and the oppressor's knife sinks into his live flesh.

Khleifi's films have enjoyed popularity and critical acclaim within Palestine, but the debate surrounding them has incessantly returned to the question of his treatment of the Israeli citizen and to his representation of Palestinian society.

> The Arab critics [asserted the *al Hasnaa* journal (M.CH, 1987)] did not conceal their uneasiness with the movie's message of unconditional coexistence with the Israelis within the Occupied Territories, in view of mil-

itaristic oppression forces. The spectators can easily see the contrast between the film *Wedding in Galilee*, which calls for coexistence, and the operation dubbed "Peace for Galilee." That military operation trampled upon the people and the land of southern Lebanon and during that act of aggression, the Israelis, for the first time in the history of their racist country, entered an Arab capital . . . how can there be peace in the Arab Galilee when war, destruction and savagery take place in the Galilee of the occupation?

It is not only the status of the Israelis in Khleifi's films that has provoked harsh reactions among Arab reviewers, but his perception of Palestinian society as well. Samir Farid (no date) summarizes this criticism and objects to it in his book, *The Palestinian Cinema in the Occupied Land*. Writing about the Palestinian journalist, Wassim Abdallah, Farid claims:

Abdallah expresses the viewpoint shared by a group of critics and writers who question Michel Khleifi's integrity. He attacks Khleifi for displaying the ignorance and backwardness of the Palestinian society that is bound by the shackles of tradition rather than sufficing with describing the occupation. According to Abdallah, Khleifi forgets the main Palestinian context of the struggle with the Zionists.

Egyptian reviewers went even further in criticizing Khleifi's film, when it was shown at in the Cannes festival, for not demanding the destruction of Israel (Farid, no date: 21). In contrast, Farid suggests that, precisely because it is produced on occupied land, Khleifi's work expresses true Palestinian resistance.[51] The film was released during the outbreak of the First *Intifada*, and therefore was not shown in the West Bank or in Gaza. It was, however, presented in the Nazareth Community Center, and has reached the Arab audience in Israel through retrospectives of Khleifi's work in cinematheques in Jerusalem, Tel-Aviv, and Haifa.

In fact, when ignoring the complexity and the heterogeneous aspects of Khleifi's films and praising them solely for their contribution to the Palestinian struggle, some of the positive reviews reflect essentially the same outlook as the negative criticism does. Farid applauds *Fertile Memories* for the fact that "woman here is a symbol for the earth and an image of motherhood and rejuvenating fertility" (no date: 11). Abed al-Wahab al Moadeb elaborates: "It is not surprising that Michel Khleifi chose to present a world of women. He did it in order to represent Palestine. He listened to the otherness of the oppressed women in his own society in order to embody his oppressed, helpless nation struggling to survive" (Farid, no date: 54).

Western critics, however, praised the stance taken by the director for determining in the film that the armed struggle to retrieve Arab rights is ineffective and that the solution is in dialogue.

Shohat and Stam (1994) suggest that the women in Khleifi's early films fore-shadow processes which were to become essentially more apparent in the reality of the First *Intifada*, when women went out into the streets and played active roles in the uprising, which led toward symbolic liberation and a change in traditional female roles in society. However, it should not be forgotten that during the era of the *Intifadas*, the voices of Islamic forces also grew louder, including those of resistance movements such as Hamas and Islamic Jihad that rose in opposition to the PLO and Fatah leaderships. Consequently, about a year after the outbreak of the *Intifada*, all the women in the Gaza Strip, except for a handful of objectors, were wearing the traditional *hijab* (head scarf) (Kimmerling and Migdal, 1993). Michel Khleifi reflects both these contradictory facets of women's status in his films.

The favorable reviews overlook the differences between the various kinds of oppression expressed in Khleifi's films. They enlist them all in favor of the united Palestinian struggle: "Michel Khleifi has endeavored to represent [in *Fertile Memories*] all the aspects of the Palestinian personality," says Samir Farid, "and all of those object to the occupation" (no date: 12).

Two elements which reappear in all of Khleifi's films, and which he mentions in reference to his first film, *Fertile Memories*, were not always identified by critics: the blurring of boundaries between fiction and documentation, and concern with the relationship between the oppressors and the oppressed, whether they be Israelis and Palestinians, or different factions within Palestinian society itself.

Elia Suleiman

Elia Suleiman was also born in Nazareth, in 1960, to an engraver father and a schoolteacher mother. When the boy was 14, his father was accused of planning to smuggle arms from Lebanon and arrested on his way to fish off the coast of Giv'at Olga. Three years later Suleiman himself was arrested while walking about the streets of Tel Aviv. The Israeli security forces asked him to sign a statement and confess to belonging to the PLO. Suleiman refused, and some time after the incident he left for London.

> I escaped. I needed to go to a place where I could find myself . . . Nazareth is as confined a place as a little Harlem. I knew that there was a more interesting life somewhere; I knew that not too far from Nazareth, people were living better lives. (private interview with Suleiman, by Alon-Olinik, Tel Aviv, November 1998)

In London, he worked in temporary jobs as a barman and a cook, then flew to France and after a year returned to his parents' home. In Ben-Gurion airport he was once again detained. This time, he was asked what he did in London and whether he had connections with suicide attack and guerilla organizations.

Upon his return to Nazareth, his interest in cinema was sparked. He read books on the topic and shot films on his home video camera. He wanted to make a movie about the Bedouin village of Bir al-Maksur, situated between Nazareth and Shafa 'amr (Shfaram), and received permission from the village's inhabitants to do so, on condition that he would film a wedding that was to be held there. With the tapes, he traveled to a film studio in Jerusalem, barged into the office of producer Micha Shagrir, who was in the middle of a meeting, and announced that he wanted to edit his film but did not have any money. "He looked at me and said: 'Really? Excuse me, but am I supposed to give you an editing studio for free?' " Suleiman relates the event in an interview with Kapra (1998: 60), "and I told him: you stole my country, at least give me this." Suleiman was granted what he asked for and managed to edit 15 minutes of the film, but was not able to raise money for its completion; it was never concluded. Two years later he flew to New York as an illegal immigrant, and settled there for the next twelve years.

In the United States, he became interested in the manner in which Arabs were presented in the Western media in general and the Israeli media in particular. This was also the subject of his first film, *Introduction to the End of an Argument* (1990), which won, among other awards, the prize for best experimental film in the Atlanta Film Festival in 1990. In his second short film, *Homage by Assassination* (1991), he continued to examine the representation of Arabs in the West. In this film, an element which will repeatedly recur in Suleiman's works makes its first appearance – the director himself is the protagonist of the movie, not as an actor as in Jacques Tati's films, for example, but as an observer; through his viewpoint, the reality of the film unfolds. The on-screen persona, referred to as E. S., has developed and matured in Suleiman's two fictional films, *Chronicle of a Disappearance* (1996) and *Divine Intervention* (2002).

E. S. is a silent, expressionless observer who does not open his mouth from start to finish. It seems that events render him mute and wipe the expression off his face. There is a close resemblance between this figure and a politicized cartoon character created by caricaturist Naji al-Ali, a refugee from Galilee who grew up in the Ein-el-Hilweh refugee camp in Lebanon. Al-Ali was a leading Palestinian political satirist and was murdered in London in the late 1980s. The character he created, Handala,[52] is a Palestinian child raised in the refugee camps. Handala observes the events delineated in the caricatures with great astonishment, which is expressed even though his face is not seen. In the caricatures, Handala represents the caricaturist himself, just as in Suleiman's films, E. S. represents the director.[53]

The fate of Elia Suleiman's *Chronicle of a Disappearance* was harsher than that of Khleifi's films. The film was reproached for being sponsored by the Israeli Fund for Quality Films (Ibrahim, 2000), and was boycotted, in fact, by the whole Arab world and by critics who accused the director of treason,

Zionism, and cooperation with the enemy (Bourlond, [1999] 2000). The main cause for the boycott was a very ironic scene in which the director's parents are seen sound asleep, while on the television screen the Israeli flag flutters and the Israeli national anthem, *Hatikva*, is heard. The critics claimed that waving the Israeli flag in Palestinian cinema is a "form of submission" (Kelly, 2002). "The problem is not only that the Palestinian director is making an Israeli film," Samir Farid claims, "but that he has received support from the Israeli government" (no date: 78).

Elia Suleiman explains these critical views, when referring to his film *Chronicle of a Disappearance*, thus:

> There is a fear of anything perceived as destabilizing in a period when unity is considered essential. A large portion of the Palestinian audience waits for the meaning to be immediately obvious. When they critique a movie, they actually evaluate in terms of its being good or bad for the Palestinians. (Bourlond, [1999] 2000: 100)

In Israel, the movie was received with mixed reactions. According to Suleiman, Israeli television's Channel One refused to air it, claiming that it might be too difficult for the public to swallow (Haluzin-Dovrat, 1999). It received warm praise, however, from the reviewers of the International Film Festival in Jerusalem in 1997, and enjoyed a long run in the cinematheques. "Yet," Suleiman qualifies the success, "this section of the public is generally left-wing and liberal" (Erickson, 2003). The movie was not commercially released, since "no distributor wanted the movie. If not because of financial reasons, then why? It was not because they didn't like it . . . it had been playing for months in Paris already, but not here. I think this question is an interesting one" (Haluzin-Dovrat, 1999: 7).

Divine Intervention (2002) was filmed under extremely difficult production conditions. When Suleiman and his crew arrived to film in Ramallah, they discovered that the Israeli army had preceded them. The entrance to the structure where the movie theater was located had been bombed, the cash registers had been robbed, and the Dolby stereo system had been stolen (Brooks, 2003). Many scenes were shot in hit-and-run style, literally meaning a quick shot followed by a hasty flight back to the production vehicle. As Suleiman recalls,

> It was very difficult. As soon as the authorities understood that you were a Palestinian and that the M16 rifles that the actors were carrying were real, then forget about it. East Jerusalem was problematic to shoot in and Nazareth even more so, with all the unrest there. In every place where we began shooting, they began shooting. (Brooks, 2003)

One of the key scenes in the movie, the detonation of the Israeli tank with a peach pit, was filmed in an out-of-the-way alley in France.

Many of the actors and production crew members were Israelis, including the producer Avi Klienberger, a fact that often facilitated production. In an interview given to Jason Wood (2003), Suleiman relates how he cast Israeli actors for the part of soldiers in a roadblock:

> The casting was done in Tel-Aviv, and naturally I wanted Israelis who served in the army. Most of the people I met with were not actors. They were extras and not actors. I asked those who auditioned for the parts whether they had served in roadblocks and if they had experience with weapons. The audition had the air of an interrogation when I began asking whether they had only checked ID cards or whether they had also hurt people and used their guns. Some had done so and were ashamed to tell me of the brutal things they had done, because they wanted the part, while others exaggerated in their accounts, also because they wished to get the part. I was a little sadistic in the examination of their moral background. (Wood, 2003)

Divine Intervention won the Judge's Choice Award in the 2002 Cannes Festival, the second most important prize after the Golden Palm. It was received with enthusiasm by the Palestinian public, and secured Suleiman's position as one of the top Palestinian directors.

Rashid Masharawi

Rashid Masharawi was born in 1962, to a family of refugees from Jaffa, and was raised in the Shati refugee camp in the Gaza Strip. At the age of twelve he moved to Tel Aviv in order to help support the family of seven siblings, after his father was struck by diabetes. He worked as a construction worker, as a waiter, and at washing dishes. Once in a while, he painted and sculpted as a hobby. At the age of nineteen, he had already directed his first short film, only four minutes long: *Partners* (1981). The partners in question are an Arab from Jaffa who drives a garbage truck, and a Jewish man whose job is to indicate to the driver where to stop. Their partnership, however, ends there. Masharawi directed his next short film, *Passport* (1986), at the age of twenty-five. Ied (Salim Daw) and Mona (Eti Ankri) are a married couple who get stuck one night on a bridge which is a crossing point between Israel and Jordan, without being able to cross in either direction since the man has lost his passport. Masharawi chooses to have his protagonist step on a mine at the end of the movie. Similarly, in his short comical movie, *The Magician* (1992), he elects to have the Palestinian vanish. A conjurer walks into a restaurant and makes the Palestinian worker disappear as if he had been never there. When he tries to bring the Palestinian back, the magic does not work, and in his place appears a young violin-playing Russian, who refuses to wash the dishes.

Between films, Masharawi earned a living by building sets in the Israeli film industry, working on *Behind Bars*, *Rage and Glory*, *Sahara*, *Alex is Madly in Love*, *The Dreamers*, and other movies, including the Palestinian film, *Wedding in Galilee*. He also participated as an actor in the film *Afflicted* (1982).

Masharawi's films have been internationally acknowledged. *Curfew* (1993) was screened during Critics' Week at the Cannes Festival and won several prizes, the most distinguished of which was first place at the 1994 Cairo International Film Festival. *Haifa* (1995) was screened as a 1995 Cannes Festival "official choice,"[54] and British television invited Masharawi to direct documentary films.

Masharawi received recognition from the Israeli Film Institute as well, and the Jerusalem International Film Festival has screened his work. Despite this honor, however, the whole time that Masharawi resided in Tel Aviv, he was living there illegally. His only way of entering Israel proper (within the 1967 borders) during the 1990s was through an agreement he had with a food supplier from Gaza, from whom he received a permit which authorized stays within Israel from four o'clock in the morning until seven in the evening (Levi, 1991). When his film, *The Shelter* (1989), won first prize at the International Film Festival in Jerusalem in 1990, his producer announced that, "Rashid could not make it, to his deep regret, because of the curfew in Gaza" (ibid. 46). Actually, Masharawi was in Tel Aviv and not in Gaza at the time, but the reason for his absence was the delay in receiving permission to enter Israeli territory.

Although he lived in Tel Aviv for many years, the most profound experience shaping his cinematic vision was daily life in the refugee camp. In his films, he depicts the everyday struggle for survival of the camp inhabitants, an endeavor, starting from the moment of relocation from their village homes to the refugee camps, which takes place in a gradually diminishing space.[55]

In 1993, Masharawi moved to the Netherlands, where he lived for three years. There he collaborated with the Palestinian director, Hani Abu-Assad, in establishing a production company called Ailul Films. In order to produce two movies, Ailul Films cooperated with Arkus Films, a Dutch production company. In 1996, Masharawi relocated to Ramallah and founded the Cinematic Production Center there, as well as initiating a mobile film unit. He attempted to produce local films while cultivating Palestinian technical and production crews, in order to lessen dependency on foreign film crews and consequently reduce production costs, thus limiting dependency on foreign funding. A number of films were produced within this framework, including the medium-length feature film, *Rabab* (1997). The enterprise, however, was not successful and Masharawi soon renewed the employment of foreign crews and financial resources, especially European ones.[56] His films, including the documentaries, are not explicitly political or social, but focus on the characters' incessant existential battles.

The movie critic, Samir Farid, has compared Rashid Masharawi's œuvre with Michel Khleifi's; just as Khleifi began a new era of original Palestinian cinema that differed greatly from the documentary works of the Palestinian organizations, so Masharawi inaugurated a new epoch of films made within the Occupied Territories by exclusively Palestinian production crews. For that reason, Farid considers Masharawi's film *Curfew* to be the first Palestinian movie. *Curfew* won the Golden Prize in the 1993 Cairo Festival, and was screened during Critics' Week in the Cannes Festival of 1994.

Ali Nassar

Ali Nassar was born in the village of Arrabeh in 1954, the sixth son of twelve children in a family of peasants. His future was predetermined – he was to cultivate the family's plot of land. According to Nassar, what altered his childhood and the rest of his life was a television set, the only one in the Arabe village of the 1960s, belonging to a man called Abed al-Farid. Those who wished to watch programs on the magic box bought tickets, drinks, and snacks, and gathered in the improvised theater of al-Farid's porch. Whether showing Egyptian movies or Lebanese operettas, the magic box took eight-year-old Nassar away from life under a military government, and far from the family's fields. He had no money for tickets, but al-Farid, who noticed the passion in the little boy's eyes, allowed him to sneak in without paying.

Nassar was so influenced by television that it inspired him to put on plays for himself. Every morning, as he walked out to the family plot in the Battof (Beit Netufa) valley, an hour from the village, he would compose monologues in his head and roll around in the dirt, hoping that the antenna would detect him and that he would be transmitted on the television screen. The road that led from the village to the fields, the same road where he dramatized and acted his little plays, was called by the villagers Darbo-t-Tabbanat, the Arabic name of his second film, *The Milky Way* (Becker, 1999).

Nassar's love for the cinema continued beyond the experience on al-Farid's porch. He spent the weekly allowance that he received from his mother on movies, and when he had seen all those available in his village he went to Acre, to search for yet more films. In 1975, his dream came true and he received a scholarship for academic studies in Moscow from the Communist Party. When he notified his family of his intention to use the scholarship in order to study cinema, they were furious. Cinema does not guarantee a livelihood, they asserted, and demanded that he study law, medicine, or engineering. In 1981, he completed his second degree in cinema and television studies and returned to Israel. By then, his parents were no longer living.

Nassar was the owner of a video studio that filmed weddings; he founded an acting school; for three years he worked as a photographer for the DFPE (Democratic Front for Peace and Equality) party newspaper, *al-Al Ittihad*; and he directed the Arabe theater company, Ein el-Balad (The Village Spring), putting on three plays. Using the original play, *The Fool*, as a foundation, he later wrote the screenplay for his second feature film, *The Milky Way* (1997).

His first film, *The Story of a Coastal Town* (1983), was a political work made on a meager budget in the Ajami neighborhood in Jaffa, which had lost its splendor and turned into a poverty-stricken suburb of the city of Tel Aviv. The film was not released to the public. That was also the fate of his second movie, *The Wet Nurse* (1994), which was shot in Romania and left him heavily in debt. This film was shelved for many years. At a certain stage, Nassar managed to complete it, but the film was aired only once, at the Arabe village soccer field: "There just isn't a movie theater in the village," he explains (Karni, 2003).

His movie, *The Milky Way*, was financed, as Suleiman's first feature film was, by the Israeli Fund for Quality Films and played at various art-house theaters for a long time, which constitutes a relative success. When shown to Arab and Palestinian audiences, the film was received with slanderous accusations similar to the ones hurled at Khleifi and Suleiman. The Tunisian Ministry of Culture, for instance, refused to distribute *The Milky Way* because the director was Israeli. The left-wing Egyptian opposition newspaper, *al-Ahali*, moreover, claimed that the film "smelled of Israeli money," and accused the director of selling out on the Palestinian problem for a fistful of shekels which he received from the Israeli government (Becker, 1999). Nassar remembers the mixed reviews thus:

> Many told me that I took them back 30 years and made them relive the era of the military government. I played the film in Nazareth, after which people there told me that they felt that I had stuck a knife in their hearts. Others claimed that I showed the situation in an overly mollifying manner, and were angry because of that. (Timen, 1999).

His last film, *In the Ninth Month* (2002), was nominated for seven Israeli Oscars, but did not take a single prize. It was presented at the Jerusalem Film Festival, and Nassar refused to receive the "consolation prize" that was offered him – the Judge's Decision Award. He was enraged:

> Any Arab-Israeli film, good as it may be, does not stand a chance in the Oscar festivities. The Israeli Oscar is not only about cinema. It's Ali Nassar against an Ashkenazi Jew from Tel Aviv. There is a racist atmosphere here, and as long as it exists, Ali Nassar, the Palestinian director, won't receive any award. (Karni, 2003).

Hani Abu-Assad

Hani Abu-Assad was born in Nazareth in 1961. His father claims to have built Tel Aviv: "Even before Israel was established he owned a company and a factory for manufacturing and retailing cement in Nazareth, and later also a distribution company that transported the construction material to Tel Aviv" (Fynero, 2002: 51). A great part of the boy's childhood in Nazareth was passed in the local movie theater, overlooking his home. "There was nothing to do there except go to the movies. I would spend the whole week in the Diana Theater, where a huge drugstore now stands" (Fynero, 2002: 51). He recalls his first visit to the cinema, which ignited the magic:

> I didn't know what to expect, but the moment it became dark, and the huge screen glared in front of me, I saw the horses coming out of the camera. I was sure that they were really coming at us. I was so frightened I hid under the seat, until my uncle crawled down beside me and promised me that the horses had gone.

He later went to look for the horses in the rear section of the theater: "To this day I don't always understand where they really come from" (Fishbein, 2003: 56).

When Abu-Assad was twenty, he decided to study abroad. He took up aeronautics and settled down in the Netherlands, where he worked as an aircraft engineer. Upon returning to Nazareth, Abu-Assad met Rashid Masharawi, with whom he established the Ailul Films production company in 1990. Abu-Assad served as assistant director on Masharawi's documentary film, *Daro-w-Dour* (*House-Houses*, 1991), and produced Masharawi's films, *Long Days in Gaza* (1991) and *Curfew* (1993). At that time he also began directing. In 1991, he made a short documentary called *To Whom it May Concern*, which examines the reasons for the pro-Iraqi inclinations of the Palestinian citizens of Israel. In 1992 he directed a short film called *Paper House*, about a child who, after the army has demolished his home, dreams of building a house made of paper. He does indeed construct it, but then his angry mother destroys it. Abu-Assad reflects,

> Half an hour, one hundred percent pure fiction, about an experience I had as a boy. I had built a house, and my mother thought that it was dangerously put together so she wrecked it. Even back then she didn't trust me as an engineer. She understood herself that I was better at storytelling. (Fishbein, 2003: 57)

From the moment he had decided that his real calling was as a filmmaker, he returned to the Netherlands and sneaked into film classes in one of the colleges, without paying and without sitting the exams. His first fictional film was written in collaboration with a Jewish-Dutch writer by the name of Arnon Gromberg. The movie, *The Fourteenth*, was crowned by some critics as "the worst film ever made" (Fishbein, 2003).

Like Khleifi, Abu-Assad tends to blur the boundaries between the documentary and the fictional in his films. In 2000, he returned to his native city and made the film *Nazareth 2000*, which describes the rift in the city's population following disputes over the construction of a mosque in close proximity to the Church of the Annunciation. The film, which has the semblance of a documentary, is in fact staged. Even the interviews with public figures from both sides were scripted. Adaniya Shibli, a young writer who produced the script and dialogues, assisted Abu-Assad. The lead roles in the movie, those of two workers in a Nazareth gas station discussing events in the city, were given to people who had never acted before.

His two most important films, *Ford Transit* (2002) and *Rana's Wedding* (2003), are concerned with roadblocks.[57] In a telephone interview he gave to Anthony Kaufman during the Sundance Festival, Abu-Assad said: "When I go to Park City, I am a filmmaker. A car waits to pick me up at the airport. But when I arrive in Israel, I need to stand in line for 3 or 4 hours in the sun just to arrive at my destination. You turn into a dog. Even a dog has more rights" (Kaufman, 2003).

Roadblocks for Abu-Assad are not just a symbol of the occupation, but an actual, tangible obstacle that stood in his way when he was directing *Rana's Wedding*. The production caused a commotion on the very first day of filming, when a border patrol unit passed by the set and detected Palestinians wearing the uniforms of border guards and carrying weapons, which they had obtained from the G. G. Film Studios. The border guard commander was called to the set and only after some hours did the Israeli defense forces realize that it was just a film being shot. In the mean time, the real border guard soldiers fixed the actors' uniforms, and one of the soldiers even scolded a Palestinian actor whose shoes were not properly polished (Fishbein, 2003).

The movie was mostly shot in East Jerusalem and Ramallah during the Second *Intifada*, when entry to the Occupied Territories was restricted and the production team was not allowed to enter with private vehicles. Abu-Assad insisted on filming in an authentic location, and therefore the crew was obliged to enter the area riding Ford Transits, the vehicles that Palestinian workers use when going to work in Israel. Abu-Assad declared in interviews that the character of the driver, Rajai, inspired his next film, *Ford Transit* (2002). "He was a superman. He always said, 'no problem.' Even when we were getting shot at, he would say, 'no problem' " (Kaufman, 2003). Since the interview, the film has been released, was nominated for an Academy Award, and has been subject to controversy and discussion.

Ford Transit is a documentary that follows Rajai, a transit driver who transports Palestinian day laborers from the Palestinian Authority territories to Israel and back. However, in August 2003, Abu-Assad revealed in an interview to Goel Pinto from *Ha'aretz* that, in fact, his film includes more than a few staged scenes. The revelation that the protagonist, the transit driver, is actually an Arab news station cameraman who had acted in one of Abu-Assad's previous films,[58] provoked controversy among Israeli filmmakers, in academe, and in the press. In the same interview, he confesses that one of the most important scenes in the movie, in which an Israeli soldier in uniform stops the transit driver and beats him up, is staged.

> I wanted the confusion to be a part of the cinematic narrative [he proclaimed in a discussion about his movie in the Tel Aviv cinematheque (Yudlevich, 2003)]. I wished the audience to think that it looked like a documentary film, but to feel uncertain about it. Like a magician who doesn't reveal his tricks, I didn't disclose mine, but I never deliberately concealed them either. I'm not the first to have blended the documentary genre with fiction, but for some reason people believe that when a director uses documentary style he needs to adhere to the truth. I didn't make up events that never happened; the scenes in the movie happen every day. I define the film as being both one hundred percent fiction and one hundred percent documentary.

Rana's Wedding was entered in the 2002 Cannes Festival as part of the prestigious Critics' Week, during which seven films, chosen out of hundreds by the French Critics' Union, are shown. This led to Abu-Assad's acceptance, together with the Israeli director, Dror Shaul, into a respected directing workshop at the Sundance Festival. *Ford Transit* won the Spirit of Freedom prize for best documentary film of 2003 at the International Film Festival in Jerusalem. Several months earlier, it was screened at the Canadian Hotdocs and the Dutch Idfa, two of the most important documentary film festivals in the world, with great success.

In an interview with Einat Fishbein, Abu-Assad reveals that he intends to direct two new films. The first is a joint Israeli-Palestinian film co-directed by Dror Shaul and produced by an American company. The second is a full-length feature film, *Paradise Now*, which would focus on suicide bombers and do for their image what the Mafia movies did for the image of the gangsters: "I believe that they are victims, of themselves and of the society in which they live," he claims (Fishbein, 2003: 58).

Nizar Hassan

The paramount Palestinian documentary film director of our time is Nizar Hassan. He was born in 1960 in the village of Mashad in the Nazareth area. Following a series of minor works at the beginning of the 1990s, he made his first important film, *Independence* (*Istiklal*) (1994), in which he returns to his

native village to reveal how the Israeli Independence Day was initially celebrated by the Palestinians after the founding of the state. These reminiscences
document contemporary life in the villages, including the various survival
mechanisms used in the face of a determined and sophisticated regime. These
personal testimonies, which add a layer to Palestinian history and to the collective memory, display the Arabs' need to imitate the hegemonic Israeli discourse. Examples of the survival strategies include the case of the head of the
village council, who has completely internalized and embraced Israeli culture,
bragging to Hassan about his distinguished position in Israeli society and the
free access that he has to the leaders of the country. Another strategy is demonstrated by people who have adopted Israeli identity through lack of choice
while secretly preserving their own identity. Finally, there are those who parody
the emulation of Israelis and the adoption of their identity, such as the director's friend who shows up in class wearing a skullcap.[59]

Hassan's second film, *Jasmine* (1996), deals with the position of women in
the Palestinian family and society, an issue which has become central in
Palestinian cinema after Khleifi's *Fertile Memories*. Hassan chose to focus on a
controversial topic, murder for reasons of "family honor." The central plot
revolves around an interview with Yasmin, who is incarcerated for being an
accomplice to the murder of her younger sister, a woman who has "disgraced
the family." Hassan interviews religious authorities, public leaders, students,
common people, and even members of, his own family, confronting them all
with bold, penetrating questions concerning women's status in Palestinian
society. At the end of the film, however, Hassan entraps himself in a web of his
own design, when his sister, a university student, turns the tables, accusing him
of maltreating the women in the family.

In *Myth* (*Austoria*) (1998), he follows the fate of a family from the village of
Saffouria near Nazareth, where the Jewish settlement of Tzipori was built after
the village had been destroyed in 1948. The family members were separated
from one another and Hassan's camera wanders to Jordan, Lebanon, and
Germany in order to meet them all. The camera dwells mostly on two men who
were separated in their childhood, Mahmud and Salim. Mahmud was raised in
Lebanon, fought the Israelis, and was pursued by them for the death of an Israeli
soldier in Lebanon in 1982. Eventually, he left Lebanon and settled in Germany,
becoming a film director. Salim was raised in Israel, studied in Jewish schools,
and developed relationships as a friend and colleague with Jews, keeping in
touch the whole time with his disowned and divided family. The contradictions
in his life turn him into an introverted and taciturn person, similar to the characters of the survivors in *Independence* (*Istiklal*) (1994) and in Emile Habibi's
short novel, *The Pessoptimist* (1974), a type that gains prominence in the
Palestinian literary and cinematic quest for self-discovery in Israel.

In his film *Cut* (2000), the director attempts to reverse the order of things, and instead of being represented by the Other, he tries to be the one who represents the Other. The film delineates a long-term feud between two "clans" of Jewish settlers in one of the settlements on the northern border of Israel. This is the first work by a Palestinian director that deals exclusively with Jewish people.

May Masri

During the period under discussion, other young Palestinian directors have begun working alongside the more eminent filmmakers. Among them is the documentary filmmaker, May Masri, who focuses mostly on social and political issues, mainly pertaining to children. She was born in Amman in 1959 into a grand old family, originally from Nablus. She studied film in the San Francisco University film department, and after completing her studies moved to Lebanon, where she met and married Jean Sham'oun, a Lebanese director who worked in Palestinian cinema during the Beirut period. Masri directed, shot, and produced several films with her husband, including *Beneath the Ruins* (1982), filmed in the decimated landscape of Beirut that was the result of the 1982 war; *The Generation of the War* (1986); and *Suspended Dreams* (1992), which deals with the situation in Lebanon during and after the 1973–90 civil war. Her first independent film endeavor, *Children of the Mountain of Fire* (1990), is concerned with the psychological and social problems of the children of Nablus during the First *Intifada* between 1987 and 1994. She later produced *Hanan Ashrawi: A Woman in the Era of Conflict* (1995), about the Palestinian politician and academic who has been considered one of the leading and best-known Palestinian spokeswomen since the Madrid Conference in 1992. Later on, Masri made *The Children of Shatila* (1998) and *Borders of Dreams and Fears* (2001).

Subhi a-Zubeidi

Subhi a-Zubeidi was born in Jerusalem in 1961, to a family of refugees from the Lod area. At an early age, his family moved to the refugee camp of Jalazun, north of Ramallah. In 1985, he went to the United States to study for a second degree in cinema at New York University, and upon his return in 1994 began making films. In his first, *My Very Private Map* (1998a), a-Zubeidi tries to examine the two themes of which his world, as a second-generation refugee, is composed: the memory bequeathed by the first generation of refugees, and his own memory of the people he knew and the places where he was raised. By way of interviews with two elders, one who has left and another who has remained in Jaffa, a-Zubeidi attempts to analyze the reasons for leaving and what would have happened had the Palestinian people stayed. He reflects on the camp, a place of childhood and of exile, declaring that "the only good memory left of it is the solidarity and the compassion that its inhabitants showed one another." The little camps grew and turned into slums on the outskirts of the cities, according to him, and the proposed peace threatened to freeze them as they were and turn them into "monuments of Palestinian despair" (private interview with Subhi a-Zubeidi, Ramallah, 2003). In the film *Ali and his Friends* (1999), a-Zubeidi returns to the camp, this time to examine the dreams of the third generation that grew up there.

Azza al-Hassan

Azza al-Hassan was born in 1971 in Amman, to a family originally from Haifa. Her father is one of the historical leaders of Fatah. She grew up in Beirut, studied in Scotland, and has moved back and forth between Cairo and Amman. Only after the Oslo Accords was she allowed to return to her native land, and when she graduated from her film studies she settled down in Ramallah. She produced films on very small budgets, shooting some of them herself without the help of any crew members. Her film *Kushan Musa* (*Kushan* meaning land settlement registration) (1998) scrutinizes Jewish settlements; *Women Talking* (1996) and *She, the Sindibad* (1999) have to do with women in Palestinian villages; and *News Time* (2001) explores the Second *Intifada*. Her next film, *Forgotten Images* (2004), delineates the quest for the Palestinian film archive, lost in Beirut after the departure of the PLO in 1982, while examining how the Palestinians' self-image has changed since the revolution.

Liana Badr

Writer and filmmaker Liana Badr was born in Jericho in 1952. The father of the family was a well-known doctor and astronomer. In 1967, the family uprooted and moved to Amman. "Father thought it would only be for a few days, but it transpired that he never got to see Jerusalem again. He died in exile," she recollects in a private interview (Ramallah, 2003). Since then, the family has traveled through different countries. Badr began studying sociology in Amman, dropped out of school in 1971, moved to Beirut, and completed a second degree in psychology. In Beirut she joined the PLO and married Yasser Abed Rabbu, a refugee from Jaffa who became the number two man in the DFLP. During this period, she sometimes worked as a journalist and sometimes as a teacher, showed a lot of interest in refugees, and taught illiterate women in the refugee camps of Beirut. She relocated several times, moving from one country to another because of her husband's career until, after the Oslo Accords, they settled in the Occupied Territories, where Abed Rabbu became the first Palestinian Minister of Culture.

Badr has written four novels, six children's books, four collections of short stories, and one volume of poetry. In 1999, she began directing documentary films, including *Fadwa* (1999), *Zaytounat* (2002), and *The Green Bird* (2002). Hani Abu-Assad's film, *Rana's Wedding* (2002), is based on a semi-autobiographical novel that Bader wrote.

Abed a-Salam Shehada

Abed a-Salam Shehada was born in 1961 and raised in the Rafah refugee camp, by a family whose origins lie in the Barbara village near Askalan (Ashqelon). He discovered cinema after becoming involved in a joint project of the Al-Quds Television Production Company and Britain's Channel 4, in 1992. The project involved three young Palestinians, who documented their daily lives during the First *Intifada*. The film they made, *Palestinian Diaries* (1991), was aired in Britain on Channel 4 and was later distributed to other channels and participated in international festivals. Since then, Shehada has been working as a news cameraman for international television stations and continues to make documentary films, almost all of them focusing on social issues. *Small Hands* (1996) deals with child labor; *Close to Death* (1997) tells the tale of a large Palestinian family that lives close to the Neve Dekalim settlement; *Women's Rights, Human Rights* (1995) documents the condition of women, including battered wives, in Gaza; *The Shadow* (2000) looks into the escapism that Palestinians find in superstitious beliefs, such as healing through the Koran and exorcism rituals; and *The Cane* (2000) depicts discrimination against girls in Palestinian families.

Hana Elias

Hana Elias was born in the village of al-Jish in Upper Galilee. He studied film at the University of California at Los Angeles. In 1991, he wrote and directed a short, fictional film called *The Mountain*, which won the best short fictional film award in the Arab Cinema Biennial in France in 1992.

Conclusion

Despite the prolonged occupation and the fact that the Palestinian establishment ignored the power of cinema as a propaganda tool, Palestinian creativity has not dried up. That creativity bore its early fruits in the 1980s and has been continually flowing at an accelerated rate. Although they suffered from lack of support and funding at home, Palestinian directors have depicted a complex Palestinian society and have been successfully represented at major international festivals where, thanks to their films, the Palestinian voice has been heard. At a time when the national reality seems to overshadow all else, some of the directors of the fourth period have succeeded in articulating personal stories as well.[60] The road paved by Michel Khleifi with *Fertile Memories* still guides Palestinian cinema, even if national and personal living conditions do not always make a walk along it easy.

NOTES

1. As a result of the "Black September" events. For further explanation, see footnote 42.

2. Examples are Kaise a-Zubeidi's films, *Palestine, the Chronicle of a People* (1984) and *Barbed-Wire Homeland* (1982).
3. Hawal headed the Cinema Department of the Popular Front for the Liberation of Palestine (PFLP).
4. We shall base our findings mostly on Hassan Abu Gh'nima's book, *Palestine and the Cinematic Eye* (1981), and on Adnan Mdanat, in *The Palestinian Encyclopedia* (1990).
5. The folk and religious Nabi Rubin festival (Mawsim), celebrated to the south of Jaffa every year in August, is similar to the Nabi Musa festivals at the Western Wall. The pilgrimages to Nabi Musa's tomb and the attendant festivities have become a tradition and are celebrated with different social and cultural activities.
6. Such a custom still existed until recently, in Jordan, where the King's portrait is projected while the national anthem is played in the background.
7. Contrary to the Palestinian national movement, the Zionist movement utilized the new medium effectively as a tool for disseminating ideas about the national cause. By 1911, Morey Rosenberg, a member of the Zionist movement, had already filmed a movie by the name of *The First Movie of Palestine 1911*. This 20 minute film composed of two parts: the first dedicated to Jerusalem, the second to the rest of the country. It remains unclear whether the Zionist movement had funded production of the movie, but it became immensely successful throughout the Jewish world before the First World War (Tzimerman, 2001). It was screened during the tenth Zionist congress, in Basel, and was distributed in the USA, the USSR, Germany, Holland, and South Africa (Gross and Gross, 1991). More movies had begun to be made in the same fashion: see the films of Yaacov Ben Dov, considered the founding father of Hebrew cinema, and films that were funded by the Jewish organizations, Keren Kayement and Keren Ha-Yesod.
8. No reviews, film schedules' or recommendations were offered.
9. Najeeb Nassar's *Al-Carmel* was one of the first journals in Palestine to be published in Arabic after the fall of Sultan Abed al-Hamid the Second and the reinstatement of the Ottoman constitution and the freedom of creation and publication in 1909.
10. The Great Arab Rebellion, as Arabs called it, or the Riots, as Jews referred to the events, took place between the years 1936 and 1939. It began as a general strike of Arab merchants and quickly turned to guerrilla attacks against Jewish settlements, quarters, and transportation routes, ultimately assuming the form of an all-out rebellion against the Jewish population and British rule. Heading the rebellion was the Supreme Arab Congress, led by the Mufti, Haj Amin al-Hussaini (Shimoni, 1988: 47). The Rebellion is considered an important landmark in Palestinian history, and the *Intifada*, which was to break out fifty years later, was consciously compared to it (Kimmerling and Migdal, 1993).
11. Both in "school theater" and that affiliated to social and cultural institutions.
12. Who conquered Andalusia.
13. The reference might be to Ahmad Pasha al jazzar, the Ottoman governor who succeeded in warding off Napoleon Bonaparte's troops.
14. They were mostly auditoria suitable for the performance of plays, and many Palestinian theater productions were indeed performed in them as well. Two such halls are the Eden Theatre in Jerusalem and the Alhamraa (Alhambra) Theatre in Jaffa.
15. After the Great Arab Rebellion of 1936–9, for instance.
16. Hebrew moving pictures of those years did not document battles. Yet people associated with the industry were still harassed by the censors using the Moving Pictures Act. Censorship demanded that almost all allusion to the conflict or to the Arab population be pulled. The British claimed, for instance, that the film *Zabar* (Ford,

1933) was anti-Arab, and banned its presentation to the public. During the 1930s, several months before the Great Arab Rebellion, the censors restricted the Hebrew daily newsreels, *The Carmel Chronicles*, insisting on removing sections that did not relate to Arabs at all, such as the opening of Assuta Hospital and the Tel Aviv municipal elections. For an elaboration of the issue of mandatory restrictions and of Hebrew cinema, see Tzimerman (2001).

17. Faruk's government in Egypt, for example, was one such corrupt regime.

18. Such negotiations were held, for instance, by Jordan under the rule of Abdallah the First.

19. The battle of al-Karama (21, March 1968) began as a large-scale Israeli retaliatory act against Fatah bases in the Jordan Valley. The Israeli Defense Force (IDF) attacked with armored forces and carried out airborne strikes on the village, where Yasser Arafat's headquarters and the high command of Fatah were located. The battle caused both sides heavy losses; 128 Palestinian fighters and 28 Israeli soldiers were killed. Yet this was perceived as the first Palestinian victory, and brought the Palestinian resistance organizations to the world's attention.

20. The plan was also rejected by Israel, as well as by the Arab nations and the Russians who claimed it was pro-Israeli.

21. The "Black September" events occurred in 1970 in Jordan. The tension between the *fedayeen* and the resistance organizations based in Jordanian territory, on the one hand, and King Hussein, on the other, intensified as a consequence of the latter's support of the American peace proposal. On 16 September, the King announced a military state of emergency, and sent the Jordanian army to attack the concentrations of *fedayeen* in Amman and the refugee camps. Many civilians were killed in these attacks, and the Jordanian army succeeded in deporting the PLO from Jordan (Shimoni, 1988).

22. In fact, the group continued without Mirsal, who had had an accident in Jordan in 1969 and became partially disabled. She passed away in Amman in 2002. Johariya moved only in 1976 to Beirut, where he was killed.

23. The film preserves source literary characteristics but, unlike the book, depicts its characters in a rather shallow and naive manner and suffers from an oppressively slow tempo. For more on this film, see Chapter 2, "From Bleeding Memories to Fertile Memories."

24. The Fatah organization has perceived itself as the representative of the entire Palestinian population. Consequently, it has accommodated a broad range of ideologies, from the religious right to the Marxist left. The extent to which this or some other faction was dominant changed over the course of time. During most of the 1970s, the ruling ideology, at least as far as terminology is concerned, was the nationalist Marxist line. This was only natural as during those years the allies of the Palestinian national movement were the USSR, Third World liberation movements, and Arab states such as Algeria, Iraq, Syria and South Yemen, which were led by the nationalist left. Other organizations, the Democratic Front and the Popular Front, for instance, were self-declared Marxists.

25. Western movies concerned with the Palestinian question included, for example, Johan van der Keuken's *The Palestinians* (1975), Vanessa Redgrave's *The Palestinian* (1978), Costa Gavras's *Hanna K.* (1983), and even a film by an Israeli director by the name of Mario Offenberg, *The Fight for Land or Palestine within Israel*, awarded a PLO prize in 1977.

26. This discourse is discussed extensively in Hennebelle and Khayati (1977), Abu Gh'nima (1981), Mdanat (1990), and Jibril (1985), and is reflected in documents concerning the nature of revolutionary cinema and the role of Palestinian cinema, such as the report on the Palestinian delegation in Tashkent, which is quoted above.

Furthermore, Palestinian publications published articles by Western filmmakers perceived as progressive, such as the Bolivian director George Senins (1978).

27. It should be noted that most of the important directors within Palestinian Revolutionary Cinema were not Palestinians themselves. Except for the Palestinians Mustafa Abu-Ali, Ghaleb Sha'ath, and Isma'il Shammut, the important figures were Kaise a-Zubeidi, Kassem Hawal, and Samir Nimer from Iraq, Adnan Mdanat from Jordan, Muhammad Malas from Syria, and Jean Sham'oun, Rafik Hajar, and Randa Shahhal from Lebanon, amongst others. For more on this, see Gh'nima (1981) and Mdanat (1990).

28. By contrast, journalism and poetry, which are not expensive, thrived during this period.

29. See footnote 4 above.

30. The Lebanese Civil War broke out in 1975 and continued until 1991. It began as a violent clash between the Falangas and the PLO-Fatah in Beirut, and rapidly turned into all-out civil war. As a result of the continued fighting, the Lebanese army disintegrated and Syria gradually took over Lebanon, except for a small security zone which Israeli forces conquered during the Lebanon War of 1982 (Shimoni, 1999; Kimmerling and Migdal, 1993).

31. Samed performed functions corresponding to those of the Ministry of Social Affairs.

32. The Lebanese Civil War evolved into a war that focused on land dispute. Each side attempted to reinforce its control over those areas of Lebanon where it reigned. The battle over territory included the destruction of "enclaves" of the opposing side, among them Tel a-Za'tar, a Palestinian refugee camp in eastern Beirut. Right-wing Christian militias in Lebanon besieged the camp, which resulted in the massacre of its inhabitants. This led to the involvement of Fatah in the Lebanese Civil War (Shimoni, 1999; Kimmerling and Migdal, 1993).

33. The Film Institute was housed in the same building as the PLO's United Propaganda department.

34. The USSR, Cuba, and Vietnam, for example.

35. Samed had an archive as well, though smaller. It mainly included films which were produced by the institution itself, as well as various filmed materials and copies at various stages of production. The building where the archive and the film laboratory were located was taken by the Israelis, and their fate, too, remains unknown.

36. Not to be confused with "Revolutionary Cinema," which existed within the framework of the PLO organizations during the Beirut period.

37. Subhi a-Zubeidi, Azza al-Hassan, Najwa Najar, and Ghada Tirawai are examples of directors who began their career in this way.

38. See *Fertile Memories* (1980), for instance, which was pre-financed by the German television channel ZDF, and the Dutch networks IKON and NOVIB; *The An-Naim Route* (1981), which was produced by the Belgian network RTBF; *Ma'aloul Celebrates its Destruction* (1984), mainly financed by the Brussels Foundation for Audio-Visual Arts, CBA; and *Wedding in Galilee* (1987), which was a joint Belgian-French-German production that included the Belgian and French Departments of Culture, the German network ZDF, and other sources. The cost of production was $1, 250,000, about one-fifth of the budget for a European film of the same scale. Most of the financing for *Tale of Three Jewels* (1994) came from the BBC, and the money for, *Canticle of the Stones* (1989) was principally given by the Franco-German television network RTE.

39. At one point Rashid Masharawi attempted to cope with the problem of foreign financial support by founding a production company comprised exclusively of Palestinians. However, the attempt failed. More details relating to this endeavor will be offered later, as part of the discussion about artists and their works.

40. Hani Abu-Assad's films, *Nazareth 2000* (2000) and *Ford Transit* (2002), were produced mainly with Dutch funds.
41. See, for example, *Introduction to the End of an Argument* (1990), made with the aid of American funds; and *Homage by Assassination* (1991), which was almost entirely supported financially by the British television network, Channel 4, as part of the Tunisian film, *The Gulf War, So What?* (1991), consisting of five episodes, each directed by a different Arab director. *Divine Intervention* (2002) was made with French finance.
42. Nizar Hassan's *Invasion* (2003) was financed by Swedish television, the Finnish Department of Foreign Affairs Fund, the American Sundance Institute, and the Lebanese ash-Shahed company, in addition to receiving private financial support.
43. Rashid Masharawi's movies, *Passport* (1986), *The Shelter* (1989), *The Magician* (1992), and *Stress Tension* (1998), were made with Israeli funds.
44. Elia Suleiman's *Chronicle of a Disappearance* (1996) was financed mostly by the Israeli Fund for Quality Films.
45. Ali Nassar's films, *The Milky Way* (1997) and *In the Ninth Month* (2002), were chiefly financed by the Israeli Film Fund.
46. Nizar Hassan made his first important film, *Istiklal* (*Independence*, 1994), with the backing of the Israeli Channel Two. *Yasmin Jasminé* (1996) was funded by Channel One of Israeli television and the Fund for the Furthering of the Documentary Movie of the New Israeli Fund, while *Cut* (2000) was financed mostly from an anonymous European source and the New Israeli Fund.
47. Nizar Hassan's *Ostura* (Myth, 1998) was almost entirely self-funded by the director, with additional financial help from an anonymous Palestinian source and the Nazareth tour company, Nazarene Tours. His movie, *Tahaddi* (*Defiance*, 2001), was financed mostly from Palestinian sources.
48. Its production was completed with funding from European sources.
49. Concerning the ambivalent attitude of Arab critics toward the movies of Khleifi and Suleiman, see Chapter 3, "About Place and Time: The Films of Michel Khleifi," and Chapter 7, "Between Exile and Homeland: The Films of Elia Suleiman."
50. Owing to the initiative of the Arab student bodies in Israeli universities.
51. For more reviews of Khleifi's films, see the Introduction.
52. Literally, *handala* means "bitter plant."
53. For more on the character of E. S. in Suleiman's films, see Chapter 7, "Between Exile and Homeland: The Films of Elia Suleiman."
54. A special category which awards a film the privilege of using the title Official Choice of the Cannes Film Festival, but which does not bestow the right to compete for the Golden Palm award.
55. As a method of survival, the inhabitants embrace restriction as a way of life, and at times even subject themselves to a state of over-limitation by not hearing and not seeing (as in the film, *The Shelter*) or when they are busy developing communication and mutual aid techniques (*Curfew*). Those who insist on clinging to the expanses can do so only through insanity (*Haifa*). For all the strategies listed above, Masharawi displays great empathy. For an elaboration of this discussion, see Chapter 4, "Without Place, Without Time: The Films of Rashid Masharawi."
56. The Center produced a number of documentary films which Rashid Masharawi directed himself, including: *Behind the Walls* (1998), recording the Palestinians' resistance to attempts to increase the number of Jewish settlers in Eastern Jerusalem and the Old City; *Makluba* (1999), an experimental film whose subject is the examination of the symbols and images prevalent in Palestinian cinema; *Stress* (1998), a film focused on exterior shots, examining the siege-like condition in which the Israelis placed the Palestinians in the midst of the peace process; and *Here is the*

Voice of Palestine (2001–2), on the Palestinian national radio station. In the course of the shooting of this last film, the Palestinian Broadcasting Authority building was bombed by Israeli forces. In 2002, Masharawi directed a feature film called *Ticket to Jerusalem*, telling the story of a Palestinian man who makes a living by projecting movies from a mobile screening unit, and who is trying to reach Jerusalem to project a Palestinian movie in a building which has been invaded by Jewish settlers.

57. The new Palestinian cinema is often concerned with roadblocks. See Chapter 6, "A Dead-End: Roadblock Movies."
58. Rajai played the character of a policeman in *Rana's Wedding* (2002).
59. Similar parodic emulation can be found in Emile Habibi's *The Pessoptimist* (1974).
60. For a discussion of the cinematic presentation of the personal alongside the national, see Chapter 7, "Between Exile and Homeland: The Films of Elia Suleiman."

2. FROM *BLEEDING MEMORIES* TO *FERTILE MEMORIES*

A manifesto, published in 1973 by the Photography Section, Mustafa Abu-Ali's Palestinian film group, articulates the goals of Palestinian cinema thus: "to reveal the actual reasons for [the Palestinians'] situation and to describe the stages of the Arab and Palestinian struggle towards the liberation of [their] country" (Hennebelle and Khayati, 1977). The writer of the manifest maintains, furthermore, that these goals require the finding of a new aesthetics to express the new contents, and a total commitment of cinema to the Palestinian revolution and Arab causes: "The Palestinian Film Group views itself as an integral part of the institutions of the Palestinian revolution" (ibid.). The Palestinian national struggle is associated here with Marxist-Leninist revolutionary ideology, dominating the thought of the Palestinian leadership during those years,[1] as well as with the artistic expressions of this ideology, as they were formed by Socialist Realism.[2] The Palestinian cinema of the third period, created in the 1970s in exile – in Jordan and particularly in Lebanon – responded, to a great extent, to these poetics and this ideology, and to the role designated to cinema by the organizations that supported it: constructing the Palestinian national narrative as part of an international revolutionary struggle.

In the 1970s, the formative years for the PLO led by the FATAH, the image of the repressed refugee that had dominated Palestinian culture in previous years gave way to the image of the fighting Feda'ee (Sanbar, 1997; Kimmerling and Migdal, 1993). The tale of suffering and adversity evolved into a story of struggle with the emphasis on the future. As Mahmud Darwish later asserts, in a poem directed at the Israeli public: "We have what you do not like: we have the future and we have things to do in our country" (Darwish, 1978). Cinema was to depict this future and to connect it to both the past and present. As Bashar Ibrahim claims: "Cinema is a means for describing and analyzing the state of the Palestinian people, to explain the past and foresee a more desirable future, to lead a struggle and to spread awareness of the Palestinian problem throughout the world" (Ibrahim, 2000: 6). He speaks of the role of cinema in preserving the Palestinian past through folklore and culture, in portraying the present by describing current events in the "occupied homeland," and in leading to a future of "relieving ourselves of the disgrace of the Zionist enemy" (ibid.).

However, third period cinema does not, in fact, deal with the story of the Palestinian past, present, and future. It does not examine the events of the past, before or after 1948, and it does not construct a sequential national narrative that clarifies and documents Palestinian history, thus preserving a national historical memory. Instead, the films refer locally and directly to the events they document (Ibrahim, 2000) and refrain from overtly touching on the painful past, or the historical sequence of events that led to and followed it. The cinema of that period is based, therefore, on forgetting history rather than on constructing it. Yet, although it seems obscured, unanalyzed, and unfamiliar, the repressed past still surfaces in the films. It emerges as a traumatic memory, obsessively returning to two points in time: to the lost object, the pre-destruction past reincarnated in the present, as an idyll of beauty and perfection,[3] and to the 1948 defeat the cinema revives and displays as if it were occurring in the present. Thus, both the trauma and life preceding it remain unprocessed and disconnected from a historical story that progresses from the past to the present and future.

The films focus on specific events such as the bombing of Tel A-Za'tar in 1976, the battle in Kafr Shuba, and the "Black September" events in Jordan in 1970.[4] Yet these incidents, which are mostly delineated through documentary archive materials, are organized in a fixed pattern that reappears in various films and is repeated many times over in each one. This pattern leads from images of tranquillity (orchards, trees, vegetation – even if only within the refugee camp itself) to a sudden, totally unexpected bombardment. Scenes of destruction and death follow the bombardment, eventually to be replaced by shots of Palestinian fighters training, battles, or symbolic depictions of rifles, hand-grenades and shotguns. Ostensibly, this structure describes individual incidents, but since the same footage so persistently duplicates itself, using similar shots of bombardments, ruins, and the dead, that impression becomes abstract. Thus, the pattern in the films represents a single, distinct meta-text, reviving, in different variations, the 1948 trauma and the idyllic state preceding it.

This form reflects the traumatic memory of Palestinian society, yet simultaneously enables a conception of the Palestinian nation as united, sharing a common past. Overtly and bluntly, the speakers in these films demonstrate the positions of the PLO and the Palestinian organizations under the PLO's wing, and reiterate issues that consistently surface in other media as well: the description of what are referred to as Zionistic crimes, the depiction of the Palestinian people as the Zionists' victims, and the belief in the power of the organizations' military force to change the situation and return the refugees to their land.

The structure, which revives the trauma of the past and holds on to the "paradise lost" that preceded it, achieves additional effects on a national scale. One such result is the creation of a shared historical memory, founded on a collective trauma. Thus the geographically and socially fragmented society is unified around one subject while disregarding anything that might harm national agreement or pride, such as the 1948 defeat. This defeat is evoked in the films time and time again, not as a memory of what happened, but as a modified version of this event; what at the time ended in failure and defeat, ends in the present descriptions as various forms of victory. Thus Palestinian cinema creates what Anderson calls the amnesia necessary for the creation of a national narrative (2000: 240).

For years, Palestinian society was composed of regional, rural, familial, clan, religious, and pan-Arabic identities that competed with the national identity.[5] Al Khalidi (1997) illustrates this phenomenon via the example of a Palestinian from Nablus, who defines himself first and foremost as a Nablusi or as an Arab and only later as a Palestinian. At a time when the institutions that traditionally constructed collective identities (the family, religion, the village, and the region)[6] disintegrated, the shared narrative filled their place, crystallizing at a historical moment when the need emerged to integrate all the different stories of identity into a single, comprehensive, unifying narrative. The narrative was no longer that of individual villages and families, but rather bonding stories of those dispersed from there.

This narrative form invents what Said calls "a rhetoric of belonging" and attempts to "create out of the deconstructed history of exile a new wholeness" (1990: 360). Hobsbawm (Hobsbawm and Ranger, 1983) describes the invention of tradition as a praxis that served the authorities in mass societies in their endeavors to create national bonds instead of weakened links within small units such as the village and the family.[7] The traumatic Palestinian story does not strive to compromise and bridge between individual, segmented stories, since it does not in effect recognize privacy or fragmentation. It endeavors to blend these stories into a single, complete, and exclusive one. Yet, it seems that it serves, in fact, the same function as "the invention of tradition", according to Said (1990) and Hobsbawm (Hobsbawm and Ranger, 1983).

Rashid al Khalidi ([2001] 2002) wonders why the 1948 Palestinian defeat was so total. He maintains that Arabs tend to describe the war as an stubborn act of resistance against a strong, invincible enemy, and to place the blame for defeat on the military might of the Israelis, and on the support of Israel by the British, the Americans, and the Russians, as well as on the weakness of the Arab states and their lack of unity, and on the Dir Yasin affair and Israeli attacks on other villages. Al Khalidi claims that defeat was mainly the result of the conditions prevailing in Palestinian society of 1948. This was a divided, leaderless society, lacking an organized army, representative institutions, allies, or a national identity recognized abroad. He asserts that acknowledgement of these facts would compel Palestinians to take responsibility for their own fate, and would oblige them to confront the state of their still segmented society.

Palestinian cinema created in the different diasporas during the 1970s has not completely ignored the causes of fragmentation in the Palestinian society of the past and present. However, rather than isolating and analyzing those causes, filmmakers have chosen to overcome them by "repairing" the past and present reality, and by creating national unity instead of segmentation and separation. Such unity has been achieved by the traumatic memory structure that brings Palestinians back to the shock they had all shared: a shock that could, therefore, serve as a point of reference and identification. But the same unity was also achieved by obscuring references to the specific places where the events had taken place. In the films, all sites seem to be the same place, a setting for one collective Palestinian fate. The association that the trauma mechanism makes between all these places and the site of the initial defeat – Palestine – crystallizes the unity, not only around the shared event in the past and present, but also around the location that belongs to all, regardless of the different exiles in which people currently resided. Blurring the unique appearance of the locations where specific events took place achieved yet another effect. It made the perception of Palestinians as victims more poignant, presenting them as suffering repeated blows, at the hands of not only the Israelis but also of the West, defined as a supporter of Israel; this is in addition to the blows delivered by the Arabs – the Christian militias in Lebanon (Tel A-Za'tar), the Jordanians ("Black September," 1970), or the Syrians (during the Lebanese Civil War, in 1975–76). The similarity or link between the blows handed out to Palestinians by both foes and allies sharpened the unity of the people who had endured them, and expresses, as well as contributes to, the tendency to replace pan-Arabic inclinations in Palestinian society with a separate national identity.

Various historians discuss the way in which the refugee condition, the uprooted state, and the disappearance of the local identity, on the one hand, and the isolation of the Palestinians in the hosting societies, on the other hand, accelerated the crystallization of the national consciousness at the expense of the regional and communal identities that had lost their power and significance. Nassar (2002) writes of the important function that literature and specifically poetry served in this process.[8] Cinema, presumably, was to play a similar role.

Yet, the construction of the Palestinian narrative cannot be isolated from the Israeli narrative, since the latter both determined the shape the former took and silenced it. The perpetually repeated traumatic structure of return to the repressed past interfered with the Israeli narrative, which had ignored Palestinian existence and related history as a sequence in which the Zionists took root in, developed, and built an empty and desolate territory. The Palestinian trauma, evoked in films as endless repetitions of the same past events, exposes the blind spots in the Israeli story and subverts the pretense of this story to present a social totality that excludes Palestinians.[9]

Nabiha Lutfi's film, *Because Roots Don't Die* (1977), is composed of Palestinian women's testimonies recounting the story of the destruction of Tel A-Za'tar camp by the Christian militias in Lebanon in 1976 and the massacre that transpired there. Archive pictures taken by Palestinian photographers and directors, including Abu Zarif, Edward al Kash, Samir Nimer, Omar al Mokhater, and Mustafa Abu-Ali, support their story. The testimonies focus on the event itself, and so does the footage, but the editing ejects the event from the historical context in which it took place and constructs it as a series of abstract repetitions of predestined events. These repetitions place the incident within the Palestinian traumatic memory as a variation on the initial 1948 events, disrupting the idyllic situation that preceded them.

The film does not recount the Tel A-Za'tar chain of events in the order in which they occurred: first the Lebanese Civil War, then the siege of Tel A-Za'tar, the bombardment and the massacre, and finally the escape of some of the residents to the town of Damour. Instead, it breaks this chronological sequence down in order to commence with a state of relative calm in Damour following the bombardment, and then turns dramatically from that tranquillity to the bombing, destruction, massacre, and death (all of which are conjured up by the women's testimonies and are accompanied by appropriate footage). Then, the film shifts from the depictions of ruin and massacre to the portrayal of Palestinians fighting, thus amending their fathers' defeat in the past. The image of the *shaheed* replaces the image of the refugee.[10] Later, the same cycle repeats itself in a different version: the calm (this time shots of the camp prior to the bombing, images of peaceful everyday life),[11] the siege of the camp (accompanied by shots of the wounded and the dead), and the struggle (here, scenes of weapon maintenance). The pattern informing the film – serenity, destruction, struggle – repeats itself several times in various situations occurring in different places before, after, or during the battle. Thus, the event that in reality take place only once is reproduced over and over again in the film. Opening with the relatively serene image of a group of women in Damour, the film ends with scenes of women busily training for battle. Framed by these opening and concluding shots, it repeatedly shifts back and forth from tranquillity to massacre and struggle.

Such a structure appropriates the historical temporal nature of the event and transforms it into a repetitious, timeless cycle, which can relate to other specific events involving Palestinians in other regions. That repetition necessarily evokes the original event, the *Naqba*, conceived of as a sudden, sharp disruption of a calm, idyllic situation. The mere fact that the event itself is not properly anchored in time and place directs viewers' attention towards the abstract structure that can easily be attributed to another time or place: that of 1948.

During the interviews, the refugee women declare:

> We are in Lebanon because we are denied the option to return to our land – our country. Our weapons were not intended to be directed against any Arab state, only against our enemy . . . but the Phalange and the Arab reactionaries have swerved our struggle away from its initial goal and toward a civil war.

The women refer here to their country of origin, Palestine, and to their banishment from it. Homeland and deportation, however, do not constitute an actual living memory in the film. Rather, they are revived in exile, in the shape of the Tel A-Za'tar camp and its fate. The camp and the events taking place in it, therefore, serve as symbols representing the original land and the expulsion from it. "You, Tel A-Za'tar, you are the deepest, purest, clearest wound bruising our hearts," sings Sheik Imam, Egypt's most prominent protest singer, as the film commences and concludes. One of the women supports his sentiment with the words: "As long as we are alive, we will not forget Tel A-Za'tar." The film, then, continuously reincarnates the first traumatic event, but this does not appear as memory, as part of the chronology of events that have taken place within a historical sequence. It exists as a present absence, through events representing it, and even repairing it again and again by substituting the defeat and escape of the past with the struggle of the present.

The structure of *Because Roots Don't Die* is consistently duplicated in all the movies as a blueprint following which different materials are assembled. In Mustafa Abu-Ali's films, *They do not Exist* (1974), *Zionist Aggression* (1973), and *Scenes from the Occupation in Gaza* (1973), the images of tranquillity revive most directly the "paradise lost" of the past. In *They do not Exist*, shots of a grapevine on a fence or plants surrounding a small house do the same. These are images shot in the town of Nabatiya, albeit easily mistaken for ones taken from a Palestinian village. The refugees often built their environment in the camps after the model of the abandoned villages. The director chooses to emphasize this custom. He conveys the serenity of the camp, reflected not only in the trees seen nearby, but also in his decision to shoot during the afternoon hours, when people relax near their houses, children play with marbles, the grocer arranges his cucumbers and potatoes, and women bake pitta bread. A voice-over complements these scenes with information about the camp.[12] Yet, the leisure and calm, nature, housework, vegetables and pitta bread – all seem general, abstract, and therefore one can extract from these shots the essence of the old village and the peaceful life that had been led there, within nature, in the traditional home. Even though the film begins with a specific camp-based character – a girl, for example, writing a letter to a Palestinian fighter – this character immediately disappears, forgotten in the course of the movie, only to return after her death, when the fighter to whom her letter was sent dreams of avenging her blood. The actual life of the child is not, then, the subject of the film. Rather, it is the concepts of innocence and childhood, as part of tranquillity interrupted. It is not regular, flesh-and-blood people who fill the camp, but extras representing the lost past, predating the trauma of deportation.

In the films *Zionist Aggression* and *Scenes from the Occupation in Gaza*, the director disconnects the scenes of tranquillity from the town and constructs them, from the beginning, as part of a vague reality that is supposedly present everywhere, and in the "lost place" in particular. The camera wanders around across orchards and vineyards or over fertile fields. It pauses near an apple tree, lingers around a boy holding a bunch of grapes, and from there swings by farmers reaping their crops. This sequence is soundless. According to the director, the intention was to create an illusion of rushes, unprocessed and unedited shots (private interview with Mustafa Abu-Ali, Ramallah, 2003). However, the shots are still manipulated by the director; even though they were shot in South Lebanon, in the first case, and the fields around Gaza, in the second, any recognizable feature of a specific place is purposefully absent. Thus, the scenes could seem to be from any place, and particularly the site of the past: the fields, vineyards, and orchards of the deserted land.

Specific location becomes even less important as a result of the editing that cuts through the pastoral scene in order to insert the dramatic images and sounds of the bombings. The editing thus incorporates the pastoral scenes into the abstract structure of serenity followed by destruction. In *Zionist Aggression*, these images are highlighted by captions: "In September 1972 the Israeli Air Force bombed villages and Palestinian refugee camps in southern Lebanon, in northern Lebanon, and in Syria." From this point on, the pattern is familiar and appears in the same form in all of the films. The wailing of ambulances and scenes of destruction are replaced by images of the wounded and dead, which in their turn are substituted by actual or symbolic accounts of the Palestinian struggle: machineguns aimed at airplanes in the sky in *Zionist Aggression*, gunshot flashes in *They do not Exist*, repeated depictions of a hand-grenade and a shotgun in *Scenes from the Occupation in Gaza*. In every case, these images are supplemented by a matching soundtrack – a victory song, as in *With Blood and Spirit* (1971) ("The day of victory is not far off . . . when a child is born to a Palestinian mother, he will emerge from the womb holding a rifle"); victory speeches, such as the one by Faruk Kadumi, head of the PLO's political office (foreign office), in *They do not Exist* ("Our answer is more and more armed operations in order to eliminate the Nazi traits characterizing Israeli society"); or the words of one of the townspeople ("We are *fedayeen* till the end. I hate Israel and I don't care about dying. We will continue the struggle until victory"). The struggle was intended, in all the cases above, to compensate for the ever-present traumatic event, to provide a good ending for what had ended badly. The films emphasize this through different means. For example, in the descriptions of the battle in *Kafr Shuba*, in 1975, which ended with the withdrawal of the Israeli army, it is asserted that the film is about "the village that for six days taught the enemy a lesson." In this case, these six days of battle were to compensate for the 1967 Six-Day War. The "correction" of the past is also accomplished through reference to or presentation of children, who personify future and hope, in contrast to the despair of the past. In many cases images of children merge into images of soldiers, and pictures of them both are dissolved into depictions of Palestinian flags (*They do not Exist*). These are common symbols, which repeatedly represent, in both Palestinian cinema and literature, notions of hope, resurrection, and struggle.[13]

Even with incidents when the concrete event is anchored in some historical sequence, the structure of the plot disengages it from that sequence. In *They do not Exist*, Faruk Kadumi explains in an interview the background to the bombings in Nabatiya. He claims that during the kidnapping of the Maalot schoolchildren, the Israeli Government gave its consent to the release of prisoners, in exchange for the liberation of the children from the hands of their captors. In fact, Kadumi maintains, the Israeli Government took advantage of the negotiations in order to bomb the town. "The children were murdered by the Israeli shootings," he says. "Those who took hostages intended to free their friends, but the Israelis only wished to deepen the abyss between the two peoples." In this case and in others, the explanation presumably delineates the historical context of the concrete event, from the Palestinian speaker's viewpoint. But because this explanation, like others, appears only at a later stage of the film, and since the film does not deal with the concrete event in particular but rather, once again, with a repeated pattern of peaceful life suddenly interrupted by the enemy army, it does not significantly anchor the timeless event to a specific time and history.

Since it is not particular events that guide these films but the abstract structure, they alternate easily between different times and places. *Kafr Shuba* (1975), which recounts the story of the Palestinian struggle against the Israelis in Kafr Shuba, includes scenes of demonstrations in the Rashedia school, near the Damascus Gate, Jerusalem, and shots of additional demonstrations in various areas of the West Bank, while mentioning the 1936 Palestinian rebellion against the British Mandate. *Scenes from the Occupation in Gaza* focuses on the anguish caused by the occupation of Gaza, house demolitions, searches, and arrests, but transfers the struggle itself to Jerusalem, Khan Yunes, Tul Karem, or the north of the country. The intention was to expand the single-location event and depict it as part of a comprehensive struggle of the Palestinian people in both past and present. The presentation of an abstract action occurring everywhere, rather than necessarily in one particular place, strengthens the abstract mythic structure which dominates the film when the peaceful shots are situated "no place." For example, the Kafr Shuba bombings afflict not the village itself but the pastoral serenity of the cultivated land near the Litany river. The conflict over the Litany waters connects these images to the concrete event, the war in the village. However, the interchangeability of sites, the easy alternation between the Kafr Shuba scenes and those located near the Litany or in Jerusalem, associate these images with an abstract structure that repeats itself, blurring the concrete quality of the locations, which once again signify the calm disrupted by violence and destruction.

In certain cases (such as in the films *Zionist Aggression* and *With Blood and Spirit*) the voice-over, the captions, and the allegorical staging of the historical processes transform the specific event into an international one, referring to it as part of the imperialist repression, or as the struggle of the East versus the West, thus reflecting the ideology that was overtly articulated by the directors (Hennebelle and Khayati, 1977). In addition, by doing so, the films contribute to the destabilization of the actuality of the events and facilitate the connection of present occurrences to events of the past. The peaceful life in the camp, in *They do not Exist*, has a soundtrack featuring Um Kulthum's voice singing Omar Khayam's *Rubaiyat*. By contrast, Bach's Concerto for Violin and Orchestra accompanies the Israeli airplanes bombing the camp. Thus, the film presents the interrupted peace in the refugee camp as part of the struggle between two cultures: that of East and West.

In fact, even films that do not deal with the bombings, their results, and the reactions to them use the same pattern. *An Opposite Siege* (1978), for instance, tells the story of the 1973 uprising in the West Bank, but easily proceeds to other places: the bombings in Lebanon, for example. As a result, it is unclear whether the images of the dead were shot in the West Bank or in Lebanon. They are, in fact, an expression of the general catastrophe that broke the timeless, unspecifically located tranquillity.

Several films produced during the 1980s are more sophisticated and complex. Nevertheless, they still tell the same homogeneous abstract story. Kaise a-Zubeidi's *Barbed-Wire Homeland* (1982), for instance, opens with the same pastoral landscapes that viewers have learned to recognize in other exilic films. The views are shot in color and by a more skilled hand. However, they are still not presented as shots of real life. As in other films, the landscapes here are in long shot, are filtered, and still convey a fantasy of tranquillity before destruction: agricultural plots, terraces, olive groves, a wooden plow, sheep, an Arab man drinking from a flowing stream, and a family sitting on the cultivated land at sunset. Here is still the peacefulness of a paradise lost that was to be interrupted, as in other movies, by Israeli actions (land expropriation), which would then lead to the Palestinian struggle. In a manner similar to that of the other films, *Barbed-Wire Homeland* deals intensively with healing the trauma. The 1948 landscapes were lost, even if they are incessantly revived here, but in the lands of the West Bank a struggle is taking place, and in this case the film implies that Palestinians will not give up or give in.

A significant novelty of *Barbed-Wire Homeland* is its direct references to the clash between the Palestinian and Israeli positions. In the early movies, Arab speakers indirectly interpreted the Israeli stance, with the clear intention of contradicting it. Here, for the first time, the Israeli position is brought forth through a direct quotation. It is true that this quotation is obviously meant to ridicule the speaker and to negate his position, and yet the appearance of an argument is presented, which heightens the realistic quality of the abstract structure.

The Israelis speak in the film in their own voices. Begin states his belief in Israeli ownership of Judea and Samaria, Israel Galilee speaks of the country as the Jews' historical homeland, and one of the settlers articulates his position thus: "This is our home and will remain our home. We feel we have come home. Millions understand the expression 'The Promised Land.' This is the land promised to the Jews by God." The editing contradicts these notions by highlighting Arab land and life, thus constituting a winning counter-argument in this dispute.

The music expresses the same contention. It commences with neutral, pastoral tones illustrating the images of cultivated agricultural land. It is interrupted by ominous sounds representing the Israeli threat, which are then replaced by oriental melodies, on the one hand, and a distorted parodical recording of people singing *Hatikva* (the Israeli national anthem), on the other.

Although the dispute presents real, concrete positions, it also transforms actual life and landscapes into abstract arguments in an on-going contention. Thus they are denied their independent existence and become symbols for the distant past, when the aforesaid dispute had begun.

The only fictional film produced by the Palestinian organizations, *The Return to Haifa* (1982), based on Ghassan Kanafani's novel, is one of the few films alluding directly to the 1948 story of escape, through the tale of a refugee family from Haifa. In the pandemonium of the 1948 flight, the family leaves its young son behind. After 1967, the parents, living in Ramallah, decide to go to Haifa to find out what happened to him. They discover that he was adopted by a Jewish family, grew up as an Israeli Jew in every way, joined the army, and even became an officer. The Palestinian parents reveal his true identity to their son, but he chooses to hold on to his Jewish Israeli identity. The parents return to Ramallah, and a resolution forms in the father's heart to allow his other son to join the organizations fighting against Israel.

The protagonists return in 1967 to the landscapes they fled in 1948 and discover that nothing has changed. The olive groves and the orchards "are almost as we have left them," says the husband to his wife. Not only do the landscapes remain the same, but the house too has stayed as it was. So have the street, the apartment, the armchairs, and even the feathers left in a jug when the family escaped. Thus, as in all other films of that era, the past is preserved in the present.

Reviving the pre-deportation past is one part of the story. Compensating for the trauma of deportation is another. The tale of escape, portrayed in black and white, is counterbalanced by the story of honor and heroism, told by the husband to his wife during the trip to Haifa (and also shot in black and white), about a young man called Abada, who fought and was killed in 1948; his portrait still hangs on the wall of his Jaffa home. The shaming story of abandonment is counterbalanced in other ways as well. The tale is narrated twice in the film. After the first time, at the beginning of the film, the protagonist's son expresses his wish to join the *fedayeen* but his father refuses to consent. Following the second account of the same story, however, the son does join the *fedayeen* and receives his father's blessing for it. Mending the past, then, here involves aligning oneself with future-oriented actions. As the film's protagonist declares: "We were wrong when we thought that the homeland is the past and the memories. The homeland is the future, for which one bears arms."[14]

The correction of events is also achieved by shifting the point of view. The film begins with black-and-white bird's-eye images of the 1948 escape from Haifa, shot from the angle of the foreign airplanes, whose roars are heard on the soundtrack. The next shots are already in color, in the present (after the 1967 war). These shots, of Israeli soldiers patrolling Ramallah, are also filmed from the Israelis' point of view – that of the armed soldiers. The escape from Haifa, just like life in post-occupation Ramallah, is described, then, from the vantage-point of the occupying Israelis. It seems as if the Arabs cannot observe their own story, much less narrate it. Indeed, they are even unable to see the views of the land that has been taken away from them. During the ride to Haifa, the husband rhetorically asks his wife: "Do you believe that you see it [the country] now?" and answers: "They are showing it to you. In order to see your country, you must be free."

Indeed, the healing of the trauma is accomplished by repairing the protagonists' vision. Some time after the conversation described above, the passengers approach a roadblock. At first, the roadblock is filmed through Israeli eyes – the eyes of the soldier guarding it. But very quickly the camera shifts to the point of view of the two passengers, and from this viewpoint an explosion of a booby trap and the death of the soldier are recorded. The Palestinian protagonists have lost the vision with the loss of country and home. That sight is restored with struggle and revenge. The vision restored to them is the free and independent Palestinian glance through which they see, according to the film, the "correct" sights.

In spite of the differences between this and other films, it seems that *The Return to Haifa*, too, duplicates the traumatic cycle that obliterates the present in favor of the past and uses it to make that past materialize, here and now, in order to change and repair it.

A RETURN TO THE LAND

Third period cinema, affiliated to the Palestinian organizations, expresses the distress of Palestinians in exile, but only vaguely represents the growing significance of Palestinian land as a national symbol for Palestinian society, as an element that allows the dream of unity. It is Michel Khleifi's cinema, and other films created during the 1980s, that brought Palestinian cinema "back to the land."

As early as the British Mandate era, although the Palestinian national discourse evolved in the towns,[15] it was nevertheless based on rural peasant culture as a central national characteristic. Traditional village clothing, dance, food, homes, and land, naturally a part of everyday life for the majority of the Arab population in Palestine, were constructed in the political and literary discourse as symbols of the Palestinian nation (Nassar, 2002). With the disappearance of the urban centers and the severe damage done to rural life after 1948, the refugees' experience replaced the rural experience in Palestinian consciousness. Yet, just as the refugee experience generated a united national consciousness, so out of the exilic experience did rural icons obtain the status of national symbol (Kimmerling and Migdal, 1993) and the focus shifted from land as a source of life and livelihood to land as a source of emotional identification (Elad, 1993). Thus land became a symbol of a period that some of those in exile still remembered and most recognized as part of their heritage.

> Against the destruction of the homeland [says Naficy], the crumbling of previous structures of authority (the language and culture), in the face of the impossibility of return, many exiles turn to the structural authority and security that only nature can bestow: absence of time, lack of borders, a dependable universal stability. (Naficy, 2001: 159)

The era symbolized by land is the pre-traumatic period, which the exiles restore in the present, as a revival of a lost object that it is so difficult to disconnect and so impossible to separate from (Freud, [1953] 1974b). Edward Said has commented (though not referring directly to Palestinian works) that the collective memory invents the geographical space (Said, 2000), and Elia Suleiman agrees, claiming that it is "easy to develop relationships with what is lost" (Bourlond, [1999] 2000: 97).

The experience of land loss was greatly significant for the Palestinians who remained in Israel as well. The wide-scale expropriation of land in Israel, in the 1950s and 1960s, in addition to processes of modernization and urbanization across the entire region, have changed the Arab population. From a rustic population it has become one of urban laborers, transforming the Arab village from an agricultural community to a dormitory town for laborers, who leave in the morning to work in Israeli cities. Thus, in this case, too, the elevation of the land into a national symbol is derived directly from the loss of that land, just as it was in the case of the Palestinians in exile. Furthermore, since the Arab population in Israel has not fully shared the prosperity that modernization has brought with it, turning the land into a national symbol intended to revive not only the period predating the Israeli occupation, but also the era that preceded the modernization associated with Israel.

Only during the 1980s did Palestinian cinema replace the suffering and destruction, as the subject of the traumatic story, with the lost land, the place. This was first observed in a very few films created by the Palestinian organizations but was crystallized mainly in Michel Khleifi's inaugural film, *Fertile Memories* (1980), as well as in other films by Khleifi and others, produced later.

Among the early films referring to the land are Adnan Mdanat's *Palestinian Visions* (1977) and Tawfik Saleh's *The Dupes* (1972),[16] and these influenced Michel Khleifi mainly in their filming of land and desert. Mdanat's movie delineates, via interviews, drawings, and song, the story of the artist Ibrahim Ghannam, who was deported from the village of Lajoun and yet continued to paint, in his Lebanese exile, the landscapes of his native village.

Palestinian Visions is still structured according to the familiar pattern of trauma. Thus it consists of the following stages: the tranquillity of paradise before banishment, which is succeeded by disaster, and finally revenge. However, each of these individual stages, and all of them combined, are deconstructed, estranged, and altered. In the paintings we see the old pastoral atmosphere, familiar from other films of exile, reviving the idyllic, lost landscapes in which Arabs live peacefully and Jews do not exist at all. Yet here the course that the camera takes, from conceiving the painting as a whole to observing its details, gives the abstract landscape an air of reality, emphasizing concrete details at the expense of the whole. The idyllic fantasy becomes a reality both through the artist's on-screen reminiscing, confirming what we see in the picture, and via the statistical details that support it. A painting of orange picking, for example, is presented alongside memories of that particular event and added information about the different types of orange to be found in different towns before 1948. The paintings depict different locations in the country: Lajoun Village, Sasa, Haifa, Nablus (Jabel A-Naar – in English: Fire Mountain), Tiberias, Acre, the Sea of Galilee, the Mediterranean, the plain, and the Jezrael Valley – places in which the painter had lived and to which he escaped. In this manner, the film marks a wide-scale geography of the country, shaping the Palestinian map in its entirety, but as in Khleifi's works, later, it is also charged with the actual experiences of the film's real protagonist: village life and the escape from it.

Life on the land allows the film to substitute the traumatic time of the other films with the story of space, which encompasses not only the lost pre-trauma era, but also mundane time and the natural everyday flow. *Palestinian Visions* follows the sequence of the agricultural seasons, leading from paintings of sowing to those of harvest, grape-picking and gathering of the crop. The film opens with an image of sowing and ends with a wedding (preserving the rituals of the past) and a birth (signifying the future). Time in nature is also inserted into the paintings by reference to the period during which the wheat ripens, the length of time the gathering of the olives takes, and so on. This sequence of nature offers an alternative to the traumatic disruption that leads the film toward the familiar route: from tranquillity, to escape, exile, and struggle. A combination of the sequences presents past time as an absent presence, as Elsaesser (forthcoming) maintains, as something that exists both in the present and in the past.

The fixated traumatic narrative of tranquillity, loss, and struggle is further upset in this film because the story is perceived through estrangement. Serenity is evoked by paintings, and the 1948 escape to exile is narrated as personal reminiscences rather than as a repetition of the story of the past, while the struggle is conveyed only in the lyrics of the songs and not in the spoken text. Thus it appears in songs summoning the people to "rise up and wipe the shame," to "climb from Haifa to the Mountain of Fire," to be "all *fedayeen*." The familiar structure also takes on a different shape since the memory of the escape is here a true memory of the past, and not a present "acting out" of a painful past trauma. In addition, it is disrupted by everyday time and the natural flow, and also as a consequence of the division of the delineation of the events between various media: paradise lost – in painting, the escape – in interviews, and the struggle – in song.

It was to take a few more years until this change, that brought Palestinian cinema to the land and shaped new modes of memory out of everyday time and the natural sequence, would find its full manifestation in the films of Michel Khleifi.

NOTES

1. For a clarification of the connection between the Palestinian leadership and Marxist-Leninist ideology, see footnote 24 in Chapter 1, "A Chronicle of Palestinian Cinema."
2. Socialist Realism was an artistic style prevalent in the Soviet Union, where culture was expected to dedicate itself to the purposes of the Communist revolution. During the revolution and following it, Socialist Realism influenced different cultures in various parts of the world, including the Hebrew and Palestinian cultures.

3. See the Introduction.
4. See footnotes 19 and 28 in Chapter 1, "A Chronicle of Palestinian Cinema."
5. See Al Khalidi (1997), Tamari (1999a), and Kimmerling and Migdal (1993). Also, see footnote 10 in the Introduction.
6. Ibid.
7. Said (2000) describes similar processes of creating a collective memory at the expense of minor units such as the family or the village. Although he does not refer directly to Palestinian society, his conceptions seem appropriate.
8. See Tamari (1999a).
9. Concerning social totality such as this, see Bhabha (1990).
10. "You left without fighting properly. Now it is time for our struggle," says one of the young men to his father, and another sums it up: "The Palestinian revolution came to create a new, fighting, Palestinian *shahid*, who replaces the persecuted refugee."
11. This footage, like much other in this cinema, depicts the camps prior to the bombing as places of tranquillity and beauty, and to that effect, ignores the severe distress that characterized them, the crowded conditions, the poverty, and the unemployment.
12. The refugee camp near Nabatiya, situated 70 kilometers south of Beirut, was established in the early 1950s and houses 6,000 refugees, most of whom are from upper Galilee, working in agriculture and as day laborers in the Nabatiya area.
13. Such visual symbols are expressed in literature and television via the plot. For example, in the story "Bashir Mosallam Aljabaii" (Natour, 1997), the heroine gives birth to a son during her flight, an event that is narrated thus: "When the newborn first breathed the air and sounded his initial cry, the dreamy, lively, easy-tempered, fighting city turned very quiet, shedding tears and begetting children while dying" (p. 138). Likewise, the son in Ghassan Kanafani's story, "The Horizon Behind the Gate" (1963), replaces death with life when he does not tell his mother about her daughter's death while fleeing in 1948. In "Farhud's Ideal" (Khouri, 1982) each casualty in a string of battles and massacres is called Farhud, after the original Farhud who was killed in the war. With every other casualty, Farhud is resurrected and dies again, and when the village rebels, at the end of the story, the narrator remarks: "I wish that my father would have been alive and seen how much Farhud has grown" (80). Az Adin al Kassam's grave is presented in a Palestinian television broadcast in similar fashion: "In July '78, the Israeli authorities sent tractors to ruin the graveyard area and build on it a park . . . but al Kasam's bones have roots in the earth and he lives in the hearts of millions and with every Palestinian child born, al Kasam is born again." The memory of the killings in the past, as an on-going trauma, is thus reconstructed again and again in the present, but is also "repaired" by the symbols of national resurrection and hope. For a discussion of this topic, see Chapter 6, "A Dead-End: Roadblock Movies."
14. The literature of this and later periods is brimming with similar examples, in which choosing to fight makes amends for the past and functions as an alternative to the non-existent present. This is the case, of course, first and foremost, in Kanafani's work, on which the film is based, but the same pattern can be found in many other places as well. In "The Lantern that Did not Extinguish" (Bannura, 1990), for instance, the old people grieve for lost tradition, but are consoled by their pride in the young men fighting for its restitution. See also the description of struggle as an option that replaces the present occupation in *A Sabbar* (Khalifa, [1976] 1978).
15. See Kabha (2007).
16. The cinematic version of Ghassan Kanafani's story, "Men in the Sun" ([1963] 1998).

3. ABOUT PLACE AND TIME: THE CINEMA OF MICHEL KHLEIFI

THE EARLY FILMS

Michel Khleifi's early documentary films, which were created in the course of the third period, initiated a new era in Palestinian cinema. His first film, *Fertile Memories* (1980), crystallized and was the culmination of a process that had begun in the early 1970s and which was to be continued in later films. On the one hand, place in Khleifi's film, as in others, is an imagined place that revives the past, drawing on the pre-traumatic era and, thus functioning as a national, unity-constructing symbol that presents an idyllic home and homeland created out of an exilic state.[1] On the other hand, the abstract space is portrayed here as a concrete, familiar, and revered place, where daily life occurs in the here and now. In Michel Khleifi's own words (private interview, Paris, 2003), "In order to defend something one must love it, and to love it, one must know it." Furthermore, this place that preserves both past and present is meant to function in the future as a relic, as the foundation of the historical memory of what is doomed to be lost in the Israeli reality, in an ever-changing world. These films, therefore, freeze the traumatic time, replacing the existing present with the absent past. Yet, they also preserve the sequence of the actual present and of the future and of both the remembrance and the forgetfulness embedded in them. In this way, they preserve the traumatic memory, and at the same time attempt to work through it, to put it in a historical context. Either way, here, as in much of Third World cinema, the presence and importance previously attributed to plot are attached to place, which becomes a "hero" in its own right.[2]

Fertile Memories is the creation of a director who lives between cultures and countries,[3] merging various identities in a montage of styles and points of view. "I like exile," Khleifi reflects. "I like the dialectic perspective that it imposes on you. People who live in a place are subordinate to an idea and experience it. I try to create a synthesis" (private interview, Paris, 2003).

The main significance of the film lies in its original focus on the private, individual story, rather than on a collective, national one. In *Fertile Memories*, the catastrophic time that had been the driving force behind earlier films, was replaced by another time, flowing between catastrophes, the everyday time that is spun out of the organic connection with the actual place[4] and shapes local, diverse life.[5]

The mundane time is linked to the real, concrete place in which it flows. These two elements are bound together, as they are in many Palestinian stories, such as Nafaa's "The Camel" (1989), which begins thus: "We left that day the house and the village and the children, the guest rooms and the wedding plazas, the tabun ovens and the barns, filled each season anew and saturating the house for many days with the scent of the new hay." The long sentence, which is loaded with the minute details of existence, gives that life breadth in terms of landscape (by listing the places) and in terms of time (many days). However, "that day" is the day when all of this is destroyed ("each time I remember all this, I simultaneously see the valley frowning and sinking into heavy mourning"). The detailed description thus revives what has been ruined.

Within this setting of daily time, Khleifi's film evokes class, gender, ethnic, and other identities that earlier cinema silenced. By doing so, the film also allows regional, village, familial, clan, religious, and pan-Arabic loyalties in Palestinian society to be expressed. Neither space nor time is homogeneous here; the movie is anchored in different spaces from which the various narratives and memories of those living in them are observed. The accounts of individual people are revealed in the course of the film to be fragments of the collective narrative. The collective, then, exists here but is taken apart, divided into different identities based on gender, class, generation, and locality. Thus the single narrative that had directed spectators, in the early films, toward one past and a sole place, is deconstructed. The new narrative is told in numerous times and places, suggesting diverse and sometimes contradictory identities alongside the single, united national identity that is still being carved out of the lost past.

The film tracks the lives of two women. Romiya Farah, an elderly Yefya woman, who preserves the Arab village tradition in food (baking bread in a tabun oven, preparing stuffed vegetables), farm chores (washing wool in a basin), conservative views (against the remarriage of her widowed daughter and against modern women's attire, such as swimsuits), and, in the main, in her stubborn objection to receiving monetary compensation for her plot of land, which was expropriated by the Israelis. The second character, a young woman named Sahar Khalifa, embodies the new, modern era in her job (at a university), her vocation (writing), and her feminist views (she has divorced her husband and challenged conservative society by asserting her right to live in dignity as a spouseless woman). The decision to depict two such different women also infers a choice of dissimilar geographical areas, one in Israel and the other in the territories occupied in 1967; of different ages; and of different classes (the urban working class versus the intellectual author). It is also the director's choice to concentrate on those who live on the fringes of patriarchal male society and whose marginality is dual: as a woman and as a widow or a divorcee.

The decision to deconstruct the national unifying narrative in the film, therefore, also involves a transition from the masculine story that dominates history, even if it is only a mythical history, to the feminine point of view. That viewpoint is shared by the two main characters, as well as by the other women caught by the camera while observing life, from within the houses, from doorsteps, from the roofs overlooking the balconies. Such a viewpoint constructs a feminine alternative to the masculine narrative recounted in earlier films.[6] It is free of the linear progression toward the achievement of a national goal, basing itself instead on place and the life unrolling in it during everyday time, in the natural rhythm of the passing hours and seasons: from morning to evening, and from the glaring light to twilight and darkness. The film is based here on the ancient association of woman and earth, but this association is divested of its symbolic, stereotypic status because it is broken down into the details of the real lives of women in motion, between the inside and the outside, between family and work. Rather than embodying generalizations, these women deconstruct them.[7]

Thus, one might say that Khleifi deconstructs the abstract unity that previously revolved around the traumatic historical narrative, and replaces it with different narratives, times, identities, and spaces. He therefore defies the national totality, which was created at the expense of an ignored variety of identities and individual stories. However, the director does not stop there. His film not only deconstructs national unity but also reconstructs it based on a new foundation, centered first and foremost on space. Out of the space,[8] the movie identifies the separate stories embedded in Palestinian society. At the same time, within that space, it also incorporates the individual narratives, constructing a multifaceted, complex reality, heterogeneous and homogeneous, tangible and symbolic, private and public.[9] Such a reality had not existed in earlier Palestinian cinema.

The heroines of *Fertile Memories* inhabit places that are geographically and psychologically far apart. The film links the two women, who do not even know each other, by situating them in one setting and giving them a common denominator: the soil, the cultivated landscape that they crisscross as they move from place to place, the olive trees, the terraces, the grapevines, and the prickly-pear hedges. It is a broad landscape unfolding in the film like a road map. The borders of this map are marked by long shots and its coordinates are plotted by the movements of the camera over the landscape (panning, tracking, zooming in and out, and traveling). The map is presented not from a top-down omniscient angle[10] but from the angle of the characters, who inhabit the filmed landscapes, move within them, walk and travel in them, and contemplate them.

The women's viewpoint is often supported by the director's impartial perspective. Thus the objective existence of the map is suggested, although it was, in fact, drawn from the point of view and lives of its heroines. In one of the film's scenes, the woman from Yefya is on a journey to visit the land expropriated from her. The traveling sequence opens with a wide panning shot of the fields cultivated by Jewish Kibbutz members in the Jezrael Valley while the soundtrack features Arab music. The gaze, in this case, is the director's "objective" gaze, using the eye of the camera to "reconquer" the landscape and the music to "translate" it into Arabic, granting it an Arab existence. Later, in a reverse shot, the woman's point of view is presented, while she is observing this landscape. This is the same plot of land taken away from her by the Israelis and it is retrieved first by the director, who has "appropriated" it with his camera, and then by her own gaze.

Throughout the film, the director merges the women's gaze with that of the "objective" camera, positioning the heroines' actual daily life in the setting of the entire, non-partitioned country, which constitutes a national collective entity. Thus, Khleifi reconstructs what he had earlier deconstructed, by integrating fragmentary personal experiences into the national whole. By means of the camera, he restores to the heroines that which was taken away from them. In addition, however, the heroines also "recover" their loss through their own exertions. The very fact that they live in and gaze on the landscape gives them a claim to it. Their movement within the landscape serves as a fine example of the concept of *sumud*, a term "which the Baghdad conference in 1978 coined in regard to the million and a half Palestinians who live under Israeli occupation" (Shehada, 1982: 9). The term denotes steadfastness and the realization of one's connection with one's location, even if it no longer exists and even if one has become a stranger in it.[11]

The disappearing, invisible Palestinian landscape has thus become visible. Palestinian eyes that lost the power to control the environment have regained their strength. In this respect, Michel Khleifi's revolutionary outlook, introduced into Palestinian cinema with this film, parallels the earlier revolution in Palestinian prose and history books. The traditional historical chronicles were replaced, as Sanbar (1997) claims, by inventory lists that articulated and testified to everything that the homeland consisted of: the flora, the fauna, the climate, the geography, and more. "The inventory has become an ideal form lending itself to the narration of the story of the land that had vanished and to resurrect the reality, the places, the times and the people that had become invisible and that nevertheless still remained in the heart of every Palestinian." (23). Like the history books, Khleifi's film points to the concrete place, revealing what has become invisible to the world, and particularly to the Israeli eye, thus asserting its existence.

The house here, like the landscape, is a junction where the private and the public, the current and the historical, the individual stories and the unity that binds them to each other intersect. Like space and tradition, the house is celebrated in the exilic Palestinian culture (Said, 1990: 359). In it, the family lives, the woman bakes her pitta bread; here children and parents gather around the dining table. The house has always been the bastion of Palestinian private life and also the epitome of the national past and tradition. It grants personal security and gives national identity its form. "A person without a house is a person without an identity," says one of the women in Muhammad Bakri's film, *1948* (1984). The house is perceived as a place where past and present, idyll and trauma, as well as family and nation, meet. Therefore, a person who has lost his or her house, as in *The Return to Haifa* (1982), has also lost family and country. In a society that has been deprived of its national symbols, the house, like the village, the land, and the family, serves as a symbol that incorporates the various social and personal identities into the national identity and transfers them, *en bloc*, from relics of the past to present entities. The house signifies what no longer exists (the idyllic past, as well as its disintegration) and transforms it into something that does exist (and that has been revived in the present). Thus, like other symbols, it enables the construction of the homeland within exile, granting a sense of peoplehood and tradition from the distance and out of estrangement (Said, 1990: 359).

The house is depicted in *Fertile Memories* as a circle whose core is the family, the children, the shared meal, and the pitta bead being baked in the tabun oven. It is a closed, secured place, but is also open to the outside, to the expanses surrounding it.[12] It is a private place of everyday life in the present, but also a place that represents the national experience and the people's tradition. At its center is age-old tradition; surrounding it, fields cultivated for generations – land conquered by the camera and presented, as mentioned earlier, as Arab land. In a television interview, a Beit Jalla resident whose house was destroyed by an Israeli missile said, "The thing they destroyed wasn't a house. It was all of history." The movement directed, here, as in all of Michel Khleifi's movies, from the inside to the outside and back – from the house to the yard, from the yard to the immediate environment, from there to the fields and expanses and vice versa – emphasizes that contact between the mundane and the private, between the national and the historical. The cinematography, then, situates the characters within a protected, intimate, private place, which is nevertheless part of a wide open territory, a national space.

Like the landscapes and places, the flow of daily life that reflects the heterogeneity of Palestinian society also represents Palestinian unity, the struggle to cling on to the land and to life in the face of threat. The everyday "performance" of the minute details of life constitutes a way of clinging on to place and even grants permanency and stability to a Palestinian identity that is still to be defined to the full.[13]

However, beyond everyday time, the film consists of another time carved (as suggested earlier) out of space. This is the lost past, preserved in the terraces, the olive trees, and the stone houses, in the family atmosphere in the house, and in the agricultural practices in the fields. This is the time embodied in the childhood home of the elderly Yefya woman, of the old pictures hanging on its walls, of the wedding ceremony she observes – in part a recollection of the past, in part a current event. This is the time of folklore – songs and traditional tales that the woman sings and recites to her grandchildren, and that the educated woman collects. This is the past, predating urbanization, modernization, and the Israeli occupation. And the film holds on to its vestiges, reviving it as one revives a distant past obliterated by traumatic events,[14] making it into an emblem of the non-partitioned homeland. The movie still expresses, therefore, that same trauma presented in other films, although it chooses to revive what has been lost rather than depict the event of the loss itself. Yet, by choosing to focus on everyday life, concrete landscapes, and diverse individual fates, the film can work through that trauma, as well. Cathy Caruth (1991) argues that to cope with trauma, there is a need to find a way to express it, to fit it into a narrative continuum. The diverse daily lives that Khleifi recounts provide the narrative continuum into which he inserts the pain of loss, and in which he finds a remedy for it.

Mustafa Abu-Ali and Hassan Abu Gh'nima, interviewed by Guy Hennebelle and Khemais Khayati in Beirut (1977), explained the role that they believed revolutionary Palestinian cinema should play: "Sometimes a revolutionary film can be more important than a successful military action" (43). *Fertile Memories* was produced three years after this interview. It ends with military action, with events of the Palestinian uprising in the West Bank, which connects it to the cinema that preceded it, the genre that documented the Palestinian armed struggle. (Indeed, this part of the footage is in black and white, strengthening in this way the impression of authentic documentation.) However, *Fertile Memories* wages war on the Israeli story via discursive, not violent means.[15] This struggle takes place here, as in earlier films, by suspending the dominant narrative and halting it. This time, it is not the cyclical story, but the spaces and the Palestinian daily life and past embedded in them, that halt it. Thus the fields, the stone fences, and the trees are designed to "insert" into the landscapes of the past, as described by the Zionist narrative, the very traces that it had purged from it: the existence of the Palestinians. As Sanbar suggests, by means of this device, they seem to say to the nations of the world, "We haven't vanished yet. We haven't become invisible yet. We still have our names, our soil, our trees, our songs, and our faces. Why don't you see us?" (1997: 30). The camera expands these landscapes, populates them with Arabs, and imposes on them the Arab gaze and the Arab voice instead of Israeli ones. Thus, it not only halts the progress of the Israeli narrative but turns it upside down and replaces it with the Arab narrative. The concrete and native quality of the setting and the positioning of the heroes in it make these substitutions authentic. In this way, what is referred to as the disappearing land, "the underground land that was covered by another land" (Sanbar, 1997: 22), has become real and visible.

While editing *Fertile Memories*, Khleifi discovered that part of the footage he had accumulated from the destroyed village of Ma'aloul was not connected to the plot of the two women. It belonged, in fact, in another film. This film, *Ma'aloul Celebrates its Destruction*, was consequently made in 1984. It continues the efforts previously carried made in Adnan Mdanat's film, *Palestinian Visions* (1977), to resurrect Palestinian memory using different kinds of media. In *Ma'aloul Celebrates its Destruction*, these means include a mural of Ma'aloul village on the wall of a refugee's house, documentary and semi-documentary footage, and testimonies of the refugees themselves, as well as a historical delineation of the conflict narrated by a schoolteacher. In addition, a stroll among the village ruins and the time spent there on Israeli Independence Day, when Arab families were allowed to leave the areas under the rule of the military government and wander around Israel, add another layer.

As in Mdanat's film, the combination of these means enables both the preservation and the deconstruction of the harmonious image of the idyllic past. Khleifi's film, however, takes this a step further, anticipating trends that would only take root several years later. Alongside the static preservation of an enchanted past image, it also excavates the layers of memory. Thus it transforms the static narrative of the past resurrected in the present into a story of the remembrance of the past, its recognition and processing, as a working through, as a stage toward a return to life in the present and its continued progression to the future.

The film opens with a "reminder" of the 1970s propaganda films – sequences of collapsing houses, wounded people, ruins, and personal testimonies. All of these constitute the familiar documentary footage of which the cinema of the 1970s made much use. This footage is replaced by documentary images from the 1948 war, beginning with house demolitions and followed by battle scenes and finally shots of refugees. This introduction not only situates the Ma'aloul story in a historical context, but also presents an argument in the dialogue with early cinema. The concrete narrative of actual time and place now replaces the abstract, repetitive story that appeared in the documentary footage in the film's opening. Alongside the revival of the past in the present, there is an endeavor to construct a sequence of time and memory.

Directly after the titles, to the sound of a pendulum ticking and later of children's voices, the camera captures, in static shots, the details of the demolished village of Ma'aloul: a wall, a window, a tree. This static condition captured on film is upset by the appearance of a walker's legs, clad in blue jeans, on which the camera focuses. Next, a mural of the village is shown – church, houses, and trees. The painting is described by the owner of the house, who is explaining how the mural came to be. And then, in a sharp cut, the painting dissolves into a kind of an old, yellow-tinged picture, and the camera moves slowly in strobes, as if simulating the effect of an old film. The village apparently leaps out of the painting and receives a here-and-now life of its own, right in front of the viewer's eyes. The image of the village is then replaced with documentary shots of the founding of the State of Israel and with the teacher's voice recounting its history.

These are the elements with which Khleifi will toy throughout the film, and through them he will, on the one hand, arrest time in a perpetual never-changing past, and, on the other, lead the film towards remembrance, shaping the distance between the time periods. With the help of these techniques, he will both express the fixation of trauma, and work through the grief, thus allowing a revival, a return to life.

While the director resurrects the demolished village via the enacted scenes, appearing in the present at any given moment, the refugees revive it through recognition; they observe the mural and point to where each family lived, where the church was, where the olive tree grew. They stroll amidst the ruins, searching for the sweet-water spring, the raspberry shrub, the prickly-pear hedges, detail after detail. The search itself and the pointing gesture grant these places current existence.

While bringing the past alive in the present, the film also indicates the gap between these two periods of time. It is the length of time passed by the walker in the village, who is searching for the remains of his home and finds them whilst walking, the distance between the ruins among which Palestinian children play during the course of Israeli Independence Day, and the village, which they do not know. It is the gap between history, as the village teacher recounts it to his students, in compliance with Israeli Ministry of Education requirements, and the subjective destiny of those defeated by it, including that same teacher, who is a Ma'aloul refugee. Above all, it is the distance between the two histories: the history of the Jews as quoted by the teacher and reenacted by the director, and Arab history as documented through individual reminiscences. *Ma'aloul Celebrates its Destruction* thus indicates the differences necessary for the recounting of a full historical narrative. These are the differences between time and time, between memory and memory, between the place that was and the one that is, between the two peoples. The film integrates the traumatic story and the story of the attempt to overcome it. Thus it offers a history of trauma as well as another history – that comprised of the double image: present/past, two representations simultaneously illuminating and obscuring each other.

KHLEIFI'S LATER FILMS

Michel Khleifi's later films consolidated the transformation his early documentary films had sparked in Palestinian cinema. As in the early films, their point of departure is a Palestinian space, closed and obstructed by the Israelis. That Palestinian space remains blocked in all of Khleifi's later films, of which we will mainly examine two: *Wedding in Galilee* (1987) and *Tale of the Three Jewels* (1994). It is blocked within the domain of the Israeli military government, within the bounds of the refugee camp, within the confines of the prison. Yet, just like *Fertile Memories*, these films do not accept this condition. Rather, they reconquer the territory. That territory is the local sphere where the daily life of the protagonists unfolds, yet it is also the national arena[16] that revives the pre-occupation past in the present, as an object that is lost but continues to exist in people's consciousness.

Just as in *Fertile Memories* and *Ma'aloul Celebrates its Destruction*, the places where the protagonists of these films reside are real: a village in Galilee (*Wedding in Galilee*), a Jerusalem hotel (*Canticle of the Stones*, 1989), a refugee camp (*Tale of the Three Jewels*). And again like *Fertile Memories*, the later films tend to expand those places, to refer to them as a part of a spacious land and an echo of the landscapes of the past, which are resurrected in the present, although they have in fact been lost.

Here, too, the expansion of space is accomplished first and foremost through the camerawork. Khleifi's films deal with borders; they are trapped within, challenge, cross, discuss, and re-discuss borders. By depicting border crossings and border inspections, the frontiers erected by Israel and those of Palestine in the past, they give shape to the Palestinian experience of growing dependency on borders, those within and those outside of Israel (al Khalidi, 1997). Khleifi's films breach borders and progress toward open spaces in long takes and slow pans, in camera sweeps across and up, in takes that span people and places. And they do so in a flowing stream, using invisible editing, or the eye of the camera that passes from minute details – a leaf, a bough of a tree, a bird – to the entire space, from the Palestinian house to its courtyard, from the courtyard to the garden, and from the garden to the fields that lie beyond. These sites are separated from each other, but the poetic camera creates a flow between them and, in so doing, also creates a link between people and nature and between reality and imagination. The protagonists, who refuse to remain prisoners in their places of quarantine, burst into these spaces of poetry, nature, and imagination. Thus the films sketch a map of the entire Palestinian space that does not recognize Israeli borders and checkpoints and marks the separate, specific features of the landscape, weaving them into one harmonious whole.

Although the Israelis control the landscape with their cars, barbed-wire fences, watchtowers, and towering phallic buildings, the films point to ways of eluding this domination by constructing a different space, one in which Palestinians define themselves apart from and outside of the domineering Israeli gaze. As a consequence, even though the Israelis are in control of it, those looking at the landscape and moving freely within it are Palestinian.[17] The control of the camera and of the Palestinian characters over the landscape compensates, then, in these films, for the distress of the Palestinians living in exile or in the narrowed-down space.

This other space also contains another time. In Khleifi's films there are few recollections of the pre-1948 past. Here and there, and in occasional brief, random and fragmented sentences, the protagonists speak of their lives before the 1948 war. However, although this past is gradually becoming blurred in their memories, it is brought back to life, as in *Fertile Memories*, through Khleifi's use of space. The reenactment, for example, of a traditional marriage ceremony occurring in the present in *Wedding in Galilee*, or palms, wells, and orange trees in Gaza, reminiscent of the Palestinian landscape in *Tale of the Three Jewels*, preserve the past in the present. Thus, what has been lost, the pre-1948 Palestinian place, its connection to nature and the land, the traditional lifestyle dominating it, the freedom of movement and action within it, are all evoked in different versions in the present. The past is imposed on the present,[18] and what happened there is imposed on what is taking place here. Khleifi's cinema, therefore, constructs "the invisible within the visible,"[19] thus expressing the post-traumatic Palestinian consciousness.

Khleifi's late fictional films accomplish in this manner what his early documentary films achieved, and what has often characterized Palestinian literature: the retrieval of the past place, which was previously seized from Palestinians, its enlargement and its revival in the present.[20] This is a space which, in many instances, does not in fact exist and is removed from its original time and place.

Such displacement of time and place occurs, for instance, in Ghassan Kanafani's *Men in the Sun* ([1963] 1998) and Anton Shammas's *Arabesque* (1986). In Kanafani's short novel, three Palestinian men who live in Iraq attempt to cross the desert in the container of a water-carrying truck, in order to reach Kuwait and find work there. During the border crossing, the driver is delayed, only to find on returning to the truck three bodies roasted in the August desert heat. Ibrahim (2000) and Yussef al Yussef, as quoted by Jean

Alexsaan (1999), claim that the story warns against forgetting the homeland and against the choice to migrate elsewhere: "The desert contradicts the homeland. There is no flora except for the homeland flora and there is no life without it" (Alexsaan, 1999). Muhammad Siddiq (1984) argues that the theme of the novel is the replacement of Palestine with the pan-Arabic dream, and the realization that this dream is false. Kamal Abdel Malek (Abdel Malek and Jacobson, 1999b) reminds readers how persistent those adhering to the concept of return are, although there is no Palestine to which they can return. However, there seems to be an additional element in the novel; in a series of replacements and displacements, the desert space, the dream about Kuwait, and the journey there imply the dream of Palestine. Thus, for example, the book describes its protagonist contemplating the junction of the Euphrates and Tigris rivers (the Shatt al Arab):

> He raised himself, placing his elbows on the ground, and stared directly onto the great river as if he had never seen it before. That is Shatt al Arab, then, a vast river in which large vessels cruise carrying dates and straw, much like a busy street in the middle of a city, in which many cars travel. This is how his son, Kais, replied in a cheerful voice when he was asked by his father at night what Shatt al Arab was. (Kanafani, [1963] 1998: 18)

The vast river, in which the Euphrates and the Tigris merge and which the protagonist observes, contains the memory of a past Palestine. It is the memory of a distant conversation with Kais about the teacher Saleem, who had taught the boy about the river and who died in Palestine before the occupation. The current space includes the former space, and present time contains past time.

Similarly, here is the dream of the protagonist, Abu Kais, about Kuwait: "Certainly, there are men and women and children in the alleys and streets running among the trees." And later: "No, no, there are no trees. His friend, Sa'ad, who had worked there as a driver and returned with sacks full of money said there are no trees. The trees are in your head, Abu Kais! In your old exhausted head. Ten, thick-trunked trees producing an abundance of olives . . . there are no trees in Kuwait" (22). The journey to Kuwait certainly emphasizes the alienation Palestinians feel in the Arab expanses that become increasingly barren the further away they are from their homeland, and it accentuates the belief that the pan-Arabic notion is no replacement for home. Yet, this is also the story of the expansion of space. The reality in which the protagonists live is constructed of impassable borders – between the characters' place of residence and Kuwait, between themselves and Palestine. The structure of the sentences in *Men in the Sun* and the structure of the characters' consciousness link these distances and bridge them. Consequently, a continuity and fluidity between areas is created, similar to the fluidity formed by the camera in Michel Khleifi's *Wedding in Galilee*, where the eye of the camera moves from the village to the olive groves and from the olive groves far away to the horizon. This is also the continuum created by the sentence structure in Anton Shammas's *Arabesque*, which fluctuates between various temporal and spatial reference points. For example: "They passed through El Mansura gate, through the fence erected at the beginning of the Arab Rebellion, which came loose around the founding of the State of Israel, and then reappeared many and good years later in the shape of the Good Fence" (Shammas, 1986: 29). Or,

> "The bride was mounted on a white mare and shots of joy echoed in the air that cleared after a week of violent rains and these are the shots that reminded her, the bride, the shots that had ended the lives of the three white horses at the end of October 1936. And she was to remember these shots again two days before Christmas of 1946, when she is already a mother of four." (29–30)

Either way, the lost land has not dissolved into a remote memory. It continues to exist everywhere and at any given moment. In other cases, the differences between works of art created in the homeland and describing the lost place and those created outside it and mainly restoring its loss will become apparent.

Yet, Khleifi's films send a double message. On the one hand, they make peace with loss and revive what has been lost "as if it is fully present, rather than a representation in memory of something that has already passed and is gone" (LaCapra, 1997). On the other hand, the focus on the particulars of reality as well as the cinematic working through of that past constitute an attempt to overcome loss and regain control over reality, in terms of time and space. It is an endeavor to proceed from the past to the present, from dream to reality, without obliterating either.

In his later films, as in his first, Khleifi not only "enlarges" the national boundaries, but also examines the fragmentation and the heterogeneity of what is bracketed by these boundaries. The films delineate a national Palestinian collective united against the Israeli enemy, while simultaneously deconstructing that collective and examining the identities comprising it: the village, class, gender, family, and so on.[21] These identities have vied, as described above, with the national identity. Since 1948, the Palestinian discourse, and Palestinian cinema within it, have been striving to make them representative of nationhood, thus blending them into the national identity. Khleifi's films restore the independence of the various identities and, as in the case of *Fertile Memories*, for instance, construct the national identity through them. This is a unity that is based neither on imposing a single identity on many nor on imposing one time on different times.

Of all the identities that fragment the national identity, Khleifi's films focus on three: women, the elderly, and children. *Fertile Memories* first positions Palestinian women at the center of the screen and examines them in view of the differences between their various classes, regions, ethnic identities, religions, and generations. Thus the film creates an alternative to the option of male dominance in construing Palestinian nationhood and struggle. Subsequent films depart from the premise of a patriarchal Palestinian society, which views the national struggle as a masculine matter,[22] by focusing on women, alongside children and the elderly. All three groups offer an alternative that is based not on a "we-them" dichotomy but on hybridity, difference, and a variety of identities and loyalties. Khleifi explains the change in the point of departure thus:

> Back then, we thought simplistically that the whole world is against us and that the Zionists are everywhere. It may be so, but since childhood I've had my own outlook on the matter and I wanted to place it at the core of my cinematic expression. This outlook consisted of the belief that the Israelis derive their strength from our weakness and that our weakness, in turn, is not derived from Israeli strength but from the archaic structure of our Arab society: tribalism, patriarchy, religion, and community life. A person isn't recognized as an individual: men, women, and above all, women's rights [are disregarded]. (Khleifi, 1997)

Furthermore:

> The Palestinians, while being victims of oppression, are also guilty of oppressing others: the rural population, the laborers and the women. I have attempted to make a film about zero oppression . . . The oppressing Jews, who are they? They are themselves the victims of inhuman persecution. However, they still oppress another people, the Palestinians. And the Palestinians, are they merely victims, or are they victimizers as well? The answer is that they are both. Their society oppresses the women and children . . . Things should be taken at all levels, there is no point in merely discussing the wrong done. This will not determine who the victim and who the oppressor is. We must unveil the systems and the logic that cause us to become potential oppressors and victims. In order to reach the depths, there was a need to penetrate the characters' inner world, and for this purpose, one needed to disregard the borders between the documentary and the fictional. (private interview, Paris, 2003)

The men in Khleifi's films are those who take action, fight, and rebel against Israeli rule. The Israeli occupation has humiliated them and has denigrated their manliness, and so the struggle against this occupation is meant also to rehabilitate their masculinity. It will enable them to shake off their passivity and submission, traits considered weak and effeminate, as well as the label of femininity which colonialism (and, later, Israeli culture) has imposed on the Arab male.[23] While doing so, the struggle allows them to present in the current time a new version of the defeat of the past. Even when women join the national struggle, as in *Tale of the Three Jewels*, it is still viewed as a purely masculine matter. Khleifi's films link masculinity as an expression of domination over the land and the homeland with manliness as an expression of patriarchal rule over the family. They also examine how the two affect each other, thus weaving an Oedipal story in which sons attempt to establish their masculinity by rebelling against their own fathers. Facing the traditional authority of the fathers, who are weak, submissive, and sickly, the sons try to find their own paths. This struggle reflects the position of those belonging to the second generation of the *Naqba*, who blame the national catastrophe on the leaders of the previous generation, accusing them of failing to set up an army, to form representative institutions, or to recruit allies. Another objection to their fathers was on the grounds of their incompetence in asserting their independence from the Arab regimes, some of which were considered corrupt (Faruk's, Egypt), some considered British protégés, and some accused of conducting clandestine negotiations with Zionist institutions (Abddalla the First's Jordan). This older generation was thus reproached for failing to crystallize the disintegrated Palestinian people around a joint active struggle. Following the war, parents were criticized by the younger generation for their passivity and cooperation with the Israeli regime. The young people's struggle suggested an alternative to all of this.

Against the Oedipal plot, which creates a coherent and unified state of nationhood and repairs and restores its past, the films, by means of women, children, or the elderly, present a different narrative. It is a multifarious, ambivalent narrative that, to paraphrase Bhabha (1990), attempts to fracture categories, to open national, class, generational, and gender borders, and to merge past traditions that are revived in the everyday life of the present itself. This narrative exceeds the binary opposites of men and women, young and old, Palestinian and others, replacing them with a range of voices that the unifying male nationhood cannot silence. In this state of affairs, it is the men who delineate the borders between masculinity and femininity, and who struggle against Israeli rule, while the women and children strive for greater heterogeneity and a more ambivalent definition of nation and gender.[24] They lean towards a third space that lies somewhere between the masculine and the feminine, between the archaic and the modern, between the young and the elderly, between the Israeli and the Palestinian.[25]

One might conclude, therefore, that Michel Khleifi's cinema breaches the boundaries of space and time, exceeding the limits of the narrow areas in which the characters live. Thus it allows them to extend themselves to other spaces and times, untouched by the Israeli occupation, including the times and spaces of the past, revealed again in the present. Yet, implied in this challenge to the national borders is a desire to obliterate those borders completely and with them also those of gender, in addition to creating alternative time sequences. The films end with the victory of the masculine, national narrative and of national time and spaces. The Israelis are the ones imposing on the Palestinians, in these films, a national binary division based on unequal power relations. In the given situation, there is no possibility of breaking these power relations and replacing them with "a game of multifarious identities" (Ferguson et al., 1990: 181). Yet the films still suggest the prospect of such a game and with it the potential to merge narratives, times, and spaces.[26]

Wedding in Galilee

Woven into the plot of *Wedding in Galilee* (1987), a struggle evolves between Israeli control over space and the camera aligned with the Arab characters' gaze, creating a different relationship with the same space. At the beginning of the film, the camera ascends to the top of the Governor's phallic building, which symbolizes might and power. Inside the building, a conversation is taking place between an Arab village mayor and the Israeli military governor of the district. The mayor wishes, despite the curfew, to celebrate his son's wedding with the traditional elaborate ceremony, and the governor, who initially refuses to allow the wedding to take place, finally yields, provided that in return he and his staff are invited.

As the father rides back to his village, open spaces – fields and olive groves – unfold in traveling shots projected through his eyes. This bus trip is both a journey across stretches of land and a response to the Israeli phallic dominance of it. It is also a journey through time since, during in the course of the trip, the father imagines what is about to occur when he reaches his home and announces the wedding to his family and to the entire village.[27] Such confrontations between Israelis and Arabs over ways of interacting with space recur throughout the film. The Jews declare a curfew and the Arab inhabitants are ordered to stay within their homes, but the camera rebels against the command and in two slow shots captures the space to the horizon, in daytime and afterwards in the evening. Thus it restores the relationship, which the Israelis have severed, between indoors and outdoors and between village and fields. A woman's voice is heard, singing in Arabic, and the camera slowly pans the garden at night; suddenly, a violent shout in Hebrew – "Shut up, you whores" – silences the voice and renders the camera motionless. Throughout the film, the Arabs' point of view, through which the camera observes the space, is confronted with the violence of the Israeli penetration of the village and the fields by means of jeeps, motor vehicles, mines that have been strewn in the fields, and shouting.

The Israelis confine the Arabs to the village and then, by imposing a curfew, to their houses. The film defies this confinement not only by employing long shots of the horizon but also by creating a continuous flow among house, court-yard, orchard, and fields. In the course of the wedding, the camera circulates freely among these places. In doing so, it turns the cramped space that the Palestinians actually possess into an infinite one, connecting house and village with the whole country and integrating them into a whole harmonious space – a spacious land. Most Palestinian films try to reconstruct this natural whole-ness, which is a site of nostalgia and yearning. This is why so many of them, such as *The Return to Haifa* (1982) or *Place, or Outside of Paradise* (2000), situate even urban houses in the heart of blooming fields.

The film subjects time to the same treatment. Life in the Israeli Arab village is divided into periods between curfews. These sections are linked by the wedding, where old traditional ceremonies, rarely performed in the modern reality in which the film is set, are re-enacted. The ceremonies revive the pre-occupation and pre-modernization past of the village in the space of the present. "How do you make a film about a non-existing space?" asks Haim Bresheeth (2002a, b), and answers: "By telling stories," by replacing the phys-ical territory of the house with narrative icons of the homeland. The wedding ceremony in *Wedding in Galilee* uses such icons, which resurrect the pre-occupation village and its space within the space of the present. It thus consti-tutes a parapraxis of sorts, enabling the past to permeate through the present and to retrieve that which has been lost.[28] The lost thing is the landscape unfolding in front of the camera. It is an agricultural and rural landscape, of the village's stone-built houses surrounded by olive groves, a landscape that has nearly ceased to exist around the Galilee villages. In fact, shots of five different villages, some in the West Bank, were required to restore that view. With the revival of the past landscape, the film also evokes the distressful living condi-tions under military government. Such a government had operated within the Israeli borders until 1966. However, the film insinuates that it is still in effect during the period of filming, in 1987.[29] Thus the film revives the past and expands it over wide areas, through the camerawork and the characters' move-ment and point of view.[30]

While, through its appropriation of time and space, the film constructs the national story of trauma, it also deconstructs that traumatic narrative by observing the personal experiences of those participating in the wedding in the course of everyday mundane moments. In Khleifi's own words (private inter-view, 2003): "The West does not see the Arab town, only the ignorant villages. I try to do the opposite. To transform the village into a town." The urban expe-rience, he believes, is a heterogeneous, multidimensional one, of various classes, generations, and genders "challenging the idea of the nation as an abstraction." That is the experience of the third space, in which Khleifi focuses mainly on female activity.[31]

The attitude of most of the villagers is: "there is no festivity without dignity and no dignity under army boots." This is especially true for the young men, who object to the father's decision to invite the Israeli military governor to attend his son's wedding. The dignity involved is a male one, unifying the villagers in the Palestinian national narrative and tested during confrontation with the Israeli Other. In the name of honor, some of them refuse to take part in the wedding. In the course of the celebrations, moreover, a few secretly organize an attack on the Governor, which, like the battles in Palestinian films of the third period, is, among other things, an attempt to revive and repair, in the present, the failure of the past – the 1948 surrender of the parents' generation. Thus, although the attack against the Governor foreshadows the First *Intifada*, it also encompasses the trauma of the past. The film tests the national masculinity and its narrative by presenting the groom's lack of virility; he cannot consummate his marriage on the wedding night, ostensibly because his father has surrendered to the Israeli Governor. The connection between masculinity and nationhood is confirmed when the bed sheet, stained with the blood of the bride (who had ruptured her own hymen), is exhibited in front of the guests, an incident which is directly followed by the villagers' general, though controlled rebellion against the Governor and his men, who are driven out of the village.

Manliness and nationality are, therefore, associated with each other even though, to a certain extent, the masculine stance, imposing its power and its will on others, is common to Israelis and Palestinians. While the Israeli military governor imposes his presence on the village as a guest of honor, the mayor imposes his fantasy – a lavish wedding for his first-born son, in spite of the hard times – on his family, and a group of youths decides to use the wedding to conduct an act of opposition and resistance that may potentially be devastating.

The film subverts masculine and national power when it places opposite the nation, both Israeli and Palestinian, the family, the village, the region, class,[32] and daily life mainly of the women, all occurring in the present tense. That female life does not strive for a definite narrative goal and is not a replacement for or a revival of the lost past. In their lives, an entire dynasty of women undermines, in various ways, the masculine order and its control over women and their sexuality in the service of patriarchal social interests.[33] The grandmother describes her erstwhile relations with her husband and with men who were not her husband. The groom's sister teases Jewish and Arab men and dreams about leaving the village. After the groom fails to do so, the bride tears her own hymen, in ambivalent, parodic imitations of the male patriarchal role.[34] In all of these instances, the women breach the limits of the masculine order, defining themselves and their bodies, not through the male gaze nor in view of female roles as delineated by men, but rather as representing fertility and as keepers of the family purity.

As already stated, the plot of the film is Oedipal. The young men of the village rebel against the father's authority and refuse to accept his submission to the Governor's order, and his son, the groom, dreams about murdering his father but fails in rebelling against him in any way. Consequently, he also fails to become man enough to fulfill his conjugal obligation on his wedding night. This Oedipal plot is related to the national narrative; rebellion against the father is also rebellion against the Israelis with whom the father cooperates.

However, while the men play out the Oedipal story of failure to rebel against the father and failure in defining their national identity, the women re-enact a different, fragmented, mundane, non-causal plot. They stretch and even cross the national borders between the Palestinian "I" and the Israeli Other by crossing the boundaries between masculine and feminine. They breach both kinds of border when they remove the Israeli army uniform of a young woman soldier who has fainted at the wedding, clothe her in a loose Arab dress, and hug and caress her. Thus, they create a feminine bond that takes place in the sphere that lies between reality and fantasy, a sphere that oversteps national borders as well as the heterosexual binary division. The boundaries are further crossed when the groom's sister provokes an Israeli soldier by telling him: "If you take off your uniform, we will dance with you." Crossing the borders also involves finding a neutral language with which both can conduct a dialogue – the language of silence and music in the women's chamber or the language of signals and sounds that the *Mukhtar*, the village mayor, uses to communicate with his mare, who has run away. The parallel editing of the women's assembly and the pursuit of the mare insinuates a female presence into the language used to bring success to a Jewish–Arabic joint endeavor to catch the runaway mare. The various meanings of the film become apparent in this scene of pursuit and capture of the female horse. The galloping, escaping mare is a symbol preserving a heroic Palestinian past that is characterized by freedom and domination over the unoccupied spaces. But it also indicates an acknowledgement of the Israelis' ambivalence concerning the occupation of the Arab villages in 1948. The scene alludes to a very similar incident in S. Yizhar's story, *Khirbit Khiz'aa* (1949), in which the conquering soldiers try to catch a foal escaping from the occupied village of that name. The Israeli soldier's contemplation of the runaway foal discloses the pain of the ambivalence he feels. He who has driven the Arab villagers out of their homes also protests against that same act and deeply identifies with their longing to return to their village. Similarly, as discussed earlier, the fleeing mare also parallels the rebellion of the women against male domination. In addition, as Naficy says (2001), it is also living proof of the possibility of creating a third space, one of dialogue between Jews and Arabs. It embodies, then, something that has been personified by the women in the film: the possibility of numerous options. It is a situation in which one truth does not obscure other truths; one time does not negate other times; and one nation does not refute the existence of other peoples.[35]

The women also overstep the barriers that separate masculinity from femininity by behaving in ways that combine both male and female traits. Examples of this tendency range from the grandmother's stories about her love affairs, to the wanton behavior of the groom's sister, or even her gazing at herself barebreasted in a mirror while wearing a man's *Kaffiyeh* (Muslim headscarf) and *akal* on her head. Thus the women rebel against both the patriarch's archaic orders and the young fighters' modern ones, and create a border zone, a third space, where sexual and national identities intermingle, and where dream rubs shoulders with reality, as do past and present.[36]

The film expresses the fluidity of female identity and its openness to the Other and to the world by designing the feminine space in a special way. In the Jewish-Arab confrontation, the film extends the Arab space to the horizon. Within the masculine-feminine confrontation, the film divides the Palestinian space in two. The men, unlike the women, are filmed mainly in the courtyard and in the village alleys, in condensed areas, burdened with the atmosphere of suspicion, while dancing, stamping their earth-shaking feet, in front of a phallic architecture. In contrast, the feminine space seems to have no borders, either between people or between person and place. This space unfolds by means of slow, poetic camera movements, panning or tracking from the women to the festooned walls, the objects in the room, the curtain and the pictures, to the colors, perfumes, and incense to keep the evil eye away. Inhabiting the house, the women are nevertheless associated with the outside when the editing cuts from the rooms to the trees in the orchard, accompanied by delicate music that is totally different from the raucous music at the wedding. The poetic motions of the camera and the lyrical music accompanying them also link the women to the elderly people sitting in the orchard, with young children and with the mare liberated from the stable, escaping to the open fields. These movements conflict with the abrupt cuts used for the editing of the men's shots, especially those who are planning the attack. The slow movements place the women (and others) in a different space from that of the men – in an open, fluid, flowing space preserved in the editing, a space in which people and objects flow and the different identities of Jews and Arabs, men and women, in a constant fluid state, are open to change and to the possibility of intermingling. The film confirms this fluidity by integrating traditions from the three religions – Jewish, Christian, and Muslim – into the wedding ceremony and by casting Arab actors (Makram Khoury and Juliano Mer, the son of an Arab father and a Jewish mother) as Jewish army officers. A year prior to the screening of the film, in 1996, the director Shimon Dotan expressed the same sentiment, granting Makhram Khoury a similar role as an Israeli officer in the film *The Smile of the Lamb*.

The association of the actor with his role thus links Jews and Arabs, and the connection between this film and the Israeli film strengthens that link.

At the end of the film, the entire village unites in the struggle against the military governor. Yet, the core of the film emphasizes the differences that are evoked rather than a collective national unity.[37] The central episode of the wedding brings the Palestinian Arab past to the surface. The camera expands the borders and the men's activity intends to atone, through the violent struggle in the present, for the defeat of the past and the loss of the land. However, female activity in the village, taking place in the present and in the mundane details of the daily past, surpasses national borders. Thus it presents the possibility of a different space existing between groups, genders, and peoples, and of another time: one reviving the lost past while integrating the daily sequence of life in the present and creating a flow and connection between tradition and modernity, between the past revived in the present and the actual present occurring separately from it. As noted, the restrained, nonviolent rebellion against the governor eventually occurs after the bride, instead of the bridegroom, has broken her hymen. The plot itself, then, bases the national solution not on the masculine battle occurring in the causal, dynamic plot but in reference to the feminine option, taking place in mundane daily life.[38]

Tale of the Three Jewels

Khleifi's film, *Tale of the Three Jewels* (1994), is set in a refugee camp in Gaza, a nonplace where people live for the moment, remembering and yearning for the places from which they were deported, or dreaming about other places. This is the liminal space, in Bhabha's terms (1990), existing in the "territory of not belonging" (Rogoff, 2000) in an area of exiles who were displaced and lost their roots. This is a place where one does not wish to live and from which one dreams about other places, in particular about Palestine. In this respect, Michel Khleifi's second fictional film is entirely different from his first and from the rest of his early films. Yet, the refugee camp is also where the daily lives of the protagonist, Yussef, and his mother and sister run their course. Yussef's father is in prison, his brother, wanted by the Israeli army, has gone into hiding, and the currently small family lives as ordinary a life as it can in the shadow of the Israeli army, the fences, the watchtowers, and the curfew orders. The boy attempts to escape from this nonplace into other spaces, and the camera accompanies and supports him. The "other spaces" consist mainly of the idyllic Palestine of days gone by.

This space usually resurfaces as part of the concern with traumatic memories of the occupation and the expulsion. A blind old man, Yussef's friend, remembers how his father had clung to the soil and refused to abandon it and escape with the rest of his family. His mother recalls how the occupation had begun as her mother was bathing in the sea. His girlfriend's father recounts a story about how the jewels in his mother's necklace were lost when the family fled from Jaffa, and so on. The film reports the memories of this trauma but also holds on to the time and place that preceded it. Thus, it materializes the absence in the presence and transfers what has occurred in its place – Palestine, and time – the past, to the wrong time and place in the present of the camp.

What is missing now is the landscape of Palestine, which is reflected as though existing in the spaces around the refugee camp: in an oasis, in the sea, and in an orange grove. The blind old man, the boy's friend, speaks longingly of the land from which he escaped and, in this context, recites a poem about a date palm; as he does so the camera cuts to a date palm in the Gaza oasis, under which the boy is walking. Yussef's father, who has been released from prison in a deranged state, rants about the oranges that surround him on all sides. These oranges, symbols of the country that the refugees have left, appear in the present, in the orchard where the boy hides after he has decided to run away to America.

In this respect, the camera and the boy's wanderings along the sandy landscapes of a desert oasis, on the seashore, and in the spaces around the refugee camp weave a fantasy of a large space reminiscent of that created by the camera in *Wedding in Galilee*. It is not a real space but a post-traumatic reflection, a representation of the past in the present.

The narrow, obstructed place is opened up in this film, as in those preceding it, by means of the camera and the editing. Shots of a barbed-wire fence, a soldier in a watchtower, and military vehicles are replaced with shots of the oasis, the sky and the palm trees, the sea and the beach, the moon and the birds, seagulls on the waves. The camera and the poetic editing of the film hurdle the obstacles, burst into open nature, and construct a large space in lieu of the cloistered and cramped one where the characters live. This space is further expanded by the camera's movements: descending from sky to earth, panning or tracking across landscapes, or contemplating the characters, a moving wagon or a galloping horse, as they pass from the right side of the frame to the left. The shots are taken from various ranges – from medium to long shots and extreme long shots. The accumulation of such shots creates the harmonious space in which the near at hand is a part of the distant, and the high, like the birds in the sky, touches the low, such as people on the ground. The Israeli army has dictated a particular map with military compounds at its core; the camera, in contrast, delineates a center-free, non-confining map.

The open nature of this map is accented by a major element in the film: motion – the motion of the horse galloping in the distance from one side of the screen to the other; the motion of birds in the sky; and the motion of a far-away wagon. These cinematic images, and others like them, express the dynamic quality of the Palestinian world, and contrast with the static nature imposed on it by the Israeli army. The continuous movement, replete with beauty and poeticism, is usually accompanied by a delicate musical motif associated with the calm and tranquil world that lies outside the clamor of gunshots, shouting soldiers, and roaring military vehicles. The birds, which soar to freedom from the cages where Yussef has kept them, also illuminate the same point symbolically.[39] The boy's wanderings and the camera's movements thus become part of the national struggle to break through the Israeli-imposed borders and to create a large space which reflects distant and unattainable Palestine.

Yet, as in *Wedding in Galilee*, while the film expands the national borders, it also deconstructs them, building on what is left of them a fantasy of a borderless world. Yussef aspires to obliterate all borders. He crosses the boundaries of the refugee camp and wanders around, reaching the oasis, the orange grove, the seashore, the wealthy part of town, and the place where his gypsy girlfriend, A'eeda – who belongs to an inferior, if not a shunned class – resides. Neither Gaza's internal borders nor the external borders constructed by the Israeli occupation seem to hinder him. The map delineated by Yussef's endless roaming does not only enlarge the borders of the siege at the national level, but also defines an open, wide area where a love story, one that has nothing to do with nationhood, can take place. It even goes beyond the limits of Palestinian culture, extending its fixed traumatic time span. This is especially evident in an episode in which the two young protagonists leave the vicinity of the riots, the shooting, and the stones, and head for the oasis. There, A'eeda spins tales of demons, spirits, and fairies. These include "The Tale of the Three Jewels," and are folk stories from various cultures and religions, from numerous past traditions. For Yussef, however, it is not enough to escape the cramped confines of the camp and its traditions. The borders he wishes to rupture are further away. According to the story that his gypsy girlfriend's grandmother tells him, three jewels from a precious necklace were lost in America. A'eeda promises to marry Yussef if he recovers them. In order to accomplish this task, he tries to cross the border into Israel and to find work there. When he fails, he hides in an orange crate in the hope of reaching Europe and subsequently America when the oranges are exported. The borders he crosses are not only regional and national; they are also international frontiers, which metamorphose at a certain stage into pan-Arabic borders: for example, when his sister shows him a map and points to Palestine, in an area marked as Southern Greater Syria. These borders eventually become metaphysical when, in Yussef's dream, his blind friend appears and explains to him that God has set borders for time, space, and the body, and warns him that they must not be crossed. Khleifi explained in an interview the background for the breaching of national time and space borders:

> I based the script upon the prevalent, cultural, and religious traditions of the region: legends, folklore, belief in spirits, and so on. A historical

space cannot be divided into community and religious segments – Jewish, Christian, Muslim – and I would add atheist, as well. I believe that everyone is entitled to inherit the legacy of the region, including the pre-monotheistic legacy of yesterday and the secularism of today. (Khleifi, 1997)

By crossing borders, Yussef embodies the complexity of Palestinian society with its diverse classes, regions, and ideologies – a complexity that is not confined to national identity alone but recognizes an intermingling of perpetually changing identities, exiles, and borderless cultures that intertwine with each other.[40] This distinct heterogeneity is linked, as in *Wedding in Galilee*, to the heterogeneity of the different time sequences, replacing the uniform national time that reconstructs the static paradise of the past in the present.

In addition, here, as in *Wedding in Galilee*, national and masculine identities are connected. The occupation has caused harm to all the men in Yussef's family. His brother goes into hiding as a fugitive and comes home with a wounded friend; the head of the household is thrown into prison and returns deranged; the man next door, Yussef's friend, is blind.[41] Against this defeated masculinity, Yussef, the film's protagonist, wishes to pave a path for himself, which will lead him to a different kind of manhood. But to that end, he must distance himself from his surroundings – the camp, the *Intifada*, and the prison – and find a place removed from the national struggle; "I must grow up; I must marry you," he tells A'eeda. With that cause in mind, he wishes to travel to America to retrieve the lost jewels. The association of a different notion of masculinity with a different idea of space emerges from a picture that Yussef draws during a school lesson. The drawing shows a man in a woman's form, an androgynous creature of sorts, surrounded by the word "borders" repeated over and over again. Thus, the borders that Yussef attempts to obliterate in his wandering are not only those of space, class, and race, but also gender boundaries between the feminine and the masculine. These boundaries are blurred, too, by the women surrounding him, in whose shadow he has grown up – the mother, the sister, and his friend A'eeda. These women dominate the world that Yussef inhabits, at home and outside of it, and what is more, he interrelates with them, and especially with A'eeda, in a symbiosis;[42] he seems to unite with her in nature, among the animals, against the background of the fables that she tells him.

At the end of this film, as in *Wedding in Galilee*, the national theme resurfaces and returns to the fore. Israeli soldiers shoot Yussef, after he emerges out of the crate in an orchard and turns to run towards the bird that his mother released from the cage. A'eeda's father explains that the jewels were lost, in fact, not in America, but in Jaffa as the family was fleeing the town. And toward the end of the film, Yussef's dream about metaphysical boundaries concludes with an image of Palestinian and Israeli flags scattered on the ground by the dozen. The final note of *Tale of the Three Jewels*, therefore, is sounded around the national narrative of repression and occupation that leads Yussef back to his national identity. However, during the course of the film, other themes, ideologies, and identities are presented and dealt with. In *Tale of the Three Jewels*, as in *Wedding in Galilee*, then, Michel Khleifi breaks through the external restrictions that have been imposed on Palestinian society and creates a fantasy about a large space that encompasses other places and times. The film resurrects the Palestinian past, plants it in the present, and allows its protagonists to reassert control over it by dominating the entire space. Yet, as in the earlier film, *Tale of the Three Jewels* also examines what has been contained within the boundaries of Palestinian society and within the fixated time, restoring the past in the present. Khleifi has peeled off the perceived illusory homogeneity of this society by examining class, regional, and gender dimensions separately, and the imagined homogeneous time by addressing different memory sequences. In the struggle between genders, regions, times, and classes, the film offers unfeasible options (as the end of the film indicates) of both an internal and an external border-free existence. Such an option has been suggested and questioned in all of Khleifi's other films. This is the possibility for a "third space," one which is neither Jewish nor Arab, neither masculine nor feminine, neither at home nor in exile, and is at the same time all of these together. Such a space indirectly reflects, perhaps, the space in which the director himself resides: between cultures, nations, countries, home, and exile, by way of co-productions with many countries that sponsor his films and by way of the various styles that characterize them.

Michel Khleifi's cinema uses the cinematic language of the Third World, as Gabriel (1989b) described it – a cinema that breaks up the structure of plot by inserting shots of space, and focuses on the collective rather than on the individual, using medium and long shots rather than close-ups, and folklore rather than individual stories. Yet, Khleifi's films also use the language of Western cinema, especially the lyrical Italian or French cinema.[43] Thus one might conclude that his work operates within Western culture while subverting it in the name of the Palestinian culture it expresses. At the same time, it operates within Palestinian culture while criticizing it and deviating from it by giving voice to "others" who have previously been excluded from it, and presenting spaces that have been ignored in it. Khleifi's films also utilize the Israeli narrative, with which the director is well familiar, in order to withhold its progression, bring to the surface what has been repressed, and replace it with the Palestinian narrative. It is an exilic cinema, to use Naficy's term (1999) – situated between the zones, at once inside and outside of them, deconstructing the various languages that it uses,[44] and thus constructing the Palestinian national narrative as an open, fluid, and diverse one.

That story had already been presented in Michel Khleifi's early documentaries. In his late films, however, it is comprised of plots that unfold as a polemic between various options. In this dispute, in this cinema, there are no winners.

NOTES

1. For the tension between home and exile, see Peters (1999).
2. See Gabriel (1989b) for the significance of space in Third World cinema.
3. As Bresheeth defines other Palestinian directors: "Conceptually and ideologically, they operate on the interstitial space between cultures: the Israeli and Palestinian, the Palestinian in Israel and the Palestinian in the occupied territories, the Palestinian in Palestine and the Palestinian in the Diaspora, Palestine and the Arab world, and Western vs Oriental discourse" (Bresheeth, 2002b).
4. As is revealed in Palestinian literature. In the words of Farid (no date: 11), for instance, "the real resistance is of the ordinary man performing his everyday chores." For the connection between space and time, see Naficy (2001). Also relevant on this matter is the article by Gurevitz and Aran (1991), which defines the small place as "a place that is determined and can be characterized according to a certain locality in a sense close to the state of being native – the home, street, friends, a childhood landscape" (11). Khleifi himself locates the sources of the cinema that documents everyday occurrences in the history of the *cinéma vérité* in France, a cinema that was anchored in people's reality. In 1997, he clarified the difference between his cinema and that which preceded him: "Beginning with my first television movie, I have reduced the role of the voice-over, I have given up leaders' speeches and focused on strong situations that expressed the complexity of the reality." In fact, the Palestinian literature in Israel has been interpreting, since as far back as the 1950s and 1960s, daily routine as a way of preserving the Palestinian environment in the Israeli reality that has been changing it (McKean Parmenter, 1994: 77).
5. This is the time of life itself, referred to by Bhabha (1990) as the performative time, subverting the linear, homogeneous time of the national narrative. In this case, it subverts both the narrative shaped by the earlier cinema and the Israeli narrative. Also, Marks (1994) attributes the linear, homogeneous "pedagogical" narrative, which Bhabha has discussed, to the Israelis alone, disregarding the Palestinian national narrative, which daily mundane life also subverts.
6. Certain scholars refer to cultural perceptions which define space as a passive, inanimate, effeminate component, as opposed to time, considered an active, masculine element (Massey, 1993). In this respect, Khleifi's choice to focus on space reflects a preference for femininity over masculinity. The same is true about his choice to highlight trivial daily life and the domestic sphere, perceived as feminine, rather than masculine action in history and the public sphere (Rose, 1993). Yet, as mentioned earlier, Khleifi deconstructs the accepted divisions of feminine and masculine space. On this deconstruction, see Naficy (2001), who defines exilic cinema as "accented cinema," in contrast with cinema that is accent-free, being rooted in place.
7. See an analysis of this phenomenon in Shafik (1998).
8. On the distinction between space as a neutral given and place as a culturally dependent construction of space, see Rogoff (2000), Kimmerling (1989), and Zanger (forthcoming).
9. Jameson (1986) identifies the connection between the private and the public, or between the poetic and the politic as a central component in Third World literature. In the case of Khleifi and other Palestinian filmmakers, this connection is only one

component in a complex junction of meanings, in which the individual does not always necessarily represent the national meaning. Also, see footnote 14 in the Introduction.

10. See Rogoff (2000) on the dependency of the gaze at the landscape on the subjective vantage point.

11. The dictionary definition of *sumud* is: a steadfast stand, facing difficulties, perseverance. The word has become commonly used in the description of the Palestinian struggle against the Israelis, a struggle waged through grasping on to life rather than through the use of firearms and active fighting.

12. On ways of connecting the house with the outside, see Morley (1999).

13. In Naficy's words, "We might say that ethnic, diasporic, exilic identities are performances dependent on repetitive practices that with time produce ethnic, diasporic or exilic identities."

14. This past is what turns the actual, natural place into an idea of homeland. See Gurevitz and Aran (1991).

15. This is how Naficy (2001) characterizes accented cinema. See also footnote 6.

16. See footnote 4.

17. On the issue of the Palestinian gaze, see Pinhasi (1999) and Shohat and Stam (1994), according to whom, by merely presenting the experiences of Palestinian society and landscapes, *Wedding in Galilee* asserts the existence of the Palestinians in defiance of their obliteration by the Israelis. On the time and space seized from the Palestinians by the Israelis, see Bresheeth (2002a).

18. The evoked past is the harmonious, whole past predating the historical separation from the country.

19. As parapraxis. See footnote 8 in the Introduction.

20. See the discussion above of the ways in which historical memory "invents" geographical space.

21. On this issue, see Shohat and Stam (1994), who examine the flowing movement of *Wedding in Galilee* between the characters and the fusion of types of discourse and languages that express, according to the writers, the complexity of the Palestinian nation.

22. For the connection between masculinity and nationality, see the Introduction.

23. The post-1948 Palestinian was also associated with the same image. See Harkabi (1975: 250): "For a long time, the Palestinian was teased for being weak, cowardly and lacking in self-respect. He was blamed for being lowly and despicable, and having no dignity or virility to elevate him."

24. Kristeva (1986) and Silverman (1996) identify this feminine activity as subversion of the masculine symbolic order in the name of the illusionary completeness of the pre-Oedipal phase, in which the child still has not experienced a separation between himself and the world (Kristeva, 1986; Moi, 1985). But this completeness is not uniform and in this case is based on compliance with a diversity of identities, on gender ambivalence instead of a binary method of thinking.

25. For the deconstruction of feminine stereotypes in Khleifi's cinema, see Naficy (2001) and Shafik (2001).

26. See Genocchio (1996) on the dismantling of the fixed layout of space and replacing it with other – more flexible – layouts.

27. According to Khleifi (1987), the father takes on the director's role here.

28. See the aforementioned discussion and Gabriel's explanation (1989b) of the role played by folklore in the revival of what official memory attempts to obliterate.

29. According to Khleifi, in this manner he links the hardships of life under occupation in the present-day West Bank with life within the State of Israel, in the past and the present, integrating it all into a single national experience.

30. The same occurs in another of Khleifi films, *Canticle of the Stones*. What has not yet unfolded at plot level is foreshadowed by the camera, which is first to reach the places to be discussed later on in the film, thus displaying its control over time and events.

31. For the use of the term third space, see the Introduction and Naficy (2001: 169), Soja and Hooper (1993), Ferguson et al. (1990), and others. Note also Khleifi's words: "There is always space overlapping another space, touching a third space. There is never a complete rift between the different groups" (Khleifi, 1987).

32. According to the Palestinian proverb, "The family honor precedes the national struggle and the protection of the land" (Kivorkian-Shalhoub, 1999). See Shohat and Stam (1994) on the many accents in this film, demonstrating the characters' regional differences.

33. See Kivorkian-Shalhoub (1999) for feminine subversion in Palestinian society. See also Jawwad (1990).

34. Mimicry, in Bhabha's terms (1990).

35. See Shohat and Stam (1994), who consider this scene proof of the superior attitude of the Arab, who succeeds in communicating with his mare by way of voices rather than through guns.

36. See Nassar (2002). It is worth adding to his argument that the dialogue is "saturated" here with the female presence.

37. In this matter, see Shohat and Stam (1994: 277), who discuss the simultaneous presentation in the film of both differences, gaps and tensions within Palestinian society, and the joint struggle against the occupation and a shared cultural and historical identity, whose foundations are rooted in the soil and in the past.

38. As Khleifi himself professes (in a private interview, Paris, 2004), associating modernity (as expressed in the images of female nudity and the voyeuristic gaze of the camera capturing them) and tradition.

39. The national significance of this breaching of borders is evident from the fact that the bird escaping its cage is a robin, *hasun* in Arabic; this is considered a "Palestinian bird."

40. On this topic, see Bhabha (1990) and footnote 1 above.

41. For the connection between blindness and castration, see Boyarin (1997) after Freud. Here, blindness is related to disconnection from the land and to losing the possibility of seeing it.

42. This symbiosis is reminiscent of the fantasy of return to the pre-Oedipal phase, in which there are no boundaries between mother and child, and between child and world. See Hoffman (1997), who discusses femininity as having more fluid borders than masculinity.

43. The landscapes, the way they are filmed, the merging of lyrical camera movements and lyrical music constitute a sort of homage to the cinema of the Taviani brothers, as well as to Pasolini's cinema, just as the dialogue in *Canticle of the Stones* is a homage to Alain Resnais's *Hiroshima mon amour* (1959).

44. Actions that can be described by the terms "de-territorialization" and "re-territorialization," coined by Deleuze and Guattari (1990).

4. WITHOUT PLACE, WITHOUT TIME: THE FILMS OF RASHID MASHARAWI

INTRODUCTION

Rashid Masharawi's films do not explore the enchanted past that is restored in Michel Khleifi's films, nor do they spin – as Khleifi's cinema does – a fantasy of open expanses. Rather, his cinema delineates the refugees' here-and-now daily struggle for survival within a space that has been gradually diminishing, from the time Palestinians were driven out of their native villages and gathered in the refugee camps up to the period of siege that they endured during the Second *Intifada*. Attempts to burst out to the open spaces of the land and references either to the country's past or to future plans to return to it are presented in his films in a disruptive, insinuated manner, in a dream sequence, or in association with madness.

In an interview with Ali Waked (1993), Masharawi explains:

> Jaffa is always present in my subconscious. It is true that I love Jaffa, but I do not have to mourn over it in a blatant and acrimonious way. It won't help if I shout all the time 'I am from Jaffa and this is my house!' The tedious repetition of my story as a refugee would only diminish its strength and significance. It would also lessen its reliability and would cast doubts on my beliefs and on the justice of my claims.

Yet, as is the case in so many other movies, the past is not completely missing from Masharawi's films. It does not, however, appear as an actual living memory but rather as a representation of what once was and is now so difficult to evoke in memory. Masharawi's films allude not to the pre-1948 enchanted past, but to the past of "pain and displacement" intrinsic to the occupation itself. Perhaps the difference between Khleifi's films, which reconstruct the country's past, and Masharawi's films, which resurrect its loss, is rooted in the two filmmakers' different backgrounds. While Khleifi grew up in pre-1948 Palestine, from which he departed to exile, Masharawi matured in a refugee camp, and spent most of his youth as a humble laborer in Israel.

Instead of reviving the Palestine of the past indirectly in the present, Rashid Masharawi's cinema brings the traumatic moments of the deportation itself to the surface. The protagonists in his films live and struggle in the dead-end present, enjoying no future prospects. The strong presence of the idyllic past in the current existence, the reliance on a world of dreams, and the fantasy of a border-free universal condition, all of which are familiar from Khleifi's films, are absent in most of Masharawi's works. When such sentiments do appear, furthermore, they are expressed mainly through the consciousness of an afflicted or mad person. The structure of his films, where aspirations to change the present situation invariably turn to hopelessness, where disaster is followed by an even greater calamity, where the protagonists' circumstances deteriorate from bad to worse, and from worse to even more terrible, is reminiscent of existentialist literature, which depicts the human condition as a kind of prison. In Albert Camus's *The Outsider* (L'Étranger, 1943), for example, the protagonist passes from a state of freedom to incarceration and finally to solitary confinement on death row, with the gradually diminishing space paralleled by his increasingly evaporating hopes. But while in existentialist literature the narrowing of space and the loss of hope are accompanied or compensated by an epiphany and consequently by an acceptance of human destiny, in Masharawi's films human destiny is intertwined with political destiny and leads to neither freedom nor enlightenment. This fate, described exclusively in the present, evokes the initial crisis, the distant defeat, as an imaginary echo, as the return of the repressed.

The different versions of the past demonstrated by the two filmmakers, Khleifi and Masharawi, determine the place of the future in their films. Both usually do not mention the idea of return. However, Michel Khleifi uses the medium of the movie camera to give form, through the expansion of the spaces of the past and the control of the Palestinian eye over them, to what is not mentioned. In contrast, Rashid Masharawi uses his camera to illustrate the heroic, futile daily struggle within the prison walls. The memories and the dreams that are evoked in the context of this struggle are presented from the beginning as acts of madness or as a fantasy and they are further distorted and replaced by a series of disasters, which constitute a repetition of the original disaster.

For both of these filmmakers, the past is substituted by the present, albeit in each case the present is different. Everyday life in Khleifi's films creates a different time, an alternative to the traumatic time that revives the national past and "repairs" the outcome of the national struggle. During this time, various protagonists, who are very different from each other and preserve diverse memories, live their private lives. Even though this private time is eventually linked to the national narrative, it still allows for individual space and consequently enables the construction of a more open and heterogeneous national narrative. In Masharawi's films, it is difficult to construct a private space. The shared experiences of siege, curfew, and exile make each of the individual stories an allegory of the collective experience,[1] and a representation of the national trauma and the trauma of displacement beyond it.

SHRINKING SPACES, DECLINING HOPES

The film *Curfew* (1993) opens with a high-angled long-shot view of the city of Gaza, and a series of dissolves that expand these spaces. Next, the camera is directed downward to the refugee camp. This is a very static camera, its immobility emphasizing the absence of motion in the camp, which appears as an unpeopled, lifeless world, bare and strange, a place of exile. The camera then zeroes in on a small playground where some children are playing, and proceeds to a narrow apartment into which a family is crowded, where it will remain "stuck" for the rest of the film. Group shots capture the family members in the foreground and the background confined in these tiny lodgings, but without close-ups that could create a sense of personal space. The family seems imprisoned behind frames and bars, blocked by closed compositions, always crowded together within the enclosing walls, while the camera is inside, trapped, like one of the family members. The camerawork therefore reflects a process of narrowing of the film's scope. It progressively shrinks the vista: from the broad space of Gaza city that, to begin with, is perceived by the camp inhabitants as an exilic space, to the camp itself, and from there to the playground and finally the apartment that confines its residents as in a jail. The urban expanses, seen only at the beginning and the end of the film as an establishing shot meant to indicate the location of events, also suggest an additional layer of constraint.[2] Being imprisoned in their own home, the people of the camp never come into contact with the city, next to which the camp is situated.

The house, designed in Khleifi's films as both a private and a national home in harmonious continuum with the space and the earth, is disconnected here from the space. Instead of symbolizing nation, land, and unity, the house signifies the prison of exile, the painful stories of those who live in spaces that "have vanished and in their stead, only a void remained" (Ghanayem, 2000: 15). The difficulties Masharawi encountered while making this film could be said to reflect the film's subject matter. It was shot in 1993, during the First *Intifada*. As it was not possible to film openly in Gaza at that time, the director had to shoot the panoramic views of the city from hidden lookouts or rooftops. The streets of the refugee camp were filmed in the Jenin camp in the West Bank, while the interior scenes were filmed in a house in Nazareth, in Israel proper – far from the camp-dwellers' real home, far from the expanses of the town, which not only the protagonists of the film, but its actors as well, could not reach.

The diminution and reduction process described here characterizes the entire film. The plot is simple. The family sits in its small, crowded home while a young son, Radar,[3] reads aloud a letter sent by his older brother in Germany. The brother's letters, like those of so many refugee sons, arrive periodically from distant diasporas and are shared by the entire family in their Gaza exile; the distant exile seems an extension of the exile depicted in the film, which has been shrunk to this one camp and to this single small apartment.

While Radar is reading the letter, a curfew is announced. If until now the camp's alleyways were more or less empty, now they become utterly deserted. And if before it would have been possible to leave the cramped house (although no such exit is documented), now it is out of the question. From now on the crowded quarters are the only space inhabited by the family members. They will not leave it for the entire length of the film, except for once, in the course of a military search. And then, the narrow apartment seems like a protected nest compared to the darkness outside, the wall against which people are lined up, and the fear of the Israeli soldiers. The result is a heightened sense of claustrophobia and suffocation, confinement with no possibility of an escape, an inside without an outside. What is happening outside (shots, pursuits, house demolitions) can only be imagined, guessed from the sounds or from what is reported by Radar as he peeps from behind a banister. The family's situation, then, worsens as the space diminishes, from being crammed into the house, to being placed under curfew, and finally to being immersed in total darkness when the electricity is cutoff, while the son attempts to resume reading his brother's letter. From this point on, the household members not only are imprisoned in the crowded apartment but also dwell in darkness. Afterwards, the apartment fills with tear gas, and in addition to the darkness, the family's eyes are also shut tight against the stinging gas. Later still, soldiers break into the neighbors' house during the curfew, cast out the residents, and blow it up. When Akram, a younger son, complains, "Eat. Sleep. Prison. Gas. We can't do a thing," his father replies, "Do you want to die? Do you want to go to prison? Do you want the house you live in to be destroyed?" His words foreshadow the future. By the end of the film the neighbors' daughter dies (of tear-gas poisoning) and the family's older son, Raji, is taken off to prison. Apparently every situation can deteriorate, and every decline is followed by another downfall.

The only "consolation" is that the previous situation was also terrible ("What difference does it make?" asks one of the brothers about the curfew. "We're not doing anything anyway"), or that the future may be even more dreadful ("There are people who have lost their sons and they're not crying," the father reproaches the mother, who weeps when her son is taken away). Under such conditions, the yearnings and dreams of the protagonists do not concern the distant past in Palestine or a possible future return to it. The focus is on what has just happened, the moment before the curfew, the moment preceding the darkness. Palestine has no explicit existence in the film. The places the characters of the film want to reach are more distant exiles such as Germany, where the oldest brother is living, or Israel, where there is work.

The unending series of calamities increases the camp-dwellers' hardships, which are not always caused directly by the occupation but are nevertheless always related to it – if not directly, then allegorically. The house was gloomy and ill-lit even before the electricity went out, but as a result it becomes completely obscured. The option of leaving Gaza for work in Israel is perceived by the son as terrible, but that of staying at home is worse. Similarly, everyone has been imprisoned in the camp even before the curfew, which merely worsens their situation. Raji could not leave because he had to look after the family; the daughter, Amal, was not allowed to go out due to required supervision by her parents and brothers; the father cannot move because of his backaches. The distress, passivity and confinement are not necessarily derived from the state of occupation, yet they symbolize it.

A similar downward progression is found in Masharawi's 1991 documentary, *House-Houses (Daro-w-Dour)*.[4] The film's main character is a man who had once been a metalsmith but lost his livelihood when the Israelis destroyed his shop while widening his street. He now works as a house-cleaner in Tel Aviv, far from home. The sharp cinematic transitions between his house in the camp in Gaza and his workplace in Tel Aviv emphasize the endlessness of his exile. Tel Aviv, which has absorbed the neighborhood where he had lived up until 1948 (Manshiyya), is a now a place of exile where he has to stay during the week, cleaning other people's apartments while he longs for his home in Gaza. But Gaza, too, is a place of exile, a foreign space. From this impasse he sinks even further during the Gulf War, when he loses his job and is penned up in the camp, with no possibility of leaving. This new situation of curfew and imprisonment underscores the distress of his previous state of exile and separation ("We had been under occupation even before the Gulf War," he says) and the hopelessness of improving the situation in the future ("God willing, tomorrow will be a better day," he says, before adding, "When will it be any better?"). He is troubled everywhere: in Tel Aviv, where he works, far from his family; in Gaza, where he cannot support them; in his house in the refugee camp, where Israeli soldiers threaten to seize him; and outside his house, where he has to hide from them. The continuing deterioration reflected in the narrowing of space – from the open sea, through the yard, into the house, and finally to the plate of food on which the entire life of the family is focused – only accentuates the dead-end nature of the general situation.

Unlike the films *Curfew* and *House-Houses*, in *Haifa* (1995) there are most explicit memories of the distant past, as there are hopes for a better future. The memories are those of Nabil, the camp's "village idiot," who is nicknamed Haifa because he wanders half-mad through the camp's narrow alleys shouting "Haifa! Jaffa! Acre!" The hopes for a better future, shared by many of the camp-dwellers and expressed by the head of the family, Abu Said, hinge on the coming of peace. These memories and hopes coalesce into a certain national continuity that was not present in the other films. However, the series of calamities that occur in *Haifa*, as in the two films described above, contradicts this narrative, shatters it or casts it, together with its memories and hopes, in an ironic mold. As in the other films, although the misfortunes depicted are personal, relating to individual life stories, they are also allegories for the collapse of Palestinian national aspirations.

At the beginning of the film, the madman Haifa still clings to the hopes and memories that sustain him. He remembers the past in Haifa, Jaffa, and Acre; for his aunt, he fills the void left by her absent sons; and he dreams of marrying his cousin in a ceremony set in his remembered city of Haifa. Yet, these hopes too disintegrate when his aunt dies, his cousin marries someone else, and the memory of Haifa and the dream of the marriage ceremony meant to take place there fade away. His aspirations and memories connect his individual story to the collective Palestinian narrative. His personal loss is a story in its own right, but it also projects an ironic light on the general loss – the loss of the dream to return to Haifa. The aunt experiences a similar disintegration as well. She, too, is sustained by hope; throughout the film she never stops waiting for the return of her sons. Each time Haifa enters her house the aunt is sure that one of her sons has returned, and when he leaves she is overcome by loss: "Everyone is leaving. No one is staying." The process of her escalating loss culminates with her death, the last and final loss. Abu Said, the head of the household, is similarly caught in a downward spiral. Formerly a policeman, he has lost his job and now sells sugar-candy to local children. Still, he is hopeful; he has faith in the peace process and believes that he will be able to return to his job, that his son will be released from prison, that the shooting will cease, that "there will be no more dead." However, all these hopes dissipate when, one day, he suffers a stroke and becomes paralyzed. Now that he is unable to leave his bed, he is notified that he has been accepted for a position as a policeman in the Palestinian Authority. Obviously, this announcement comes too late in the game and he is unable to accept it. Although Abu Said's personal catastrophe is also independent of the national story, it seems an ironic comment on the

Palestinian aspirations that he shares, and it reflects, in allegorical fashion, the loss of collective hopes. It confirms the outlook of Ziad, his son, who claims that the peace accord will bring no change in the lives of the refugees in the camp. And, perhaps, it also strengthens the director's point of view: "When they made the agreement they knew that it would leave us in the camps. While in the camp, my land was Jaffa. It justified my life. I would have preferred to end my life with that dream. The peace took Jaffa away from the refugee camp" (Masharawi, telephone interview, 2001).

The camp residents in *Haifa* look forward to the peace process and expect that it will lead to a restoration of Palestinian rights. The deterioration in the lives of the protagonists – Haifa, the aunt, Abu Said – is bitterly accentuated against the background of these hopes. The collision between private and public spheres is exemplified in the film's climax, when a demonstration crossing the camp from one direction intersects with the funeral procession of Haifa's aunt coming from another; in the middle, between them, stands Haifa. The camera moves in for a close-up, and the expression in his eyes reveals the totality of the collapse in both personal and collective spheres. Although these would appear to contradict each other, they are, on the allegorical level, inseparable.

As in *Curfew*, here too the general deterioration is reflected in the diminishing space. And just as Masharawi's characters do not succeed in escaping from present time into memory and dream, so they are unable to progress beyond the present space that becomes more and more condensed and reduced. In *Haifa*, two places are linked to the camp-dwellers' aspirations and dreams: Washington, where the peace talks are taking place, and Palestine, the land relinquished. Both are depicted as equally out of reach. Washington is very far from the refugee camp and the fact that it appears to the camp-dwellers through a broadcast on a broken-down television set exemplifies that distance allegorically. Palestine seems to exist only in the mind of a madman who, when trying to recollect specific details, recalls only the conquest and expulsion rather than the particulars of what had occurred prior to that event. These faraway significant places being out of reach for the camp inhabitants, the characters' connection with them is either devastating or comic. A random conversation among the youths of the camp highlights this, the boys attempting to calculate distances and the time it takes to travel between places in the country – the land they call Palestine – in which they only arrive in their dreams, without ever actually moving.

Both the spaces of the past (Palestine) and those of the future (the peace talks), therefore, seem light years away from the refugee camp inhabitants. But even the nearby spaces remain inaccessible to them. The impossibility of escape is prefigured in the film's opening footage, in which Haifa is seen sitting in an old wreck of a car, turning the steering wheel and going through the motions of driving without, of course, moving anywhere. The editing carries the camera from the car to the landscape just beyond, to the broad open spaces of the nearby desert, which Haifa never reaches. Like the other protagonists of this and earlier films, Haifa remains "stuck" in the camp, a lifeless, motionless place[5] filmed in static shots which take in deserted alleyways and passers-by that seem to float in and out of the frames, or to advance, very slowly, from background to foreground. This is a camp in a state of continuous anxiety, expressed from the start by the pursuit of Ziad by the soldiers, or by the figure of Amal, the daughter, in the desolate house, hidden from the eye.

And, again as in Masharawi's other films, the camera employs an ever-narrowing focus, passing from empty streets to cramped apartments to one small corner in that apartment where Abu Said, the ex-policeman, lies paralyzed in his bed. The broad space displayed as the film opens, evoking promise and memories, diminishes step by step as the film progresses, to close in, at the end, on the narrow confines of a sick man's bed.

The same structure of deterioration that characterized all of Masharawi's other films characterizes *Ticket to Jerusalem* (2003) as well. But here, following the events of the Second *Intifada* during which the film was made, the falls are more severe and the collapse more dramatic. The film begins and ends with traveling shots of the open spaces through which the protagonist, a film projectionist, is driving. The traveling shots allow the camera, here as in many Palestinian films, to conquer the landscape with a look and a movement. But this unfolding view closes as soon as the protagonist arrives at a roadblock. From now on and throughout the rest of the film, he will remain trapped between barriers, much in the same manner as the characters of Masharawi's other films are limited to their apartments or refugee camps. The shots of the exterior are now as cramped as the interior shots were in the earlier films, a fact emphasized by the camera, which captures the narrow streets from a superior angle, from among the narrow alleyways, from in between banisters and stairways.

From the beginning of the film, the protagonist's predicament seems desperate and even impossible, worse, perhaps, than the situation of Masharawi's characters in previous movies. The inhabitants of the West Bank, he is repeatedly told, require not movies but bread and work. Not only do they have no need for his films but he is also unable to reach them physically, spending most of his time trying to pass through checkpoints. Meanwhile his wife remains alone in an empty apartment in the Qalandia refugee camp, his parents are angry with him for leaving her by herself, and everyone around him undermines his work. From here, things become even worse. The closure is tightened, roads are entirely blocked off, the public does not attend the film screening, the electricity is cut off, the camera breaks down, the protagonist stops going to work, and his relations with his wife reach breaking point. And the background is filled with unending explosions, shootings, destroyed houses, and people who have been wounded or killed.

Within the general breakdown occurring in Masharawi's films and as an integral part of it, the hierarchy of authority and identity also crumbles. It is the adult men who decline most acutely. They have been cast out of the public sphere where they were active, cannot leave for work (because of the curfew in the film of that name, the termination of the right to cross the border in *Daro-w-Dour* and in *Ticket to Jerusalem*, or physical paralysis in *Haifa*), and can determine neither their own nor their families' fates. The people who control their lives from a distance are the Israelis. They themselves are restricted to their homes – the women's space, in a passive state, doing nothing, which they experience as a castration, as a backache, or as a paralysis that confines them to their beds (in *Curfew* and in *Haifa*) but keeps them away from their wives' beds. Although both the backache and the paralysis are private, physical, and real, they also serve as allegories for the collective situation of the adult generation: the second *Naqba* generation. As mentioned earlier, the first generation was accused of passivity and incompetence by its sons, who have matured along with the national Palestinian movement and in the shadow of the First *Intifada*. The male identity of this generation as a whole is presented in these films as a mere semblance of such, with the men clinging to manly functions that they can no longer fulfill. Thus Haifa is a soldier armed with a cardboard gun, who "drives" a car that goes nowhere; Abu Said is a policeman who is no longer on the police force; Abu Raji is a shopless barber; and the protagonist of *Ticket to Jerusalem* projects films to an audience that does not want to see them. Michel Khleifi has examined and deconstructed in his films the connection between patriarchal virility and national masculinity. Masharawi, in turn, does not deconstruct this connection. Rather, he integrates it into the theme of general collapse, not necessarily a masculine collapse.

Ostensibly, real control appears to be in the hands of the women, who run the households, determine lifestyles, distribute what little food they manage to obtain, and try to dictate how their adult children will live (one son will study, another will work, and the daughter will marry, decides mother Um Said in *Haifa*). They do not create a fluid third space like the one inhabited by the women in Khleifi's films, but they do reflect the strengthening of women's status in Palestinian society and the roles that they filled during the First *Intifada*. Yet, not only do the women remain under male control and supervision, locked within the preordained constraints of fertility and family, but they also lose whatever authority they appeared to have acquired within their families. The process is reflected in their sons' refusal to stay at home, their unwillingness to give up underground political activity, and their defiance of the demand to take on the burden of marriage. In short, they refuse to surrender to their mothers' dictates. In that respect, too, the films express processes that have characterized Arab society and intensified during the *Intifada*.[6]

Indeed, those who endeavor to break free of both the parents' rule and the rule of the Israelis are the younger sons. Relentlessly, they speak of defiance and struggle, preaching about "retrieving what has wrongly been taken away from them," as Ziad says in *Haifa*. They are active in underground operations (in *Curfew*), spend time in prison, challenge the parents' authority, and – as mentioned earlier – refuse to shape their masculinity according to the mother's wishes, through marriage and the family. Yet, the most important revolt, the sons' Oedipal rebellion, cannot be resolved, for their weak fathers do not constitute a challenge ("No one speaks to his father in such a way," complains the father, Abu Raji, about his son Akram in *Curfew*). The ones who actually dominate the young men's lives and have complete authority over them are the Israelis, who are usually not even seen, so overt rebellion against them is impossible. The young men, therefore, cannot express their masculinity within the framework of the family, either because they refuse to marry or because the woman is the one in control. They also fail to express their manhood through their political activities, which inevitably end in searches, house demolitions, and imprisonment.

The structure of breakdowns and gradual diminishing in Masharawi's films is emphasized by the vicious dead-end cycle that is manifested in them. Life in the camp runs its course as a daily struggle for survival, repeating the same actions (gathering for a meal during curfew, wandering around in the empty streets of the camp in *Haifa*) and the same calamities. In *Curfew*, the family repeatedly attempts to read the letter from the son in Germany, and is interrupted again and again by mishaps and interference such as the curfew or electricity outage. The monotonous music or noises heard on the soundtrack – the sound of a reverberating bullet, the backgammon dice rolling, and distant shots – further accentuate the sameness of daily life. This uniformity is also the result of events that occur over the course of longer stretches of time; a newborn son is named after one who died, or a birth during the curfew is reminiscent of another taking place during a previous curfew. The cyclical structure of the movie, which opens with a shot of the expanses of the city of Gaza and closes with them too, which begins with the postman delivering letters to the camp residents and ends with the reading of the letter from the son based in Germany, intensifies even further the dead-end quality of this life. Time is arrested, leading nowhere. Homi Bhabha (1990)[7] wrote about the "daily life" of a people as an on-going, cyclical, and repetitive process that breaks the national narrative, which advances in a linear route toward a defined goal. Michel Khleifi was the first to portray this life on the screen. Here, it has become static, condensed, and suffocating routine.[8]

Loss and Renewed Control over Time and Space

All of Masharawi's films, therefore, present the current life of the camp-dwellers as a dead-end situation, in which neither past nor future seems to exist. Yet, beyond the harsh descriptions of the present, it seems as if something of the past reverberates. This is the trauma of war and deportation which the films do not mention directly, but which nevertheless resurfaces as a vague memory.[9]

For an explanation of the particular role that the past plays in Masharawi's cinema we might consider, among other things, the "second generation" narrative. The new directors living in exile have inherited from their parents or grandparents memories of the deserted land. Their association with that land is not derived from a direct, first-hand experience of someone who grew up in it (Harkabi, 1975). Rather, it is an indirect connection dependent on inherited memory and imagination. Marianne Hirsch (1996) calls this phenomenon "postmemory."

> Postmemory (or, the memory after the memory) [she writes] is the strongest form of memory, precisely because its connection to the object, or the origin, is not mediated by memories but by investment and imagination. The memory after the memory characterizes the experience of those who grow up dominated by narratives that preceded their birth, whose own belated stories are evacuated by the stories of the previous generation, shaped by traumatic events that can be neither fully understood nor re-created (659).

This memory "creates where it cannot recover. It imagines where it cannot recall" (664). Hirsch's ideas about postmemory refer to the experiences of the second generation of Holocaust survivors, yet they are most appropriate when discussing exilic directors, belonging to the second and third generations of the Palestinian *Naqba*. "I am from Jaffa, from Manshiyya," says Rashid Masharawi (telephone interview, 2001). "Half of the 'Dolfinarium' [a waterfront recreational facility] is ours. I grew up in Gaza, in a refugee camp, but all along it was clear to me that I am from Jaffa, that we are poor since we are not in Jaffa." These directors do not refer directly to the past defeat and occupation and refrain from delineating it as a living memory. Nevertheless, they do not replace the present with that traumatic past, as third period Palestinian films did. Instead, they attempt to construct a double-layered image: of contemporary time and of the past, of the currently present and of the memory that remains hidden beyond it. Such a twofold picture can be found in Michel Khleifi's cinema yet, in his films, the past is the idyllic past of the land and not the painful past of its occupation.

In Masharawi's films, it is not the protagonists who remember but rather the entire film, over which the past devastation dominates without actually being present, permeating through the general disintegration and the various reductions. Several reminders reveal the past, exposing the lurking trauma: for example, the madness of Haifa, who has replaced the pain of loss with a crazed monotonous listing of the names of abandoned places. The past also resurfaces through the deterioration that is manifested on several levels, which, like the filming of the blocked-off spaces, creates a general impression of disaster and exile that goes beyond a specific time and place and thus evokes an atmosphere of total, all-embracing disaster and exile. Such a transgression beyond the specific allows viewers to see in the disasters of the present not only incidents that are harsh in themselves, but also a duplication of the past catastrophe. The structure of pain, spiraling downward to an abyss, in itself revives the first step, the initial anguish, even if it never mentions it; if the trauma is experienced through forgetfulness, as Cathy Caruth (1995) claims, then paradoxically, one of the signs of its existence is the lack of any signs of it.[10]

Masharawi's cinema is a desperate cinema. Interestingly enough, though, his bleakest, most desperate film, *Stress*, was created during the Oslo peace accords of 1998. It, too, begins and ends with long shots, opening with a view of the Erez checkpoint at the northern exit of the Gaza Strip and concluding with the refugee camp in Gaza. This documentary film, however, does not pause on the shrinking processes that have characterized the other films. Instead, it delineates their end result: life in diminished places – at checkpoints and bypasses, and across internal borders that intersect and divide Palestinian society into fragmented sections: between one Jewish settlement and another, between settlers and soldiers.

The entire film takes place out of doors; unlike Masharawi's earlier films, there is no indoor location and therefore no place within which the film's characters can feel to be a safe haven. But even the out-of-doors expanses disappear. They are disrupted by the camera when it perceives, in close-up, high-angle, or medium shot, cut-off partial images of a stomach, face, hand, shirt, ID card, and distorted, broken-down images, disconnected from any organizing framework and not preceded by an establishing shot. The space is also repeatedly truncated by images of soldiers, settlers, and settlements that dissolve into, or are cut off by, images of Arab towns and refugee camps. While Masharawi's earliest films deal with the diminishing borders themselves, *Stress* deals with the already shattered reality dictated by these borders. It is an entire reality, which has faded away, leaving only the part, the section, the detail. Whereas in *Haifa* the Oslo accords were presented by one of the characters, Ziad, as a surrender of the dream of the broad boundaries of a return, *Stress* presents these accords as the setting of new boundaries that assault Palestinian identity and shatter it from within. It documents what happened in the seven years following the signing in Oslo: the expanding and proliferating settlements; the splintering of the designated Palestinian area into small fragments scattered among road-blocks and bypass roads; the cutting off of Palestinian urban areas from rural ones, of villages from their lands, with the ever-increasing travel restrictions between the West Bank and the Gaza Strip, and between both these territories and Israel (Hamami and Tamari, 2001). The distress that is expressed in the film clarifies to a great extent the background to the outbreak of the Second *Intifada* two years later.

Along with space, time in the film also disintegrates. Ostensibly, ordinary routine Palestinian life is described here. It is much like the suffocating daily life portrayed in Masharawi's other movies: vendors in the market, carpenters, construction workers, blacksmiths, humble laborers passing through roadblocks, children playing. However, here daily life loses even the little continuity that it enjoys in the director's other films, since it is cut off from its various contexts. We are presented with isolated moments, without past and without future. The fragmentation of the images of space parallels the disruption of life itself: a man hammering metal, a man carving a stone, a young woman at the checkpoint, someone dismantling a wooden construction. These people have no complete life that gives purpose to their actions. They live within segments of a sequence that was broken.

Thus the lost harmonious wholeness of the landscapes of the past is not a part of Masharawi's world, as it is not a part of the world of a whole new generation of Palestinian directors making films during the 1990s and who, for the most part, grew up in diasporas or in West Bank refugee camps, in spaces divided and fragmented by borders, settlements, and roadblocks. A considerable number of these directors have nevertheless tried to recreate this harmonious wholeness by holding on to details of the past that have become abstract symbols: traditional food, typical clothing, stone houses, Al-Aqsa mosque, and other emblems representing the past in the present.[11]

But in Mashwari's bleak world there is no room for reverential treatment of these symbols. His short film, *Upside-Down* (Maklouba, 2002), parodies them by turning them into surrealistic fantasies, thus both trivializing and revitalizing them. The film opens with an old woman in traditional village dress climbing the stairs of an old, ruined stone house. The walls of the house are painted in faded colors typical of rooms in the old houses abandoned by the 1948 refugees and which fill the new Palestinian cinema as recollections of the distant past. The woman prepares the traditional Arab dish called *maklouba*, with the camera lingering on the ingredient – rice, chicken, lemon – the kitchen utensils, the stone, the wall. Occasionally, the camera shifts from the woman to the view of the landscape seen through the window. At first this seems to be an inventory of shopworn Palestinian symbols: village woman, stone house, traditional food, cleaning of rice, dreams of open spaces, the bird's-eye view of the Al-Aqsa mosque – all representative of the destroyed Palestinian past and the hope for a future revival. However, all of these elements are misplaced or are seen from an unlikely angle, much like an unfinished puzzle whose pieces are scattered around every which way; the *maklouba* is seen from below, through the bottom of the transparent pot. The views from the window are constantly changing – mountains, fields, refugee camp, a city (perhaps Jerusalem), the sea. As the film nears its end, the *maklouba* is ready, the camera showing it from below, and is then upturned on to the serving platter – so that it is now right side up. But the serving platter, instead of being placed on a table, begins to soar above Jerusalem and above the mosque, the empty pot floating above it. The *maklouba* is a national symbol representing and restoring the national past. But when it is floating in the sky, like Arafat's picture on the balloon in Suleiman's film *Divine Intervention* (*Yadon Elahiyya*, 2002), shot some time later, it looks ridiculous and loses the symbolic meaning it used to have. Yet at the same time, it regains that meaning by being revitalized through the effect of estrangement. Thus, while the two films, like others to be discussed later, expose the trivializing of Palestinian national symbols, they also grant them a surreal, hallucinatory, imaginary dimension, thus reviving them and enabling their continued use.

In addition to resisting other comforts, then, Masharawi's films do not rely on the comfort that the national symbol offers. These films do not give their protagonists much room for hope. Only a marginal place is dedicated in them to the national narrative of memory and struggle, which then remains extremely abstract or is negated by the events taking place. Yet, the protagonists in the films do not give up. While they do not rebel overtly against Israeli rule, they express their opposition to it by maintaining some semblance of normality under the noses of the occupiers. And while doing so, they ignore the presence of the Israelis,[12] in an unyielding struggle to survive, in everyday acts of defiance, by mutual assistance of neighbors and friends, by supporting each other, in joined work. In *Daro-w-Dour* the resistance is expressed in minor, insignificant activities; the protagonist, a Tel Aviv house-cleaner, goes fishing in the sea facing Manshiyya, which was his home town. Thus, he conquers in action that which is unconquerable. Watching from a distance a television report of *Intifada* rioting (on his Israeli neighbor's television set), moreover, he hears the then Israeli prime minister, Yitzhak Shamir, say, "We will withstand this," but achieves a kind of victory over the Prime Minister by fastening his penetrating gaze on him.

In other films the protagonists' even less significant triumphs are reminiscent of the Sisyphean, purposeless victories that different existentialist thinkers have described:[13] for example the conquests of Rieux, the protagonist of Camus's *The Plague* (*La Peste*, 1947), or those of the protagonist of Solzhenitsyn's *A Day in the Life of Ivan Denisovich* ([1962] 1963). These are triumphs based on stubborn resistance, on the ability to continue, day by day and day after day, simply to survive. Rashid Masharawi grants these conquests sharp and clear national significance; daily life in the camp unites the Palestinian family beyond the quarrels and the friction, presenting the existence of the family and of the Palestinian people which it represents as a *fait accompli*. Daily life also indicates another option of struggle against the Israeli oppression – one fought by maintaining a long-term perseverance, a strong hold on life itself, *sumud*.[14] In Masharawi's films, the space to which the heroines of *Fertile Memories* (1980), for instance, clung does not exist. Space has diminished here. Mundane everyday life has also lost its power to weave the thread connecting characters to place. Yet, this hold on life still constitutes a passive form of opposition for the subjugated, endowing them with an independent sphere of their own where they can both evade the hegemonic power of the rulers and undermine it (Bhabha, 1990). They continue to give the threatened Palestinian identity the validity of an existing solid fact.

The more severe the suffering in the camps becomes, the deeper the opposition designed in the movies, and the more diverse the manifestation of that opposition becomes. In *Stress*, it is the resistance of the director, who pieces together all of the parts of the picture, the sights, the faces, and the fragments of life that were shattered, which amount to a single theme: the ever-increasing tension before the explosion. This theme unifies all of the sections and parts in a single whole, above and beyond the borders blocking and dividing it. The tension is reflected in the facial expressions of the silent people and the muted soundtrack that creates a sense of helpless dumbness. It is also apparent in the substitution of the intra-diagetic cinematic voice with Arab ex-cinematic music that bridges the separate images with one elegiac lament, then broken by the commotion of gunshots, screeching, sirens, strokes on iron and stone, shouting in the market. These are everyday sounds that have lost their mundane meaning,[15] and when seen together, they create a distinct atmosphere of tension and violence. This atmosphere is not unlike that just prior to the explosion later portrayed in Tawfik Abu Wa'el's *Waiting for Salah A-Ddin* (2001). It is the same atmosphere that culminates in the image of milk spilling over a pot or of a pressure cooker in Elia Suleiman's films, *Homage by Assassination* (1991) and *Divine Intervention* (2002).

Masharawi's later films capture the enclosing borders, like other Palestinian films produced during the Second *Intifada*, through fantasy, imagination, and art. In *Haifa*, art is used by two children bound to a deserted house, painting pictures by themselves, telling stories, and spinning dreams. This outlet, however, is closed toward the end of the movie, with the general desperation affecting all of its characters. In *Ticket to Jerusalem*, the outlet is the movies that the protagonist projects for the benefit of the Palestinian residents in Jerusalem and with which the film concludes on a kind of happy note.

Out of the desperation of the camp in *Haifa*, as from within the constant anxiety, the gunshots and explosions, the dead and the injured in *Ticket to Jerusalem*, the protagonists insist on clinging on to the imagination in art: to paint, to tell stories, to project films. That insistence is in itself a kind of a victory, whether it fails, as in *Haifa*, or succeeds, as in a *Ticket to Jerusalem*. The triumph of the protagonist of a *Ticket to Jerusalem* lies in is his success in attracting an audience to a friend's yard, which religious Jews have invaded, and in projecting a film for them. This is indeed a very minor victory, however, since the invaders stay and would remain in the yard, the roadblocks are in operation, and the violence in the streets continues. The significance of this victory diminishes even further once we realize that the film screened is, in fact, Masharawi's own previous film, *Haifa*, that ends in utter despair. And yet, the final shot of a *Ticket to Jerusalem* captures this Palestinian crowd filling the yard, while the protagonist is seen hugging his wife; the Jews observe all this from a distance.

Resistance to the hegemonic might of the rulers is expressed in the films in one other way: by driving them out of the cinematic frame. In reality, the Israelis dominate the lives of the Palestinians, their time and their space. They slice time, bracketing it between curfews, searches, pursuits, and house demolitions. Yet, the Palestinian as a filmmaker rebels against the Israelis when he drives them out of the cinematic frame and presents them as a nonexistent entity. In *Haifa*, the Israelis only appear at the beginning, seen while chasing after Ziad. In *Curfew*, they appear only once during the search, and in *Daro-w-Dour*, they are situated at the edge of the geographical map whose core is Gaza, not Tel Aviv where the protagonist works. Edward Said (1991) claims that for years the Israeli narrative concealed the existence of the Palestinian Arabs.[16] Masharawi demonstrates this notion in his short film, **The Magician** (1992), in which an Arab worker in a Jewish restaurant is made to disappear by a professional conjurer, who is then unable to bring him back.

In an interview (with Urri Lotan, in 1993) Masharawi explains this idea as follows: "One-hundred thousand [Palestinian Arabs] work [in Tel Aviv] and as if with a magic wand they are made non-existent, they are not there . . . nonexistent. It's like with a television remote control . . . as if someone from the government came and went 'click', and that's it." This assertion reflects a general state and not necessarily the personal biography of Masharawi, who for a long time cooperated closely with Israeli artists and with the Israeli cinematic establishment.[17]

Two films, *Curfew* and, to a lesser extent, *Haifa*, reverse this picture. They eliminate the Israelis or turn them into some blurred "Other" – an invisible, incoherent, deconstructed entity subjected to the Palestinian gaze. They are viewed exclusively by children and remain unseen by the rest of the family, as by the film audience.[18]

While it is the Israelis who dictate the cinematic narrative – they are the ones declaring the curfew and determining its outcome – they still exist only in fragmentary form; only the sound of their gunshots is heard, making them a disembodied voice in the cinematic framework (Pinhasi, 1999). Although the Israelis dictate the cinematic narrative – the Palestinian life story – they themselves lack a narrative, when no reasons are suggested for their existence, both in the specific place where the film unrolls, Gaza, and in the wider space, Israel/Palestine.

This absence from the screen does not conceal the power the Israelis wield and the oppression they impose on the Palestinians. However, it makes it possible to undermine these power relations and to construct a definition of Palestinian identity as an autonomous one, independent of the ruler's vision (Lubin, 2000).

In Michel Khleifi's films, the camera defies the Israeli "closure" and conquers areas and spaces outside the refugee camp and the Arab village. Rebellion in these movies is also expressed in the domination of time, in the cinematic fantasy that is meant to retrieve a world that has disappeared. The reality in Rashid Masharawi's films is an existential rather than a fantastic one. It is a reality of distress and siege, of a perpetual, hopeless downfall. In such a reality, it is the trauma of occupation that is revived, not the past preceding it. And when his films do turn to fantasy, it becomes a more desperate kind. It does not seem part of "actual" reality, which the film captures, but rather part of rather fictitious world to which the protagonists cling.

Yet, within this reality, there is opposition: the Sisyphean resistance expressed in the futile, perpetual act of pushing the rock up to the mountain summit again and again. The rock associates Palestinian fate with human fate, and the passive Palestinian struggle with the destiny and aspirations of the existential "rebelling man."

NOTES

1. The personal story is thus revealed as an allegory of both the national and the exilic condition. See Jameson (1986) and Naficy (2001: 31). See also footnote 14 in the Introduction.
2. Masharawi makes unusual use of a familiar convention. Uncommonly, the establishing shot intends to present here the places where the film will not, in fact, take place. Elsewhere, Masharawi makes conventional use of this device. In the film *Long Days in Gaza* (1991), for instance, the establishing shots of the space and the transitions between shots of the space and the entire refugee camp, on the one hand, and the streets and interior shots, on the other, intend to locate the film and facilitate the transitions between the different interviewees' monologues.
3. As actual radar does, the child observes and perceives all army movements and informs his family and neighbors about them.
4. In Arabic, *daro-w-dour* means "house-houses," the name of a children's game.

5. Since refugee camps are particularly crowded and condensed places, for the purpose of creating this emptiness, the film was shot in Aqbat Jaber, a deserted refugee camp near Jericho.
6. For women's status during the *Intifada*, see Tamari (1999b). Also see Chapter 1, "A Chronicle of Palestinian Cinema."
7. See Chapter 2, "From Bleeding Memories to Fertile Memories."
8. As in Suleiman's films. See Chapter 7, "Between Exile and Homeland: The Films of Elia Suleiman."
9. The imagination functions, in this case, as an outlet for what Freud calls "acting out": that is, an imitation in present action of a traumatic past experience. It is a persistent, repetitive enactment, evoking the past as if it were occurring in the present. On this issue, see the discussion in the Introduction.
10. According to Elsaesser (forthcoming), a special method is, therefore, required to decipher them.
11. See Chapter 6, "A Dead-End: Roadblock Movies."
12. Lubin (1998) describes a similar phenomenon occurring in an Israeli short movie by Dina Zvi-Riklis, *Point of View* (1991).
13. Albert Camus explains the philosophical background to these ideas in *The Myth of Sisyphus* ([1942] 1978).
14. See footnote 10 in Chapter 3, "About Place and Time: The Films of Michel Khleifi."
15. This phenomenon becomes most prominent when the vendors in the market are filmed in extreme close-up and the sound of their shouting is disrupted. What is now seen on the screen does not appear to be the selling of market products but a mute, voiceless outcry.
16. See also Sanbar (1997) and Bresheeth (2002b).
17. For Masharawi's biography, see Chapter 1, "A Chronicle of Palestinian Cinema."
18. For an analysis of this phenomenon, see Pinhasi (1999).

5. THE HOUSE AND ITS DESTRUCTION: THE FILMS OF ALI NASSAR

Ali Nassar's two films, *The Milky Way* (1997) and *In the Ninth Month* (2002), are constructed, to a great extent, along familiar lines. They may be defined as epigonic films, deriving their plots and styles from contemporary cinema and literature as well as from those of earlier periods, while simplifying and reversing them. Thus, the complex, deep, and multidimensional has become simple and flat, the implicit has become explicit, and what, in earlier films, had reflected the place and *Zeitgeist* has remained here unchanged, even when transferred to a different time and place.

It is precisely because of this characteristic that Nassar's films can serve to illustrate the different periods in Palestinian cinema, both those discussed previously and those to be considered in the following chapters. His films function as a useful reference point both for the examination of what has become commonplace and familiar in Palestinian films, and for the illumination of attempts to renew it.

The Milky Way was Ali Nassar's first feature film to be screened to a large audience. It combines the two types of past that feature in Khleifi and Masharawi's cinema – the memory of the relinquished land and the memory of its traumatic loss. In persistent and diverse ways it returns to the moments of trauma. Similarly, it also looks back to the golden era preceding it.

The film depicts an Arab village in 1964. "This is the same village," says Ali Nassar, "that existed prior to 1948. Nothing has changed in it" (private interview, 2001). The village atmosphere and the details of reality projected in the film fit not only the 1960s but the 1950s as well, reviving both the reality of that period and the prose published during those years, mainly in the Communist Party journal, *al Jadid*. The *al Jadid* stories largely deal with the struggle of the Arab population against the military government and the emergency defense regulations that came into effect in 1945 and remained in use until 1964, mostly in the Arab towns and villages. The stories describe the expropriation of Arab village land and discuss the Arab population's right to organize against the Israeli regime. These stories describe cases of arrest and deportation without trial; they depict the involvement of the military government in all aspects of life, including handing out travel passes, construction permits, and teachers' employment permits, and even meddling with matters such as romantic alliances and marriage. They also describe the control the military government exercised over the population through clan leaders who functioned as a branch of the regime and served as its informers, in exchange for favors such as travel passes, construction permits, employment of family members as teachers and so on.[1] All these details of everyday life, portrayed minutely in the stories of the 1950s and 1960s, appear in *The Milky Way*, yet they do not blur the memory of the harmonious golden age still experienced in the post-1948 village. That memory is evoked by the beauty of the Arab village and the lives playing out there. It is an enclosed but vibrant place, full of movement – movement of men, women, and children, donkeys and sheep. It is a protected place, a home. Although people leave the village to work in the Jewish settlements, and despite the Israeli army that penetrates it and disturbs the tranquility, the film still clings to that calmness, restoring it as something that was never lost, that still exists and is tangible.

The landscape here, as in Khleifi's films, is what revives the pre-1948 past in both the present of 1964 and that of 1997, expanding the past in the temporal as well as the spatial dimension. The time unfolding in this place is an ordinary time: people walking to work and returning from it, a shepherd guiding his flock, children going to school and coming back. This is the time of routine, granting a constant and stable existence in the present progressive to what had already become a thing of the past. As in Khleifi and Masharawi's films, the routine of daily life in *The Milky Way* intends, among other things, to fracture the dominant future-oriented narrative dictated by the Israelis[2] and to demonstrate the *sumud*, a firm, persistent hold on the land.

The existence of the past landscape in the present is shaped not only by the expansion of time but also by the extension of space, which includes in the film both the village's remote pre-1948 past and 1964, when the events of the film take place. Geographically, it encompasses the village itself, the desert, the Samarian hills, and the luscious green Wadi El Bathan, abundant in water. (The film was shot in the village of Mughayyir, on the edge of the eastern, more barren slopes of the Samarian hills.) As in Khleifi's cinema, *The Milky Way* links a specific small site with a larger place representing the entire homeland as an idea of completeness.

The landscapes, therefore, allow the film to retrieve what has been seized, expanding it, moreover, across a large territory for a long stretch of time. This is a territory that became a sign and a substitute, a symbol of an absent unity. What existed in the past is displaced and disconnected from its original period, appearing here in the present, where it is reestablished and enjoys new life – the life of those who represent the other time and place.

Nassar's film reconstructs the fantasy of the lost Palestinian paradise through a melodramatic structure that divides the settlement unequivocally between those who guard the purity and harmony of the traditional Arab village and the Palestinian people on the one hand, and those who harm them on the other: the Israelis and their collaborators. The film denounces the latter and allows the former to triumph. In that respect, Nassar follows the Socialist Realism model, which dominated Arab literary circles in the 1950s. That model aimed to document the struggle between the proletariat and the bourgeoisie, depicting it as a battle between positive and negative forces in society leading to a revolutionary consciousness.[3]

The corrupt *mukhtar* in *The Milky Way* collaborates with the Israelis, distorts justice, pursues and enjoys bribes, and relishes the pleasures of power; he owns a large house, his son drives a car (apparently the only one in the village), and both terrorize the other inhabitants and each other. While the *mukhtar* conducts a biased Muslim religious procedure, his son breaks Muslim law with his untamed, indiscriminate drinking. The village teacher and the blacksmith, Mahmud, represent opposite poles in Palestinian society. The two live the life of peasants, their apartments are small and modest, and their means of transportation are the donkey and their own feet. They personify a pure and just lifestyle, living in harmony with the natural rhythm of the agricultural village, enjoying warm relationships with others, and confronting the Israeli authorities as political activists in a secret cell. They are inspired by the Communist Party that dominated the Arab village in the 1950s and 1960s, and by the nationalist ideologies linked to Abed A-Nassar, whose image is displayed several times in the course of the film. The friendship between the two men reflects the Communist Party ideological agenda and the alliance that indeed existed at that time between the proletariat and the intelligentsia.

The plot ends with the triumph of good over evil, a conclusion that reiterates and preserves the harmony created by the film's melodramatic, Socialist Realist structure. The central struggle in the film is the one between the blacksmith, Mahmud, and the corrupt *mukhtar*'s son. The latter lusts after Mahmud's fiancée and, following a series of clashes, decides to burn Mahmud's house down. However, the blacksmith arrives just in time, and in the struggle between the two, the *mukhtar*'s son is killed by the knife with which he intended to hurt

Mahmud. Yet, in the village, people are not aware of the details of the case and, as a result, they pursue Mahmud in order to avenge the blood of the deceased. Toward the end of the film, Mahmud returns to the village from his hiding place, tells the *mukhtar* the truth, and convinces him of his innocence. The solution to this private dispute is mirrored by a solution at the national level of the plot. This story revolves around friction between the representatives of the Israeli military government and the village teacher, who is suspected of counterfeiting work permits (a deed executed, in fact, by the *mukhtar*'s daughter). The *mukhtar* solves this conflict by putting the blame for the forgery on his dead son. Consequently, the teacher is released from jail. The melodramatic plot intends to lead the film toward a sealed and just solution, and to progress in a rational, coherent, causal manner toward a harmonious future,[4] based here on the idyllic image of the past which merges class, family, and national values.

The *mukhtar*'s "repentance," after he is convinced of the blacksmith's righteousness and consequently saves him from imprisonment, enables him to participate in the harmony of man, land, and nation that he had previously damaged, and which the film restores.[5] That harmony has been a cornerstone of Palestinian literature. "I am the earth," wrote Rashed Hussein, "Do not withhold rain from me/I am all that is left of it." Similarly, Abad Ellatif Akel wrote: "In times of drought you are my figs and my olives,/Your wilderness is my aromatic gown."[6]

In many cases, such as in *The Milky Way*, this harmony reconstructs a precious past, threatened by the occupation, greed, and individualism. In the story, "The Visit" (Baidas, 1987), the protagonist's decline into private life and into the accumulation of property closes the national path, and does not allow him to share with his sister her memories of places lost. In another story, "The Immigrant" (Jahshan, 1997), the greedy bridegroom attempts to convince the father to abandon his land and depart for America, but the father refuses. He is the one preserving the national flame, identified with the agricultural heritage of the past.

The unity of man, nation, and land is intertwined in these stories with man's harmony with his family (either the family of origin or a future one, represented by ties of love). The sibling relationship in "The Visit" withers away because the brother refuses to reminisce with his sister about their shared pre-occupation past. In yet another story, Samira Azzam's "Another Year" (1982a), the mother longs for both the homeland she has left and for her daughter. Azzam's story ends with the following words: "I shall die with two sighs on my lips – one for my country and one for Marie [her daughter])." In Emile Habibi's "At Last the Almond Tree Blossomed" (1968b), the protagonist forgets his lover, his identity, his national affiliation, and his past. He lives under Israeli rule and cooperates with it. Only after the opening of the borders, in 1967, after revisiting people and parts of the country from which the Israeli Palestinians were separated in

1948, does he remember that the man who promised his lover that he would meet her in springtime, and who gave her an almond tree bough as a token, was none other than himself. The unification of the two segments of the people is connected not only to the merging of the two parts of the land, but also to the reunion of the family and to the renewed alliance of the man with his own past. All of the above are part of one harmonious whole, connected to the past, the time before the crisis, the fall, the separation.[7]

It is men who rule this harmonious whole that includes both family and nation. Manhood, therefore, is tested by loyalty to nation and by preserving the wholeness and honor of the family, which go hand in hand.

The *mukhtar* in *The Milky Way* is unable to control his disintegrated family. He deceives it, and vice versa – his daughter rebels against him, counterfeiting work permits for the village people. His son, too, disobeys him and approaches him only when he needs money, and both father and son share the sexual favors of the same married woman (the son does so in the back seat of a car). In contrast, the village teacher and the blacksmith are paragons of stability, as each one's family life suggests – the teacher is a married man and the blacksmith is engaged to be married. Several family scenes illustrate the love and friendship between each couple.

As mentioned in a previous chapter, Michel Khleifi's films both construct the patriarchal combination of family and nation and deconstruct it. They do so by positioning the men – the keepers of the old patriarchal order – at the margins while creating another border-free world, where the women act independently and in which sexual, national and class differences are recognized but at the same time are separated by fluid borderlines. Ali Nassar's film sketches, albeit ever so lightly, this feminine rebellion; the blacksmith's beloved exercises the option brought to the surface by the women in *Wedding in Galilee* (1987) when she teaches her students a song about peace. The *mukhtar*'s daughter subverts her father's authority by counterfeiting work permits, and the poultry vendor does the same when refusing to obey the *mukhtar*'s instructions to give his wife merchandise free of charge.

Although the film implies new possibilities of liberating the women from male domination, it realizes them neither in the plot nor in its cinematic expression, both of which preserve the old structure that has guided so many Palestinian narratives.

For example, when the protagonist of *Returning to Haifa* (Kanafani, 2000)[8] loses his home once the Jews occupy Haifa in 1948, he is simultaneously separated from his homeland and his city too, all of which are connected to the disintegration of the family – to losing his son. In fact, the father loses both his sons. His first son was left behind in Haifa and now the father threatens to break off his relationship with his second son if he joins those fighting against the Israeli regime. At the end of the story, however, he changes his approach, thus retrieving his paternal authority, at least as far as the second son is concerned. Family, nation, homeland, and land are, hence, linked here to paternal authority. Their loss is its loss; their reconstruction is its reconstruction.

The same principle also typifies Hanna Ibrahim's story, "Holiday Eve," (1972). The man who has lost his honor in addition to his family, who do not acknowledge him, along with his livelihood too, is requested to distribute leaflets opposing Israeli rule. Consequently, he reconnects with his father-in-law, who now accepts him as a member of the family. The national effort, then, results in him regaining his honor as a man, as a family member, and as a citizen. The connection is similarly reflected, in Samira Azzam's "Because He Loves Them" (1982b), in the character of the man who lost his lands in 1948, and who also abuses his wife and eventually kills her. In *Men in the Sun* (Kanafani, [1963] 1998), the man's ability to protect his family as well as the nation is related to his potency. Abu al Khayzran, the water-tank carrier, lost his manhood in the war, with the loss of the homeland, and has become impotent. As a replacement for homeland and manhood, he dreams of monetary profits. And as in other cases, a bourgeois lifestyle, money, decay, and corruption replace a harmonious world in which the man controlled a united family, the village, and its associated orchards and olive groves, in the intact homeland.

A similar structure is found in *The Milky Way*. Here, too, the national struggle and life in nature, on the land, correlate with moral and family purity, all of which together preserve the image of an idyllic paradise. Loyalty to the nation, to the family, to the village, and to religion, elements which in the reality of that period were separated,[9] merges here to form a single completeness maintained by the men, who dominate the family and lead the national struggle.[10]

This remembered image thus tends to be homogeneous and uniform. In the words of Elia Suleiman: "Unfortunately many think that the period of construction of the nation in which we are living requires one story, a single voice, a national art" (Bourlond, [1999] 2000: 98). Or, as Yazid Sayigh asserts: "The individual stories of my father, his parents, the family, his brothers as well as the collective state of being uprooted from '47 to '49, all focus on what seems to me to be one event from which the details and the texture of a much richer fabric are missing" (Sayigh, 1998).[11]

In interviews that Amira Habibi conducted with 1948 refugees, the explanation that the mass escape was caused by rumors of Jews desecrating Arab women's honor is reiterated (Balas, 1978). The imperative to guard the wholeness and honor of the family overcame, in these cases, the need to cling to the soil of the homeland. This sentiment emerges in Abu Shaur's "Palestinian Men," when the woman proclaims: "We should not have escaped." To this, her partner replies: "Honor [el 'Ard] is dear, woman. Should we have left our daughters to the Jews? They have slaughtered the Gaza youth and desecrated their honor." The woman, however, answers: "This is better than exile . . .

don't you see the disgrace in which we exist?" Literature and cinema remember the sin of this disgrace and "amend" the split between the land, the nation, and the family, creating among these various elements a harmonious unity ruled by the man. He who is loyal to the land and nation, like Mahmud in *The Milky Way*, is also true to his wife and family, and he who betrays the nation, like the *mukhtar* and his son, also violates the integrity and honor of the family with casual betrayals.

Yet the fantasy of a long-lost harmony does not remain untouched in the movie. It is fractured by the traumatic memory of the massacre and deportation evoked in its very midst. Therefore, it is not only the idyllic pre-crisis past that is revived in the present, but also the crisis itself marring that same past. In this respect, too, the film restores the combination characteristic of many Palestinian stories. For example, "That Village, that Morning" (Haniya, [1979] 1989) tells the tale of a dead man who is disturbed in his grave by Israeli shovels, ruining his cemetery for a Jewish settlement in the making. The dead man, who climbs out of his grave, observes his village which, it seems, has not changed at all since his death; the children are at school, the men at work. The deceased man "looked toward the east and saw the village houses calmly slumbering at the foot of the mountain." But what seems like tranquility also appears to be deadly silence: "quiet and stillness not unlike the stillness of his grave surrounded the randomly scattered houses." Indeed he does not find among them his son's house, which was demolished by the Israeli army. The village, then, is steeped here in the same idyllic calm that encompassed it in the remote past, before death. But destruction and death are embedded in this calmness and they bring back to the dead man memories of the destruction of 1948.[12]

In *The Milky Way*, two mentally disturbed characters, Jamilla and Mabruc, do not fully experience life within the harmonious present (which, as mentioned earlier, reconstructs the past) because memories of their parents' violent deaths, in 1948 and 1956 respectively, haunt them in a series of cinematic flashbacks that drive them away from the idyll and back to the traumatic event. The idyllic time is everyday time, through which the past becomes a constant, safe, and perpetuating present. The flashbacks apparently steer the movie toward the wars of the past and make them a part of this harmonious present. Nevertheless, Jamilla and Mabruc cannot function in the present because the horrendous incidents in their past are experienced, in the consciousness of each of them, not as memories belonging in the past, but as if they are currently happening.

However, the trauma of the massacre not only disrupts the idyll but also coalesces with it, to the point that the two are indistinguishable. The title, *The Milky Way* (*Darbo-t-Tabbanat*), refers to the name used in the Arab villages for the path along hay was traditionally transported from the fields to the barn.

This path is the symbol of a clinging on to an existence farming the land. But on that same path Mabruc is seen in a flashback to his childhood, walking further and further away from his slaughtered parents. Here, the slaughter does not disrupt the tranquility. Rather, it resides at its very core.

This scar on this pastoral existence is also indicated in the film by the instability of the home. The home, like the land, has been constituted in Palestinian culture as an answer to the exilic and uprooted condition, a utopian sign of the homeland untouched by time[13] – a symbol of the unity of the nation, the land, and the family. Therefore, those who lost their houses, as in *The Return to Haifa* (1982), also lost their homeland and family, and anyone living alone in an empty house, as in "The Visit," is punished for betraying the memory of his or her pre-1948 town, home, and homeland.

Michel Khleifi construed the home, for the first time in Palestinian cinema, as a shrine to both family and nation, as a crux around which the life of the family and the nation revolves. He also linked the house to the spaces around it. Nassar's film mainly deals with the destruction of that house. The private house has a special significance in *The Milky Way* since the public *mukhtar*'s house, is a place of corruption and squalor. The private house is the one preserving the family and national heritage, the private and the public legacy, and it represents the harmonious unity of the past. But this house is repeatedly violated, in many different ways, all of which echo the primal violation: the demolition of the first house.

The village blacksmith, Mahmud, embodies in the movie the insistence on national and personal values, intertwined with each other and creating a single ideological completeness. He devises acts of resistance against the Israeli military government and plans to marry his fiancée, with whom he has a relationship of love and respect. It is no accident, then, that he is occupied with building the door to the house of his lover's father; nor is it by chance that he gives Mabruc a key for him to guard his house. The door and the key symbolize, here and throughout the film, a defense against the infringement of anything externally threatening the house, the nation, and the family. But the door and the key cannot stop the intruders, in this case as in other incidents. The Israelis break into the village teacher's house, destroying everything in it, and the *mukhtar*'s son and his friend break into Mabruc's house with the purpose of using it for sexual affairs. The *mukhtar*'s son also infringes Mahmud's house and tries to burn it down, thus mirroring the Israeli act of demolishing the teacher's house. After the *mukhtar*'s son is killed in a brawl with Mahmud, the village people break into the house of Mahmud's lover, where he is hiding, in order to avenge the blood of the slain man. At this stage, the movie draws away from the present and looks back toward the past. Mahmud escapes from the village to the ruins of a demolished village and cleans a wrecked gravestone. Thus, the destroyed 1948 village is presented as a relic, a sort of origin of all the other violations, just as the key given to Mabruc seems like a duplication of the house keys the banished Palestinians took with them to exile. These are reenactments and echoes of something that, at the time and in the manner it actually occurred, was indescribable. Mabruc reconstructs this incident in disrupted flashbacks and the film reconstructs it when displacing it to another place and time – to the present.

The infringement of the houses is what creates in the movie a sense of exile in the heart of a village and its land. The house, the village, and the homeland are transformed from something familiar, known, and loved into something threatening and uncanny, reminiscent of the way Haifa changed in Kanafani's novel, *Returning to Haifa* (2000), after deportation to a wild world, a jungle, a place of flooding and fire.[14]

The sense of exile at the very core of the idyllic past is also created in the film by the division of the space. In the orderly, reassuring division, space is usually composed of three areas: the private, protected domestic sphere; the dominating public sphere that dictates both private and public life; and the outside that can be alien, threatening and uncanny, and at the same time also enchanting and alluring. The private and the public areas are divided in the *Milky Way* village between the residents' houses, the *mukhtar*'s house, and the village square. However, the traditional division is disrupted because the private houses do not protect the inhabitants, while the *mukhtar*'s house, which is supposed to represent public order and security, is corruptly run and operated by the Israelis. The village square, moreover, being a place of public gathering, is "conquered" by the Israelis. In this manner, external alienation and threat invade the village and turn it into an exilic place: an exile from home and an exile from the protected sphere. The film ostensibly sets out to revive the cherished days of the past, but the relationship with those days eventually proves to be a post-traumatic one.

Thus, the year 1964, when the film's action takes place, leaves only a minor impression on it. Actually, *The Milky Way* is a reconstruction of pre-1948 village life on the one hand, and of the trauma that disrupted that life on the other. The past that is revived here in many shapes and forms stops the "chronological clock" (Langer, 1991), takes hold of the present, and replaces it. "This present is a temporary fake present," says Bashar Ibrahim about the post-1948 Palestinian present. "It is merely an illusion, a time which is void of identity. The fighting Palestinians manifest the refusal of that present" (Ibrahim, 2000). Likewise, Shafik al-Hout refers to life after 1948 thus: "I am from Jaffa and my fate is to have been banished from the city on April 24, 1948, and to waste the rest of my life fighting for my right to return there, as a free citizen" (Al-Hout, 1998). The year 1948, then, appears not as in the past but as a present progressive dictating the direction for the future, a direction whose mere purpose is the struggle to restore the past. In a similar way, two points in time bracket the life of Um a-Robabikia, the central character in Emile Habibi's story of the same name (1988). First, her life is interrupted in 1948, when her husband and children flee Haifa, and then in 1967, when the sons who have returned are incarcerated in the Israeli jail, setting an example to those continuing to fight for their homeland – for the future. Since the present practically does not exist, the protagonist of Kanafani's *The Return to Haifa* (2000) can return in 1967 to his home that was conquered in 1948 and find that nothing has changed in it.[15] Since the present does not count, literature and the cinema can imprint descriptions of the past on it, and turn the past to the present tense. In this respect, *The Milky Way* "sums up" the different times incorporated into the present: the era of the lost homeland and the time of its loss.

In many Palestinian stories the image of the present is related to the image of the past and is, in fact, derived from it. Literary works that shaped a homogeneous, united past used it to envision a harmonious future in which class, gender, and family will all be incorporated into national values. *The Milky Way* constructs such an image of the future based on the harmonious past and yet, through an additional plot – that of the two village idiots – also deconstructs it.

The main story line in the film is a melodramatic Social Realist plot, at the end of which the just protagonist and his just causes triumph. Yet, the final scene of the film is incongruous in its conventional melodramatic happy ending. It concludes with the two fools seeking redemption, not in history or in reality, but while looking at the Milky Way, up in the sky.

The merging of plots in the film, therefore, constructs the image of the future and then deconstructs it, presents a lost, harmonious world and takes it apart. It narrates a national historical tale and casts doubt on it at the same time. The figures of the two mentally disabled characters in the film, Mabruc and Jamilla, express this ambivalence accurately. The two, like other mentally ill characters in Palestinian cinema, such as Haifa in the film of the same name (1995), the father in *Tale of the Three Jewels* (1994), or the senile in *Wedding in Galilee* (1987), are those preserving the memory of the past and, in this case, memories of the massacre. But they are also those outlining hopes for the future. In this role they function as a kind of metaphor for the Palestinian Arabs living in Israel. In fact, the 1948 *Naqba* pushed beyond the borders of Palestine not only most of the general Palestinian population, but most of the political, economic, cultural, and religious leadership as well. The Israeli Arabs found themselves living in isolated, frightened groups lacking any leadership. Their situation is commonly characterized by the well-known Arab parable, "Orphans at a tyrants' feast." In their lives and fates Mabruc and Jamilla serve as a metaphor for such a situation. Both have experienced the trauma of war and death and have lost their parents. Jamilla is motherless and Mabruc is both an orphan and a refugee. Both represent a former image of the Palestinian people facing Israeli rule: pure, decent, afraid, and vulnerable. At the same time each also plays the part of the village idiot, who has a most distinguished role in literature and cinema in general and in Arab literature and cinema in particular. The fool utters bold truths and expresses thoughts that authors cannot or dare not express through sane people. In this case, these are assertions concerning Palestinian history. The movie thus forms an outlet for shaping identity, memory, and hope. Yet, *The Milky Way* points to the problematic aspects of this identity, memory, and hope when it, like other films, designates their protection to those who have lost their memory or sanity. What does not exist, what cannot be restored, what remains vague and deconstructed in consciousness, exists through madness.

Mabruc and Jamilla command both time and space. Mabruc is the only character who can be found inside the village as well as outside of it.[16] He is the only one who passes through all the village houses, and is seen in the company of both men and women, as if disregarding all barriers and boundaries. Both he and Jamilla apparently experience, in their own way, events that did not occur in their presence, such as Israeli violence toward the village teacher, and respond to them with either laughter or tears. The pain is expressed by the editing that cuts abruptly from the forced military entry into the teacher's house to a shot of Jamilla sobbing. Laughter is the response when the film shifts from the teacher's interrogation to the mock parodic trial that Mabruc conducts for the children, his friends. The way the different characters in the film treat Mabruc reflects their moral status. Favorable treatment of him (looking after him, loving him) indicates goodness; mistreatment (typical of the *mukhtar*, his son, and his men) indicates evil. Control over space is accompanied by a command of time. Mabruc plays with the village children as one of them. He seems to have remained immersed in the childhood that he never had, yet he dreams an impossible dream of children he will never have and of the education he would give them.[17] At the same time, he struggles, in his own way, with Israeli rule and fantasizes about a demonstration that would rebel against it. Out of this hallucinated demonstration, the camera ascends, hovering over the village, perceiving the whole scene from up above. Mabruc's domination over a time sequence is also his domination over space. He is fixated on the traumatic memories of the past but he is also the one "fixing" them, forging a path to the future. It is a hallucinated future, a doubtful future, a future foreseen by a madman.

The Milky Way, then, incorporates various literary, cinematic, and ideological models. On the one hand, it preserves old literary forms, which correspond to old social forms as well. On the other hand, integration of the models also constitutes a statement about the types of Palestinian memory: the memory of the trauma, what preceded it, and what came after it. The poetical, melancholy dimension that the insane characters, the music, and the shots of the village bestow on the movie, moreover, clashes with the simplicity of the melodramatic plot. Thus, it creates some distance between the present and the past, between exile and home, between the dream and its realization, a distance that the plot attempts to bridge.

Five years after directing *The Milky Way*, Ali Nassar's film, *In the Ninth Month*, premiered. To a great extent, the two films are similar. Here, too, we find historical memory combining the enchanted past and its shattering. We also find the same flaws, such as the use of a melodramatic plot and an epigonic use of familiar patterns. Again, repetition of well-established patterns allows us to identify quite clearly those characteristics that were shaped in a more complex manner in other films.

The film's plot is saturated with melodramatic incidents. A Palestinian warrior is secretly returning to his village to meet his wife and take her with him to Lebanon. His brother, whom he secretly meets, is seen by the villagers wandering at night and as a result is accused of kidnapping a child. Husband and wife decide to flee together to Lebanon, but the attempt fails. While the husband escapes, the wife is left behind, pregnant, and in order to save her honor, the protagonist's brother is compelled to break the engagement with his own fiancée and marry her instead. She then dies in childbirth and the brother, who is obliged to live outside the village because of the villagers' suspicions, raises the boy.

This melodramatic plot restores lost harmony and national unity through means similar to *The Milky Way*. The cinematic world is as sharply divided. The Israelis play the part of the evil characters here, alongside the religious dignitaries and the representatives of the patriarchal order who encourage the revival of village superstitions and lead the persecution of the innocent brother, and compel the woman to marry against her will. The representatives of the "evil axis," the keepers of the old order on the one hand and the Israelis on the other, together pursue the representatives of the positive alternative. The Israelis chase the brother who was exiled to Lebanon, and the religious dignitaries, followed by the villagers, pursue the other brother out of the village. In contrast, the two brothers and their two lovers embody both a national and a familial alternative, the same alternative introduced by the positive characters in the earlier film.

The movie, which describes an Arab village in the 1990s and the early years of the third millennium, was shot in the director's home village, Arabe. Nevertheless, it quite anachronistically revives the 1950s and, like *The Milky Way*, also restores the literature depicting those years. Nassar has transferred the 1950s story, told in many versions in many works of art, to recent years, when the Israeli military government is no longer in effect in Israeli villages, when residents of Israel are no longer deported, when there is no infiltration and no informers. According to Nassar (in a private interview with Assaf Grinbaum, Tel Aviv, 2003), this is not anachronism, since "nothing has changed. On the contrary, the difficulties have worsened. The military government still exists, only in a different form."

The lack of reliability and plausibility of the plot reflects, in fact, the traumatic perception of time standing still; the past refuses to dissolve, it continues to be revived in the present, even in the twenty-first century. The trauma of the crisis and the loss disturbs repeatedly, refusing to retreat to the back of memory. Similar phenomena can be found in Khleifi and Masharawi's films. In this case, it is precisely the improbability of the plot that testifies to the need to restore the past in the present, at any cost, even at the cost of reliability.

The film sums up not only a general phenomenon that crops up repeatedly in Palestinian cinema throughout the years, but also specific occurrences taking place in this cinema during the 1990s and the early years of the third millennium. As in many other films produced during the *Intifadas*, space is reduced here. The interior of the house remains almost unexposed to the camera. Instead, the only protected area, which looks like a place of warmth and love, is a cave on the outskirts of the village, where the husband who sneaks in from Lebanon secretly meets his wife, afraid of the Israeli army and its Arab collaborators. The outside also disappears in this film. The village is now mainly filmed in darkness, in pouring rain. Lights flicker here and there, but these are the lights of the Israelis, conducting searches in the village, or of Arabs seeking the missing boy, or of the man who kidnapped him, that man who, according to villagers' beliefs, "carries his bottom in a basket," stealing young children and handing them over to the Israelis. The home, then, is absent in the film, and the exterior is presented as a place of mistrust, persecution, resentment, and fear. Everyone there chases everyone else, seeking each other in the darkness. The Israelis hunt down infiltrators from across the border; the father searches for his daughter, who goes out at night to meet her husband in the cave; the father of the missing child looks for his son; and so, the returning husband's meetings with his brother, who attempts to help him and his wife, turn into violent pursuits in which those hunted down have no chance of escape.

If the village is a place of darkness and terror, then the areas outside the village are places of exile, border zones and death. This is where most of the film takes place: in the border zone, through which the brother escaped to Lebanon; in the cemetery, where the mother is buried; and in the house outside the village, where the second brother resides.

While in the earlier film it was possible to map out private and the public spheres, the space between the two and that which is outside them, although they were all bruised, threatened, or ruined, in the present film it is difficult to draw a map. There are simply not enough details to fill it in.

The missing integrity of space and home is recreated in the film by the tale of the two brothers' meeting. This encounter symbolizes family unity and national unity between the two sections of the Palestinian people – those who remained within the boundaries of the Israeli state, and those who went into exile – as well as the unity of the space, whose borders can be crossed, as the exiled brother demonstrates. The national allegory constructed by the plot is reinforced in the film by the most commonplace symbols in Palestinian cinema and culture, for the construction of the national narrative, its past and future. The film begins with an image of a child, an olive tree, and a cemetery, and ends with similar shots of the same child, tree, and cemetery. In the opening scenes, the camera pauses near the graves of those killed on Earth Day 1976.[18] In the closing scenes, it lingers by those killed in the October 2000 riots.[19] At the beginning of the film, a demonstration against the first Gulf War takes place. The end features a demonstration against the Israeli occupation. The film, then, both commences and closes with demonstrations and death, and within this repetitive cycle the movie positions the symbols of a child and an olive tree, familiar emblems of steadfastness on the one hand and hope on the other. *Wedding in Galilee* ends with a symbolic shot of a young boy, hiding from Israeli gunfire under an olive tree, watching the rising sun. In *The Milky Way*, Mabruc and Jamilla perform the boy's symbolic role. *In the Ninth Month* depicts boys and the olive trees who function as replacements and reminders of the gradually crumbling wholeness. Nassar uses these symbols in a familiar and commonplace manner, making their meaning transparent by naming the boy Amal, which means hope.

Nassar's films provide the opportunity to encapsulate phenomena examined in previous chapters, which referred to the films of Michel Khleifi and Rashid Masharawi, and allow us to foreshadow characteristics of the cinema to be discussed in the following chapters, in the "roadblock" and "*Intifada*" films of the 1990s and beyond. Here lies their place and significance for the understanding of the history of Palestinian cinema.

NOTES

1. See the stories *Asabania (Spain)* (Taha, 1965), *Abd-el-jabbar* (Murkus, 1956), and *Nazalani YaAbi (Father, Put me Down)* (Amar, 1957).
2. We refer here to the linear, homogeneous narrative, according to Bhabha (1990). See the Introduction and Chapter 3, "About Place and Time: The Films of Michel Khleifi."
3. On Socialist Realism in Palestinian literature, see Khater (1993).
4. See Judith Greenberg, who describes how the melodrama grants closure and solution to moments of trauma (1998).
5. The background to this kind of plot is possibly the policy of the Communist Party, which never broke off its relationship with the representatives of the old order. Eventually, it set up an alliance with them within the Democratic Front for Peace and Equality (Hadash).
6. See Rashed Hussein's "Laanen" and Abed al Latif Akel's "Love, Palestinian Style," both in Elmessiri (1982).
7. See Muhammad Siddiq (1984) on the connection between identity and memory. See also Jabra Ibrahim Jabra's "The Other Rooms" (1986), dealing with the

disintegration of identity and memory. Although there is no direct reference in the story to Palestinian existence, it nevertheless appears in the background.

8. As well as the protagonist of its cinematic adaptation. See the discussion in Chapter 2, "From Bleeding Memories to Fertile Memories."

9. See footnote 10 in the Introduction, and a discussion of this subject in Chapter 3, "About Place and Time: The Films of Michel Khleifi."

10. That is, as mentioned above, the lost wholeness of the Palestinian past perceived as a pre-Oedipal completeness of unity with the mother and the world.

11. See the discussion of this issue in Chapter 2, "From Bleeding Memories to Fertile Memories."

12. In very similar fashion, idyll and trauma are associated in stories that connect marriage and death: "Worry," for instance (Kiwan, 1997), in which the announcement of a death overshadows a wedding, or "Palestinian Wedding" (Nahoi, 1970), where the bride insists on going ahead with the marriage ceremony with her beloved, who was killed while attempting to infiltrate Israel. The association of the grave with the house is also often repeated in Palestinian literature. See "He Who Does Not Have a Homeland, Will Not Have a Grave, Said my Father and Forbade Me to Leave," by Mahmud Darwish (1978). See also Muhammad Ali Taha's story, "The Planted in the Land" ([1974] 1997), dealing with a protagonist who cannot come to terms with the fact that his father is buried in the ground, without a proper grave. The grave as a place of eternal life is the continuation of the house as a place of life, and both are harmed and destroyed by the Israelis in these stories and films.

13. See Chapter 2, "From Bleeding Memories to Fertile Memories," Chapter 3, "About Place and Time: The Films of Michel Khleifi" and Chapter 4, "Without Place, Without Time: The Films of Rashid Masharawi." See also Naficy (2001).

14. This is the *heimlich* turning into the *unheimlich*, according to Freud: the familiar becoming the threatening unknown. On the connection between exile and home, see Peters (1999) and Naficy (2001).

15. As described in Chapter 2, "From Bleeding Memories to Fertile Memories."

16. Mahmud, too, exits the village but does so while fleeing, finding refuge in a sort of place of exile and not while seeking an open space.

17. As in other films, *Haifa* and *Wedding in Galilee*. These are children symbolizing hope, the future, and continuation of a severed dynasty. See Chapter 6, "A Dead-End: Roadblock Movies."

18. The first Earth Day was held in 1976 following a governmental decision to confiscate about 20,000 dunan of land around the Arab village of Sachnin for the purpose of Jewification of Galilee. The Arab leaders called for protest demonstrations and a general strike, during the course of which six demonstrators were killed by the police.

19. On 29 September 2000, a day after the ascent of Ariel Sharon, then head of the Israeli opposition, to Temple Mount, riots broke in Judea, Samaria, and the Gaza Strip, swiftly deteriorating into what the Palestinians refer to as the "Al-Aqsa *Intifada*." As a sign of identification with the Al Aqsa *Intifada*, the Israeli Arabs started violent demonstrations, known as the "October Riots." During the suppression of the riots, the police used live ammunition, killing thirteen Israeli Arabs.

6. A DEAD-END: ROADBLOCK MOVIES

Since the last years of the twentieth century and up to the present, directors such as Khleifi, Masharawi, Nassar, and Suleiman, who had established themselves in Palestinian society in general and the Palestinian cinematic landscape in particular, have been joined by a large number of filmmakers, most of whom create documentaries. Some of these filmmakers belong to the generation that grew up and evolved during the period when the Palestinian national movement matured, both within the Occupied Territories and in the Diaspora. Several of them were brought up in the West Bank, in the Gaza Strip, or in the refugee camps, in the years of and between the two *Intifadas*, when the peace process was crumbling and frustration with the civil struggle for Palestinian Arabs' rights in Israel was growing. Their cinema has evolved without direct contact or relationship with outside cinematic cultures. On the one hand, "the Palestinian national option" during those years became "a central component of identity," a "source of solidarity across class, geographical and religious borders" (Rabinovitz and Abu Backr, 2002: 53). And on the other hand, these were also the years when Palestinian unity and identity appeared to many to be more threatened than ever.

To a large extent, the new directors have joined forces to protect Palestinian unity and identity in the face of the threat of extinction. Thus, they express, even more intensely than their predecessors did, the strengthening national consciousness and identity vying with familial, regional, pan-Arabic, class, or gender identities. In their films, they strive to construct a single national unity, which is strong and secured, by integrating different sections, groups, minorities, and political stances. Thus, the diversity of the Palestinian society, the everyday and the personal, all eventually unite in these films under a single homogeneous, national identity coping with collective hardships and struggles.

Yet, simultaneously, throughout that time the new filmmakers have continued in the direction outlined by Michel Khleifi, focusing on Palestinian society itself, and observing its internal diversity, its daily life, and the place where this life occurs. Their films grant independent existence to these details and particulars, even if this existence eventually becomes blurred when it turns an allegory[1] into either the reality of exile or to a homogeneous national identity. The directors also contemplate whether the rejection of the social-personal theme has not in the long run harmed, in many cases, the national cause as well. "The contemporary filmmaker understands that the personal story is missing from our collective narrative," says the director Subhi a-Zubeidi (in a private interview, Ramallah, 2003). "A director's role today is to create spaces that are suitable for the Palestinian manifold and complex existence." The new filmmakers, who strive for national unity, therefore attempt to recount realistic, documentary stories of Palestinians in Israel and in the Diaspora, reflecting differences, divisions, and distances between them. However, in the early years of the millennium, Palestinian distress has intensified, the occupation has become harsher, and the violent clashes have become more brutal. In addition, the social and economic situation has further deteriorated and resistance to the occupation has accelerated and became more violent. Under such circumstances, it has become more difficult for cinema to maintain a balance between the particular and the general. Hence, private experiences have gradually been dissolving into the great collective national fate.

The directors' oscillation between constructing the threatened Palestinian unity and deconstructing it is expressed in the ways time flows and space unfolds in their films.

Several films endeavor to show the Palestinian historical narrative from a personal angle, thus escaping the picture of an enchanted past frozen in the present. In this way, they attempt to create a flow of a vivid experience-based memory bridging between daily life, what preceded it, and what will follow it. Yet, when mundane life becomes an on-going torment, when it is increasingly characterized not by diversity but by a static, passive, and irremediable nature, time stops and the historical sequence is interrupted. This interruption, the experience of being stuck in the present, is what revives and recreates the lost idyllic past, and particularly the trauma that disturbed that idyll. If there is "no direct line from the home to the place of birth, to school," if "all events are accidental, all progression is a regression" (Said and Mohr, [1986] 1999), the imaginary past remains the only vital and enduring time.

The opposing tendencies, of unification versus disintegration, are also expressed in the nature of the space represented by the new films. Certain films still attempt to depict the whole Palestinian map, encompassing the house, the yard attached to it, the orchard and the fields all the way to the horizon, and also to delineate distinctly diverse regions and areas, as Khleifi did in his films. Yet, as the *Intifada* intensified and the Israeli occupation became more deeply felt, the more space was narrowed down or reduced, dissected by checkpoints, the more filmmakers found it difficult to create a harmonious whole map and at the same time were reluctant to deconstruct it. Therefore the filmmakers limited themselves, as Masharawi did, to blocked areas or to border zones, turning those into emblems of lost unity. The discovery of lost unity is always connected to the discovery of lost time: the imaginary past time when Palestinians inhabited their land, or the traumatic time when they were uprooted from it.

Generally speaking, although the new films start out from the ambivalent point of departure inherited from Khleifi's films, even while attempting to construct large spaces and then deconstruct them, to replace the traumatic dissected time with mundane everyday time and to shape a diverse private life, these films ultimately consolidate the national narrative, past, and identity. Historical events demonstrate why it is so difficult for Palestinian cinema to maintain the balance between the two tendencies in the first decade of the third millennium, the years of the Second *Intifada*.

The new directors perceive themselves as followers of the cinema established in earlier years. As Hani Abu-Assad defines it (in a private interview, Jerusalem, 2003): "Michel Khleifi opened a path that had not existed earlier, Rashid Masharawi distributed the gravel, Elia Suleiman paved it and I drive on it at 120 kilometers per hour." Yet, this road is still marked and full of obstacles and potholes.

THE BLOCKED JOURNEY TO THE PAST

One of the most prominent characteristics of the new films is the endeavor to become free of the traumatic fixation that presents the past as a hidden image embedded in present existence. They do so by replacing historical time with personal time, either that of the directors, who search for a cinematic way to portray the past and the present from their own private angle, or that of the characters living their mundane life. The directors try to provide eyewitness testimony, avoiding in this way the setbacks of the stagnant historical narrative. Thus they create a different time span, a duration of life in the present, out of which it is possible to search and excavate a past that has not yet frozen, a past that is gradually revealed in the course of the process of remembrance.

The personal quest enables the films to extract from reality different and distinct variations while shaping a history of distance and change. This is the distance between the director's eye and the remote events, between the various and changing points of view through which those incidents are delineated, the distance between daily life and history and between allegory and reality. In this way, the movies venture to replace a complete and sealed history that can be revived in the present with a quest that must be constantly renewed. However, in all of these cases, violent history permeating the plots of the movies requires a tightening of the ranks, a bridging over of differences, presenting national unity in the face of a threat to the nation and reconstructing the wholeness of days gone by.

Personal, biographical, investigation is the driving force behind many of the new documentary films.[2] Such a biographical quest can be found in May Masri's *Children of the Mountain of Fire* (1990) or in Azza al-Hassan's *Place, or Outside of Paradise* (2000). In both, the quest unfolds as a journey across geographical space. *Place or Out of Eden* opens with a shot of a woman sitting on an empty, deserted path, while faraway houses of Israeli settlements are seen in the background. It is a sort of a wasteland shown as a dead-end road, the same dead-end represented so often in Palestinian cinema, through images such as stranded or engine-less cars, vehicles whose destination is unclear, or blocked roads.[3] The camera this time suggests a way out, through a journey to the past, to the city and the house of the director's grandmother in Acre. It passes by cultivated fields, by the seashore, by a bay and a city, finally coming to rest in an old Arab apartment, adorned by an old-fashioned decorated stone floor and ceiling. Here the wholeness of the lost paradise is embedded: the house, the sea, and the fields. A series of dissolves merges all these details into one colorful image overflowing with old family photographs and accompanied by an old tune that revives that period, Abed Al-Wahhab's 1940s song, "You who Leave Me in My Home, Pining for You." Whereas, by playing a modern version of that song, Elia Suleiman's film, *Chronicle of a Disappearance* (1996), indicated the inability actually to return to the past, here the song appears in its original arrangement, evoked out of the faraway past. Yet, the film still acknowledges the gap between the heavenly image of that past and real memory, and endeavors to reaffirm that memory, rather than the idyll, basing it on the director's subjective experience, on the senses.

Thus, while the visual image indeed summons up a fixed past, the accompanying text contradicts it. A caption projected over a shot of the house says: "My parents used to say: 'Where ever we were, that was paradise,'" and when fields in bloom are seen, another caption asserts "In every Persian rug, there is an intentional error. Only paradise is perfect." The paradise of the past still appears here, then, but there is also an awareness of its existence as a story, as fiction, and the realization provided in the last shot of the film that time and place do change. Al-Hassan explains in a private interview in Ramallah her ambivalence to the dream of the past, her simultaneous attempt to hold on to it and desire to be free of it.

> In the aftermath of the disaster, the trauma, the *Naqba*, you hope that things would stay as they were, so you would be able to return to them. I know, of course, that this is impossible, and try to give form to a new memory, but the new memory turns sour since the problems of the refugees and the land have not been resolved. One cannot come to terms with things before resolving them. As long as the place has unsettled issues with its history, the past will remain the solution.

If, in Azza al-Hassan's film, the sequence of the journey across the expanses indicates the distance between the present and the past, in Subhi a-Zubeidi's *My Very Private Map* (1998), this distance is suggested by traveling in time. The film recounts two histories. The first is the history of the Jilazun refugee camp, where the director grew up, from the erection of the camp on rocky, barren terrain; the second is the earlier history of life in Palestine and the expulsion from it.

The two stories are ostensibly presented in a mixed-up, associative manner, lacking any order. In their interrupted and repetitive nature, they reflect a still-traumatic consciousness, "stuck" in the events of the past. Black-and-white documentary footage of the deportation incessantly punctuates the flow of the plot, as a compulsive feat, as acting out of the painful incident. Shots of the old village, furthermore, occur again and again in the midst of the camp scenes, until it becomes difficult to distinguish between here and there. We are led to wonder if this is a genuine camp or a restoration of the homeland village, whether the song of longing we hear is about life in the village or life in the camp.

Still, the movie inserts the enchanted past and the traumatic event that interrupted it into a chain of memories. It is a backward-looking sequence: from the present to the past, from the camp of today to the period when it was smaller and nicer, and from there to the time when it was "even more nice and small." And then to the rocky soil where the camp was set up, and finally to the deportation and war. As a result, what seems important here is not the past itself but the path leading back to it. It is a sort of archeological excavation that slowly exposes the past, layer after layer, the layers of the director's subjective memories attached to layers of the collective memory of his people. Thus, it is not history itself that is at stake here but the process of remembering it; not the immutable collective experience that is is delineated but its connection to the subjective, live, fluid and flowing experience.

The director, who is telling his own story, is reminded of an old woman whose son had immigrated to Venezuela. As a child, the director used to read this woman her son's letters. He recalls that she and her son would discuss events that had occurred two decades earlier as if they were taking place in the present. In one scene in the film, a young child is seen delivering the mail. Is this the director in his childhood? Is this an event occurring today? This vignette demonstrates how the subjective guides the movie – the director returns to his childhood in the camp and, with the help of his memories and the reminiscences of others and assisted by historical footage, he evokes the past. This may be the first film in which nostalgia is directed toward the refugee camp rather than toward the village. Yet, more distant memories of the village and the expulsion are intertwined with memories of the camp, summoned forth through historical footage, which is interlaced with the refugees' personal testimonies.

Those interviewed in the film tell the old story of a paradise lost that culminates with the dream of return: "Our fate is to dream of the land about which our ancestors dreamt." The director ventures to give shape to this story but discovers that this is impossible. On the way to visit his sister in Kafr Kassem, he stops by the ruins of his mother's village, Kafr Kolia. He talks about his mother's memories, but the frame remains visually empty; nothing is seen. A-Zubeidi himself admits that one had to imagine what could not be observed. The Palestinian village's past, revived in Khleifi's films, is presented here as concealed, forgotten, and imagined.[4] It becomes an unattainable object, and precisely as such, as a present absentee, enjoys a renewed existence. The personal quest unites the shreds of traumatic memory, connecting them to the memory of the refugee camp and integrating them into a single story of a subjective quest for objective history.

The story of that search, in this and other films, and the personal experience conveyed through it allow a splitting of the single homogeneous past into several personal and separate stories, thus depicting a heterogeneous society and history. The distance created in these films between past and present is linked to other gaps, between various people and memories. By way of presenting an assortment of testimonies gathered from the inhabitants of numerous villages, peoples (Jewish and Arab), and classes, all recounting the story of the events of 1948 from several different angles, Muhammad Bakri's *1948* (1998) depicts a diversified and polyphonic past. The different points of view include the perspective of the people who experienced the events, that of the historians attempting to understand them, and that of the artists describing them (Muhammad Taha, Emile Habibi). It is also both the perspective of past days, when the events actually occurred (supported by archival photos), and that of the present time, when the tale is being narrated. The gap between the past and the present, which is also featured in *My Personal Map*, is exemplified here by discrepancies between shots of the ruined villages, as they appear in the present, and accounts of life in these villages and the expulsion from them, as they are remembered by their former inhabitants. The past thus ceases to be an absent, concealed time lurking behind the present. It is no longer spun out of the suffering of the present and is, therefore, liberated from its idyllic image. Differences between the various stories of the same past suggest a more diverse picture. The interrupted editing of the film, cutting frantically from village to village, from story to story, accentuates the multiplicity of these stories, and perhaps also the disrupted, disintegrated experience of Palestinian society. Yet, all of these fragments eventually merge into a single story – the story of 1948. Historical memory is here, as in other films, a unifying cohesive factor, imagined and created out of the present. However, the film also observes the past from different angles and distances of time, and by doing so, attempts to express the diversity of Palestinian diversity and to liberate its past from the constraints of the present, to present it as a living, real time.[5]

Yet in many cases, beyond this diversity, the personal quest reveals anew images of a uniform society frozen in the past. The place of Israeli identity in these films could explain this uniformity and immutability. Several films produced during the 1990s dealt with the search for a Palestinian identity that is independent of the Israeli narrative or history, an identity that has not been shaped through exclusion.[6] If, in previous years Palestinian cinema only told the Israeli story indirectly, by revealing what that story had concealed or erased from the screen,[7] then now several movies were dealing with it directly. They do so, for example, when they focus on the process of releasing Palestinian identity from its dependence on Israeli identity. Although this narrative of disengagement from the Israeli identity strives to release the idyllic frozen picture of the Palestinian past, perceiving it as part of the process of a dynamic quest, the personal and private still remain part of the homogeneous Palestinian story that is presented in opposition to the other – Israeli – story.

The attempt to liberate the Palestinian narrative from the constraints of the Israeli one appears in its most distilled form in Subhi a-Zubeidi's *Looking Away* (2001). That is the story of a Palestinian director (A-Zubeidi himself in the role of a fictitious director) who signs a contract with a Jewish-American producer during the era of the Oslo Accords. He agrees to direct a movie about Jerusalem as the city of peace – a city in which people of the three religions live together, side by side. He attempts to make the movie but fails because he discovers neither harmony between the religions nor peace. What is conceived of as a heterogeneous "multi-religious" narrative in the Israeli discourse, as expressed by the producer of the movie, is consequently revealed as a cover story for silencing the Palestinian voice.[8]

The clash between these two perceptions emerges through a debate between the characters concerning the question of who should dictate editing policy and who should dominate decisions about shooting angles. A-Zubeidi travels with his film crew to the Nablus Gate to shoot the wall of the old city. Filming has concluded but the result revealed in the editing room is different from what he had envisioned. During the editing process, the editor has cut from a shot of an Israeli soldier at the top of the wall to a shot of Israeli soldiers shooting children throwing rocks. A-Zubeidi is embarrassed. The agreement was for him to create a film void of shootings "and the like," he tells the editor, who replies: "Mr Subhi, do you want a documentary or a science fiction film? Do you want to tell the real story or a love story?" The director is compelled to call the producer and assure him that it is just a very short scene involving "no violence, no blood, only soldiers shooting children. Seventeen seconds. Very short. Only to give a sense of reality." The producer refuses to accept it and the editor now has a problem: where to cut to after the shot of the soldier on the wall. He does not wish to solve the problem by removing this shot from the movie altogether. "Subhi," he asks his director. "Have you ever seen Jerusalem without soldiers? Is there a Jerusalem without *Intifada*? Without soldiers and without children?"

In his movie, *Happy Birthday Mr Mugrabi* (1999), Avi Mugrabi recounts a remarkably similar story, in which he is asked by an Israeli producer to direct a film about Israel's jubilee celebrations. However, he is unable to direct this film as another film that he has been asked to direct by a Palestinian producer, about the commemoration of the fifty years since the Palestinian *Naqba*, permeates the film about the festivities. It interpolates the Palestinian past and space into the Israeli story, thus disrupting the latter and emptying it of its intended meaning. Avi Mugrabi's plot is the narrative of the hegemonic culture that fails to tell a unified coherent story because the voice that had been muted penetrates this story, interrupting it. Subhi a-Zubeidi's plot follows the narrative of the silenced voice, attempting to break free of that culture. In both cases, the directors use the reflexive model of film within film, telling the tale of "the director searching for his story," in order to expose the gap between the overt story and what has been concealed behind it. In both instances, this gap is perceived as a rift between fiction and reality, between the cinematic image and what it is supposed to represent. Yet, in a-Zubeidi's film, unlike Mugrabi's film, that search has a happy ending. The director eventually decides to resign from the role of hired hand and to commence work on a film of his own, where the "real" story will be told and where the cinematic, fictitious plot will reflect reality rather than conceal it. Clearly, "the real movie" is the one we are watching, the film directed by Subhi a-Zubeidi, the real director.

The difficulties that arise during filming are all derived from the same source. The signifiers fail to portray what they were meant to signify: the story of harmony between the religions. For example, the idea of capturing a church, a synagogue, and a mosque in a single frame fails. "The director" realizes that what seemed like a synagogue, with the menorah of seven branches, is in fact Ariel Sharon's house. At the entrance to the church, furthermore, the crew cannot find priests who will talk about peace, only tourists who provide a rosy, glossy picture of Jerusalem as a city of tranquility.

However, all the discrepancies apparent throughout the film eventually smooth out. At the end of the movie, the crew films the whole city, encompassing the walls and the mosque, in a high-angle shot in which the scenes appear like tacky postcards. At this moment, the actual object of this picture, the Palestinian people who live within the walls and pray in the mosque, "rebel" against the story of harmony between religions. Information about Sharon's visit to Temple Mount and about the beginning of the new *Intifada* stops the work of the film crew and leads it to the place where the real-time incidents take place – the mosque.

The film, in fact, describes the growth of a new Palestinian story, which is independent of the Israeli and Western narrative forced on it. It is the tale of peace that is perceived here, as in so many other films, as a fabricated myth. The description of the Palestinian narrative as a dispute, as a yet-to-be-told story, allows the presentation of it as a process that is still in the making. Yet into this process the preserved past is already inserted. An unemployed actor who meets the director during the filming brings history into the movie. He does not understand that this is a documentary and insists upon being given a part as an actor portraying a historical figure. He can play the part of his own grand-father from the days of the Turks, he assures the director, or even Salah A-Ddin, and he even brings the appropriate costumes along. History, then, is introduced to the film, as to other films, by a character who does not clearly realize what is happening around him. However, he is the one who steers the director toward "actual" reality – pointing to the real story. With the eruption of the riots on Temple Mount, he scolds the director, saying: "What kind of a documentary is this, that when such a thing occurs, you remain to film the view?" Later, he is killed in the course of those same riots.

In fact, the actor who directs the film toward reality and leads the story toward its solution, through the national struggle, attempts to set the past in the present. He testifies to the recurring trauma that does not allow distinction between the times, creating a sequence and continuity between the two periods. While the unemployed actor sets history in one way, the geography of the place fixes it in another. The crew is situated east of the city and the cinematographer attempts to include the cemeteries of the three religions in one frame; but mean-while, the camera of the real film (not the fictitious one) captures something else. Next to the crew, in a green field under the terraces, a shepherd sits next to a horse and a dog, sprawled in the grass. The rustic scene, very familiar from other Palestinian movies, is inserted into the movie via one shot only, as a hint of another option or as a cornerstone to another story – the same old story of a lost idyll. The film's fictitious director perceives at that moment the falsehood of the narrative of three-religion harmony and tries to express that realization. What is now projected on frame, like what the unemployed actor brought to the frame, is the story of the imagined Palestinian past: the terraces on the mountain, the fields, and the land. These are the landscapes of the past that had populated earlier films, and here, as in those movies, they are newly revived in the present, interrupting the pursuit of a flowing Palestinian story which would replace the Israeli, Western one.

In the new reflexive films, like as Khleifi's cinema, the fixated past is overcome by way of contemplating the everyday, progressing time of the present, the duration between the events rather than the time of the events themselves: life at home, at work, on the road, engaged in cultural activities, or during play with the children. This time allows a lingering, here and in other Palestinian films, on the variety and diversity in Palestinian society. However, the more the hardships intensified, the more preservation of this time became impossible. The new time is *News Time*, like the title of Azza al-Hassan's film (2001).

The film opens with two catastrophic events: a solar eclipse and the events of the Lebanon War, which the director experienced as a child, in 1982. The eclipse and the war are not, in fact, related to the events of the movie, which takes place in Ramallah during the Second *Intifada*. They open the movie as a way of introducing the catastrophic story from which the director attempts to escape and to which she is compelled to return.

As in Subhi a-Zubeidi's *Looking Away* (2001) and many other Palestinian films, this film utilizes the familiar film-within-a-film formula, as a director's quest for the right movie that would recount the true Palestinian story. As in other works that are concerned with the filming and documentation of the *Intifada* events, furthermore, this film also oscillates between the intention to document the collective experience of the struggle against occupation and the wish to document private, daily, mundane life. In Khleifi's films, everyday life subverts both the Israeli and the Palestinian national-political narrative. In the new cinema, the story of the everyday cannot separate itself from those narratives. Although the director's friends advise her to make a movie about the current political situation, a news film, she decides to tell a story of everyday life, about peace and love. Later, in his film *Crossing Kalandia (Roadblock)* (2002), Subhi a-Zubeidi would attempt to do the same: to stop filming demonstrations, funerals, and events commemorating the *Naqba* or the *Naksa* (the Arab defeat of 1967), and search for the "simple things: weddings, games, cultural activities." Like Azza al-Hassan before him, he will also fail in the attempt. Al-Hassan begins her personal film with her neighbors' ordinary story. In a manner reminiscent of the tale of Suleiman's parents in *Chronicle of a Disappearance* (1996) and Khleifi's story of the two women in *Fertile Memories* (1980), she meditates on seemingly insignificant scenes: a man feeding his birds, a woman watering her garden, a boy playing with his dog. This is a story of life and love, the love of the partners for each other, but this "love story" stops when the neighbors fled Ramallah at the beginning of the *Intifada*. Similarly, daily life, cultural events, and family celebrations are repeatedly ruptured in a-Zubeidi's *Crossing Kalandia (Roadblock)* by the scenes of destruction and demolition wrought by Israeli soldiers in the West Bank towns. The two films attempt to cling to the everyday, to normality, to flowing natural time, and they are "halted" by catastrophic time, reviving the disasters of the past through the *Intifada* and the struggle. They try to hold on to private experiences but are prompted to relate the collective, national experience. The turning point in al-Hassan's film, when she chooses to forsake the love story and her neighbors' daily life and focus instead on the events of the *Intifada*, therefore reflects turning point in Palestinian cinema. On the one hand, the film still preserves the tradition of documenting the complexity of everyday life, but on the other, it recruits that life in favor of the collective message.

The return to the traumatic cycle is well understood when we observe the nature of everyday time. Time that flowed in Khleifi's films has now lost its sweetness. It has become static, stagnant time, such as that experienced in the narrow apartment, during the curfew, in Rashid Masharawi's *Curfew* (1993), or in Nazareth, at the entrance to the gift shop, in Elia Suleiman's *Chronicle of a Disappearance*. This is the time of waiting at roadblocks, of endless job hunts, of shopping between one curfew and another. As Raja Shehada (2003) defines it:

> It is as if life was reduced to buying food and accumulating it, so it would last long enough to feed us during our imprisonment. All people do is buy, cook, eat and wait for the next time that the curfew would be lifted, so they could buy again. Without income, work or pleasure.

Such a time of distress unites the people, merging them into a single community with one story and one hope. It unifies the separate details, integrating them into a complete national story and leaving an empty space into which the dreamed-about past time and the traumatic incident that severed it reenter. The *Intifada* that has tore daily life apart in *News Time*, leaving an abandoned, almost deserted town, revives the spirit of an earlier exilic condition and other formerly deserted towns.

In the new films, this is the time of people who wait for hours and hours at the Erez checkpoint,[9] who drag their feet along winding roads to detour IDF roadblocks,[10] or who line up at the Ministry of Internal Affairs in Ibn Shadad Street in Tawfik Abu Wa'el's film *Waiting for Salah A-Ddin* (2001). Abu Wa'el presents four separate episodes from life in Jerusalem: the police harassment of city vendors, the job hunt of a laborer who is now unemployed, the life of a family whose house has been repeatedly demolished, and the work of a cafeteria worker in the Palestinian national theater (the former Al Haquawati), who is also an amateur director. These episodes do not deal with heroic events or large-scale disasters. They focus on small everyday, on-going upsets. Everything contributes in this film to the sense of distress of the people captured within the stagnant time, a time that leads nowhere, a time that trudges again and again through the same meaningless activities. The endless job hunting, for instance, houses demolished again and again, the Sisyphean effort to maintain fruit stands opposite the city wall in spite of policemen who confiscate the merchandise. This is not just Sisyphean time, but also "marginal" time – it flows an in event-less, plot-less place and has no purpose or result. No one reaches the end of the line in Ibn Shadad's Ministry of Internal Affairs; people remain there till the end of the episode. The camera hardly depicts the show in the theater, since it remains outside the hall, in the cafeteria, where nothing happens. Similarly, throughout his episode the unemployed man passes from one workplace to another and will probably even continue his search for a job after the episode ends. The job that he is searching for is not in this film. Out of this desolate time, people aspire to find hope, a story, and a purpose. And they find those in the distant past that appears as present in contemporary time. Beyond all the purposeless expectations lurks another that is reflected in the title of the film, *Waiting for Salah A-Ddin*.

Two documentary films, the earlier produced during the peace accords and the later in the midst of the Second *Intifada*, illuminate the freezing effect that the sights of destruction have on daily life, prompting the post-traumatic time to resurface in the present. Subhi a-Zubeidi's *Light at the End of the Tunnel* (2000), produced during the Oslo Accords, documents the anguish of the Palestinian prisoners who, as a consequence of developments in the region, have been released from Israeli prison. The film depicts their economic problems and the difficult process of rehabilitation and reintegration into the family and into society as a whole. However, all of these are organized in the film within the flowing time of hope. Parallel to the harsh testimonies recorded on the soundtrack, the film follows the various characters to their places of residence, enthusiastically observing their daily lives and the particulars of their homes. Plots of cultivated land, a vegetable garden and a mulberry tree, the milking of a goat or a horse galloping on a path through the fields – every detail is acknowledged. The land portrayed here is not a remnant of the past. It is real soil, where real life takes place. It constitutes, to a great extent, a defiant response to the hardships recounted on the soundtrack. It is the promise of the happy ending that, at least partially, the film does conclude with, particularly in regard to the former prisoner, who has spent almost his entire life in prison and now lives with his new family and children on the fruit of his land. Now, at the end of the movie, the visual image and the verbal testimony unite to form a single story, that of clinging on to the land. "I have planted tomatoes," says the ex-prisoner. "Now the tomatoes are ripe, the corn is ripe and the children are eating it. I plant many things and they grow, so I do not have to buy them at the market." In the frame, he and his children are indeed seen eating the fruit of their garden. In *Light at the End of the Tunnel*, there is life and there is land and the land is concrete, cultivated and real, even if behind it the lost homeland reverberates.

In Muhammad Bakri's *Jenin, Jenin* (2002), produced in the aftermath of the invasion and destruction of the Jenin refugee camp, the conclusion is different. Life seems to have stood still and time is trapped in the past. The film avoids encompassing broad expanses: Jenin, its houses, its streets or the fields around it. Instead, it presents a single homogeneous view – the landscape in ruins. This uniform image of space is related here to a homogeneous image of the past. The camp inhabitants, interviewed by the director, mourn their ruined house, the olive tree, the grapevine or the fig tree in the yard, promising to reconstruct and restore them, refusing to forsake or forget them. The theme is the trauma of Jenin's destruction, but the language, the style of depiction, and the terms used are borrowed from another, earlier trauma – that of 1948. Thus, the house, the street, and the camp environment have become a transparent window of sorts, through which the old pre-1948 house is revealed.

Indeed, the more widespread and severe the destruction becomes, the more the presence of the old trauma is felt, and with it the presence of the lost past. In Abed A-Salam Shehada's film, *Debris* (2001),[11] the father of the family recounts how his house was demolished in 1970, and once again a short while before filming began. He also recalls seeing his own father beaten by soldiers and remarks that the experience resurfaces at the present time, when he helplessly watches his wounded son, unable to assist him. Throughout the time when these harsh testimonies are uttered by the father, his wife, and their son, the orchard in which they are sitting, including the water flowing in the irrigation ditches and the fruit trees, can be seen. Thus, a contradiction between the soundtrack and the visual image is created, becoming particularly prominent toward the end of the film. The woman remembers the past: "We lived from harvest to harvest. Twenty-four years ago we planted twenty trees, each yielding six to eight sacks of good olives." And the husband adds, "I am an optimist, I still believe in a return to our land." Serving as backdrop to these monologues are the orchard, the blooming trees, and the people cultivating the land. That is the same land in which they live – real land, in the current time. Yet, it appears that they do not perceive it or relate to it. Rather, what they refer to in their words, in their imagination, and in their dreams is the land of the past. The imagined memory and the dream of return to the land have thus replaced actual existence, which has faded away, becoming invisible.

The new cinema attempts to shape, through the directors' subjective viewpoints, a variety of private experiences embedded within several different identities, spaces, and times. Among the points of view expressed are those of children,[12] refugees, women or, as in Sa'ad Andoni's *Last Frontiers* (2002) and *Zero* (2002) and Hani Abu-Assad's *Nazareth 2000* (2000), of Christians in a predominantly Muslim society. Yet, the domination of frozen time over the fluid, flowing sequence and the domination of national unity over social diversity is most clearly expressed in the symbolic role granted in the new films to women and children as representatives of Palestinian history, unity, and hope.

In Michel Khleifi's films, women inhabit the "third space": between Israeli and Palestinian male violence, between elderly men (such as the *mukhtar* in *Wedding in Galilee*, 1987) and young (such as the youngsters planning a suicide attack in that movie), between the archaic and the modern, between dream and reality. Palestinian cinema of later years has not always kept up that ambivalence and heterogeneity. On the one hand, it has rescued women from patriarchal oppression and provided them with distinctly masculine roles in the national struggle. On the other hand, it depicts how, in spite of their significance in the national struggle, they have remained subject to archaic male laws, especially with the strengthening of the status of religion in Palestinian society.[13] In certain cases, such as in Elia Suleiman's films, despite women's active role, they still embody the male fantasy: when they stand at the forefront of the national struggle and perform what the man is incapable of doing.

To a large extent, and mainly in the later films, the directors come to terms with the differences within Palestinian society that the women exposed, by integrating them into the struggle toward the common national cause, or by portraying them as an allegory of the nation, its past and its future.

Liana Badr's film, *Fadwa* (1999), which recounts the life story of the Palestinian national poet, Fadwa Tukan, is an example of the growing tendency in Palestinian cinema to progress more swiftly and clearly from the starting point of social differences and the gap between the times to the final destination – national unity and restoration of the past.

The film opens with a journey through Nablus, its neighborhoods, the mountains around it, and the three religions that found a place there. It utilizes conventions that conceive of Nablus as a symbol of the Palestinian people's open heart, its tradition, its rich past, identifying, finally, the town where the woman loves. The poet's narrative is one of oppression. At the age of twelve, as punishment for receiving a flower from a boy several years her senior, she was taken out of school and kept at home. The film describes how she overcame this oppression with the help of her brother, the poet Ibrahim Tukan, who encouraged her to write poems. Fadwa Tukan's story, like that of the women in *Fertile Memories*, is a private tale of a woman rendered marginal in a patriarchal society. However, unlike the women in *My Very Private Map*, she is rescued from this marginality when she becomes a national poet, and when she is associated with the city of Nablus and the Tukan family's guesthouse, the Diwan, where she is filmed. The shots establish her in static poses under the curving arches of the house, next to the stone walls, among the clay pots, beyond the windows and iron latticework, under the adorned ceiling. Thus, she seems an integral part of this historic house that serves as a commemoration and a symbol of a long-lost world.

The film focuses on the details, granting them a symbolic dimension. A black scarf hanging from a branch of a tree, a familiar emblem of mourning, foreshadows the story of the brother's death; a carnation floating in the water and gradually changing from its original white color to red, symbolizes the death of a warrior that the poet has known. Other significant details include a bouquet of flowers beside a record album, indicating her love of music; a pair of doves on the roof, suggesting her dream of becoming a bird; and two lemons on a saucer with a daffodil, signifying the Palestinian poets living within the Israeli borders, with whom she met after 1967. These symbols associate national aspirations and grief with private hopes and mourning, constructing all of these as a kind of oriental ornamentation reminiscent of murals, embroidery, and pottery decorations, an ornamentation that revives the old Arab tradition of a female harem, steeped in scents and colors. Michel Khleifi, in *Wedding in Galilee*, uses this feminine adornment in order to deconstruct the national masculine unity; Liana Badr uses it to redefine woman as an allegory of the Palestinian and Arab nation, of its tradition, of lost Palestinian richness and wholeness. Palestinian and Arab critics often ignored the multi-dimensional women characters in Khleifi's films and referred to them as national symbols. The new cinema actually realizes this interpretation more than Khleifi's own movies had, since the latter features women characters who are too complex to be reduced to this one-dimensional role.

The most illuminating example of the domination of national allegory and fixated time over the private stories of Palestinian women appears in Azza al-Hassan's documentary, *Three Centimeters Less* (2002). The film is set up to follow the familiar accepted convention discussed above, that of a director seeking a subject for a film. This cinematic quest constitutes here, as in other films following the same model,[14] a kind of a historical investigation or archeological excavation. It intends to transform the past from a mythic, frozen legend that is fully present in the current time, to a flowing continuum, the time of the personal testimony and individual memory. It is the protagonists' everyday time manifested in the kitchen chores, in neighborly conversations, in cosmetic treatments and so on. However, that time freezes in the film, even before it fully unfolds, and beyond it the traumatic national time is revealed, appropriating the mundane and the personal in favor of the general and united.

The film's important innovation is the expression it gives to the frustration of the younger generation, whose private lives were sacrificed by their parents and overshadowed by the national cause. This frustration is reflected in two interlacing stories. The first is the story of Samia, who grew up, like all her siblings, bereft of maternal warmth and compassion. Her mother, who emigrated with her husband to Colombia, returned to her homeland, to Kobar in the West Bank, after her husband was killed. Ever since, she has been constantly occupied with providing the basic necessities for her children and with her efforts to acquire a residence permit that will allow them to stay in their native village. The second story tells the tale of Ra'ida, a woman suffering her entire life from the trauma of separation from her father, Ali Taha, who was killed during the Sabena airplane hijack in 1972, when she was a girl.[15]

The story of Samia and her mother, Hajar, is woven out of interviews with the mother and daughter, whereas Ra'ida's story unfolds in the course of the search the heroine conducts (with the director) for people who knew her father: the tailor who sewed his suits, his co-workers, the woman who participated in the plane hijack. Through these partial, interrupted memories, the daughter, assisted by the director, attempts to work through the traumatic memory, while internalizing the past and acknowledging it as different from the present, yet connected to it. The choice to depict the individual personal story as sacrificed on the altar of the general, national narrative is combined with the choice to relate women's stories. Men are, in fact, practically absent from the film. The two fathers were killed when their daughters were young girls. In the first case (Samia's), the daughter does not recall her father at all. In the second case, the quest for the father ends paradoxically in finding a "mother"; in an emotional interview with the female hijacker, the latter speaks to Samia as mother to daughter. The living "mother," then, replaces the absent father. As in Khleifi's *Wedding in Galilee*, instead of the Oedipal, male, national narrative, a private, female story is presented. Rather than frozen history, the film focuses on a history of flowing continuum linking the past, the present, and the future, and instead of the traumatic time, it is the everyday time of life itself that is displayed. Thus, the film continues and is the culmination of what other directors, such as Michel Khleifi, Elia Suleiman, and Subhi a-Zubeidi, initiated.

Yet, the general structure of the film, the analogies it creates between the stories, and the details it chooses to silence, enable the national allegory and frozen time to overpower and serve as an answer to the private stories and flowing time. The trauma of the grandfathers' (1948) generation, which failed by relinquishing the country, permeates the present trauma of the missing fathers. The loss of the homeland is exposed as a painful issue experienced through the loss in the family. The struggle, the healing of the wounds of the present, also serves as a belated remedy to the bruises of the past.

In fact, the two stories are not completely analogous. Ra'ida's father has hurt his family and his daughters by sacrificing them for the national cause, while in Samia's story, it seems that what has scarred the sisters' lives is the difficult circumstances in which the widowed mother lives. After losing her husband, she has apparently found it difficult to continue living with her ten children in a foreign land, submerged in an alien culture and environment. However, her troubles did not end there. When she returns to her native country, she is compelled to work hard, in order to support her children. These past and present ordeals are completely ignored in movie. So is any detail that can shed light on her past or on her relationship with her children, such as what her profession was, how she passed her time, and why, exactly, she was unable to give her children with love and affection. In place of all this, the film constantly reminds us of her heroic battles to return to the land, to save her sons from deportation, to retrieve her husband's body and ship it back to the homeland.

> I have fought for the right to place my children here. No one helped me. I nearly went mad. They told me: "Hajar, Ishmael's mother, relocated and so will you." To this assertion, my lawyer replied that this was my home and that my children and I have the right to live here, in our house.

According to what both the mother and her daughters claim, this persistent struggle to remain in the country is what ultimately has distanced Hajar from her children.

> During my childhood, my mother was away from me for eleven years [says the daughter Sara]. She was always busy wandering about and doing something for our sake. Back then I didn't realize what she was doing. Only when I grew up, did I understand that she had worked for us to obtain identity cards and to settle us down in our country. I blame the situation that compelled her to always be far from me.

The widow's specific, personal memories of private difficulties and distresses, while attempting to support her children despite loneliness and many obstacles, without the support of a husband and in the face of a traditional society that sanctifies the wholeness of the family – all of these are overlooked in the film. Instead, a single hardship is highlighted: the endeavor to cling on to the ancestral land, which is equivalent to the national struggle that conceals and mends the national trauma – the initial "immigration." The national situation and struggle overshadow all other aspects of life, so much so that even the justification for the woman's physical appearance is based on national circumstances. "Had Palestine not been what it is today," she says, "a place where my children are imprisoned and beaten, I might have looked younger than my seventy-two years." The focus on the national struggle, in fact, leaves the story of the personal past opaque and misunderstood. It is especially unclear why this struggle has prevented her from granting her children tenderness and affection. The movie, therefore, obscures the memory of the personal past and the story of daily survival, replacing them with the story of the national struggle. In this way, individual trauma becomes a memory that conceals an earlier national trauma, that of 1948. The film attempts to atone for this trauma and so the elegy to a private life sacrificed on the national altar is eventually replaced by a hymn of glory for the national deed. "Hajar," the director concludes, "is a fighter. All of us, her children and I, stand in awe, helplessly trying to emulate her." At the beginning of the film, she had mocked the image of the rural woman who revives the tradition of the Palestinian past through her dress and behavior. In the course of the movie, however, she rehabilitates this character and, with her, the past which is represented by her – the idyll, its ruin, and the struggle to retrieve it.

The second story, that of Ra'ida's search for her father, ostensibly ends in a more clear-cut manner with the daughter's complaints about her father's commitment to the national cause: "I understand that the cause turns into a curse," she tells Therese Halsa, the plane's other hijacker. "I want to see him here with me . . . to live a normal life. As long as the cause is what it is, we will pay the price. For father to be with me – that would have been worth everything." Therese responds to the daughter's accusations by advising her to judge her father in the context of the struggle and the significance of that act, which brought the Palestinian cause to the attention of the world. The film reinforces this stance, which is received as a general, final answer delivered by the two mothers: the real and the imagined (surrogate). The masculine, Oedipal story of searching for a father is, indeed, replaced here with the narratives of women. Yet, the women do not bring to the film another view of life or different possibilities, or even offer alternative angles on the national debate, such as the controversy surrounding the killing of civilians as a way of achieving national goals.[16] Instead, they sustain the national struggle run by men, which eliminates details of personal memories and adapts what is left of them to suit the national memory. Thus, the dispossession of national land is yet again reflected through the personal, closer loss – loss of the private family.[17]

A double status, similar to the one bestowed on women, is granted by Palestinian cinema to children as well. On the one hand, the films use children to "disperse" the Palestinian story across a diverse and changing life, through various childhood dreams that are not necessarily related to the national narrative,[18] and through the human, personal everyday. Thus, children function as an additional layer of the continuous historical narrative. Yet from the beginning they also act as a symbol in concrete form, preserving history as a process of handing down from grandfather to grandson.[19] In addition, they constitute the ultimate innocent victims figures. They signify the difficulties of the present and the aspirations for the future.[20]

In many cases, as the films unfold, it becomes clear how and why children have been transformed from real characters to symbols, and how their private memories and dreams have been turned into a collective national memory and longing. Azza al-Hassan had planned to recount, in her film *News Time*, a love story between a neighboring couple. The project failed, however, since the story's "protagonists," the two neighbors, left Ramallah following the city's bombardment during the Second *Intifada*. After their departure, insisting on continuing her film, the director turned to another theme: a group of children loitering on the city's empty streets. Not only did the children enable Al-Hassan to replace a narrative of disaster with a story of hope, but they also allowed her to continue focusing on everyday, mundane private time, albeit now closely connected to the collective story. The children also expressed the same aspiration that guided the director herself: to reclaim her story, which had been appropriated by the Other, the Israelis. Among all of the dreams they discuss, one recurs, reminiscent of the children's dream in May Masri's *The Children of Shatila* (1998): to make a movie, to act in a movie, to be part of a cinematic production. This is an escapist "American dream," yet it is also their fantasy to narrate their story themselves.

Reality, however, steers the director, the children, and the entire film in another direction, when games turn into disasters and dreams become nightmares. The children who had been roaming the streets now go out to throw stones at the roadblocks; they had strolled about Ramallah but the walk now becomes a funeral procession when they are confronted with Muhammad a-Durra's face on a poster;[21] the director visits them at school and stumbles against Nassar's empty seat. He was killed by a dumdum bullet. The everyday story that the director wished to depict gradually turns into a story of death, mourning, and disaster. This is the story she had previously refused to tell but she now realizes is unavoidable. It unites, in one fate, all of the separate destinies, magically reviving the past that they had tried to forget.[22]

A Journey through Blocked Space

The interruption of Palestinian time is associated in these films with the fragmentation of Palestinian space, which had not been demarcated by clear boundaries to begin with. On the one hand, it was divided into separate regions and villages where families and clans resided, and on the other hand, it was defined as part of a broad pan-Arabic territory.[23] Since 1948, the borders that delineated Palestinian space and were drawn by others have left a disintegrated identity both within the frontiers and outside them: in the areas under Israeli dominion, in the West Bank and Gaza Strip, across the Middle East, and in the diasporic communities around the world. These borders deconstructed Palestinian identity while imprisoning it, within the boundaries of the refugee camps, behind fences and watchtowers, as depicted in Masharawi's films,[24] or among mine-fields, jeeps, and soldiers, as reflected in Michel Khleifi's work.[25] In recent years, as roadblocks and checkpoints have become an increasingly grueling daily experience, as the bypass roads and settlements that crisscross the Gaza Strip have proliferated, and with the introduction of soldiers and tanks to the streets and houses, the problem of borders has become a poignant one in the Palestinian consciousness.[26] What could have functioned as a signifier of collective identity (Rogoff, 2000; Kimmerling, 1989) or might have emerged as a place of dialogue between peoples and cultures – a third space – ultimately became a signifier of repression. The border penetrated the private and public spheres, the home, the town, the entire environment, sabotaging the possibility of either setting public and private spaces apart, or creating a flowing continuum between them, like the one in Khleifi's films. The border became a sort of an aching wound for Palestinian society. This was not merely a result of the *Intifadas*, but also a consequence of the peace accords that threatened to sever the boundaries of the dream of return as well as to fragment, within internal borders, the expanses of the future Palestinian state.

Borders and roadblocks, therefore, have made it difficult for Palestinian cinema, during the years of the two *Intifadas*, to construct a harmonious space on the one hand, and to deconstruct it in order to reflect the heterogeneity of Palestinian society on the other. As suggested earlier, the biography of a large number of the directors, who were born and raised in the refugee camps or in exile, has made them even more prone to depict a disharmonious space. Consequently, following the process of the destruction of the house and the diminishing space, as delineated in Ali Nassar and Rashid Masharawi's cinema, a sort of void is reflected in some of the recent films. Thus, the house appears in ruins, the outside has been obliterated, and the only place left intact is the border, the roadblock, which splits both identity and geography into isolated segments. This reality explains, perhaps, why so many recent Palestinian films take place at border crossings and checkpoints, and have, therefore, been dubbed "roadblock movies." These films strive to reconstruct an imaginary harmonious space out of the fragmented blocked one.

In Hani Abu-Assad's film, *Rana's Wedding* (2003), home is the place from which the protagonist flees. Rana is ordered by her father to choose a suitable husband from a list of candidates that he has prepared for her. The father allows her until four o'clock in the afternoon to decide; if she doesn't do as she is told, she will have to accompany him to Egypt. The film's protagonist, Rana, lives in a grand and beautiful home, but in the film we see her escaping from it. At the beginning, Rana leaves the house before daybreak to search for her beloved. Later, when her father agrees to approve the marriage, she flees to the desert, stricken with fear. And finally, at the end of the film, all those invited to the wedding are compelled to leave the house and cross the roadblock, where the wedding ceremony is to be performed. The home thus loses its stability and reliability as a safe haven providing warmth and shelter. Rana's marriage is intended to allow her to build a new home. However, a menacing shadow hovers over this future home, too, when she visits a friend and, through the window, witnesses an Israeli bulldozer destroying a neighbor's house. "They are destroying a home on the very day that I want to build one," she remarks.

The house is set against the landscape surrounding it, which is presented by the film, in effect a travel film, through Rana's journeys. Her first journey is in search of her lover; then there is the loving pair's quest for someone to register their marriage; and finally, we see the trip back to Jerusalem, in order to convince Rana's father to approve their marriage. The journeys in the film, like so many other cinematic trips, appear at first to denote mobility, control of space, the mapping out of the landscapes, and movement toward a goal, redemption or a new vision.[27] Yet, like journeys in other Palestinian films, this one, too, leads through a devastated country and ends in a single destination – the roadblock. The city of Jerusalem, where the heroine wanders before daybreak searching for her lover, is a deserted place, frightening and threatening, reminiscent of the cities in the films of Michelangelo Antonioni or Ingmar Bergman.[28] The places she passes and those she later travels through with her husband-to-be are all destroyed, filled with ruins, piles of dirt, and concrete barriers. It seems, moreover, that couple are traveling round and round in endless and inescapable circles. Here, as in other Palestinian films, such as Hani Abu-Assad's *Ford Transit* (2002), Subhi a-Zubeidi's *Crossing Kalandia (Roadblock)* (2002), or Rashid Masharawi's *Ticket to Jerusalem* (2002), the time devoted to the journey is disproportionately long in relation to the distance of the destination from the starting point. The same dreary places are traveled through again and again, dirt bypasses and heaps of debris repeatedly reappear, the protagonists follow the same routes endlessly and get stuck on the same roads, due to a puncture, a broken-down engine, or simply a pile of stones blocking the way. In all these cases, the beginning, the mid-point, and the final point of each of the journeys is the same – a roadblock. The film ends at the A-Ram roadblock, close to Jerusalem, as the soldiers refuse to let the registrar for the couple's marriage cross the barrier and he is obliged to wed them right there.

Thus, as home no longer constitutes a safe haven and the landscape is in ruins, the most significant place in the film becomes the roadblock. It separates lovers, comes between family members who need to meet each other, splits the different sections of Jerusalem, and even divides houses into segregated spaces.[29]

This structure, loss of both public and private spaces, characterizes a great deal of the new Palestinian films. In Azza al-Hassan's *Three Centimeters Less*, for instance, landscapes and expanses are completely missing. Even when her camera is placed on the protagonist's balcony, overlooking an untamed, natural mountain view, this landscape is never captured on film and can only be inadvertently seen through a window frame. Even when the camera ventures outside, to the cities and villages, it tilts downward or is imprisoned in confined places that block the view. The only landscape appearing in the movie is the view of the sea, which is filmed in a traveling shot out of a moving car, when one protagonist, Ra'ida, travels to Haifa. A filming error suggests the problematic status of landscape in this film. On Ra'ida's way from Tel Aviv to Haifa in the north, the car is filmed traveling from north to south (the sea is to the right), rather than the other way around.[30] The director, who has turned her back on the landscape, concentrates on homes – on the interiors of apartments and on the kitchens, living rooms, and balconies of the protagonists' homes. These homes, however, are no safe alternative to the outside space. "This is the house," she states in the opening scene as she moves with her camera in the midst of ruins, "and this is the attempt to preserve a normal life," she continues, as she focuses her camera on a group of children wandering about the ruins. Her film opens with these ruins and concludes with the wreckage of her own apartment when she returns to it and moves through the rooms surveying the damage done by the soldiers who have broken into and searched it. The destruction at the beginning and end of the film and the disappearance of expanses throughout symbolize the impossibility of cinematically creating a complete harmonious space and highlight a sense of being continuously blocked.

Some of the Palestinian films concentrate on just one of these losses: either that of the house or that of the outside. In films such as Rashid Masharawi's *Stress* (1998) or Elia Suleiman's *Divine Intervention* (2002), the house either does not exist or has turned into a narrow, fractured prison. The destruction of the house is most poignantly depicted in Nizar Hassan's film, *Invasion* (2003). Here, children play among the rooms of a demolished apartment and a couple is sitting on the floor on the second story of an apartment building that has collapsed, fancy curtains, a remnant of past grandeur, still hanging within the wrecked room. What creates the strongest effect of devastation in this film is precisely the opposition between the ruined structures on the one hand, and on the other hand, life that nevertheless perseveres, as if the buildings were still intact, as if everything remained as it had been.

In Abu Wa'el's *Waiting for Salah A-Ddin* (2001), external space has turned into a narrow and fractured prison. This film indicates the connection between the obstruction of everyday life that came to a halt, and the blocked space. Together, arrested time and obstructed space evoke a strong sense of a dead-end. The camera is crowded in this film, hard-pressed between demolished walls, observing the protagonists through banisters, behind closed doors or blocked windows, from peculiar angles which are inconvenient for the viewer, in deep focus through which the wretched emptiness or density of the filmed spaces can be seen. The blocking of spaces and the continuation of the distress described above is translated into cinematic language through the slow and static camera movements, passing, for example, back and forth, along the lengthening line in front of the Ministry of Internal Affairs in Ibn Shadad Street, pausing on the face of a man whose house has been destroyed or on a man sitting, motionless, at the entrance to the Al Haquawati Theater, waiting for the show to end. The camera's stationary position is reinforced by the long takes and by the people's own static condition.

Palestinian cinema, however, not only repeatedly depicts a state of siege and enclosure, but also attempts to break out of it. Focusing the gaze on details entrapped within the space and transforming them into signifiers of the whole space, or employing cinematic means to avoid the confining borders, supports the endeavor to overcome the enclosing boundaries. In certain cases, these films succeed in thus imagining another space, free of limitations. In other cases, crossing the borders recreates the idyllic past landscapes that have frozen in their pre-1948 state, thus obscuring, as the cinema of the 1970s had done, the multiplicity of the Palestinian narrative and history.

In *Waiting for Salah A-Ddin*, there are no expanses. Two trips take place in the movie. Yet, one occurs in a car with drawn curtains, blocking the view, and the other, along the wall of the Old City in Jerusalem, is a journey in darkness. All one sees is the illuminated Dome of the Rock. However, the camera breaks open these enclosed spaces by conquering the heights. Throughout Tawfik Abu Wa'el's film, a cryptic struggle between Israelis and Palestinians for the control of space evolves. From the beginning of the film, the Israelis dominate the high places; Israeli soldiers patrol along the top of the Old City walls and over the Al-Aqsa mosque, and Israeli policemen on horseback soar over the peddlers in the markets, and so on. Although Abu Wa'el's camera, like the protagonists in the film, is placed in an essentially inferior position, by using such camera techniques as tilt-up, zoom-out and long shot, the soldiers on the city wall are made to dissolve and disappear; they are reduced in size or are lost in the distance or in spaces crowded with Palestinians. The spectacular movements of the camera circumvent what the Israelis see, but show what they perhaps fail to acknowledge. The camera moves upward, over the heads of the Israelis, or drops low, below their viewing range. It takes in the crowds at prayer in the area surrounding the Al-Aqsa Mosque, tracks lines of soldiers, rises again to the *muezzin* in a minaret, and then rises even further up, to the moon. The camera's wide and slow movements capture the sky and suffuse the protagonists' static and limited space with dynamics and height.

As in Abu Wa'el's movie, many Palestinian films dominate the air and the sky in order to control the expropriated territories from above. Camera shots of this kind allow the directors to perceive both the Israelis and the Arabs, the masses in Jerusalem as well as at the roadblocks, to give a sense of the overcrowding and commotion. In many cases, such cinematography allows directors to film in places where the Israeli army usually forbids filming. Yet, they have a clear function beyond that: "The Jew is always high up, in the place of the one in charge," says Subhi a-Zubeidi. "I create a hierarchy that leads from the ground below to what is above it and above the Israeli." In a private interview in Ramallah (2002), Hani Abu-Assad explained this point even more vividly: "In order to dictate your reality you must film it from above. You cannot change the reality; you can only overcome it. The crane allows me to ascend above the border that the officer had set at the roadblock and to film beyond it. Cinematic means enable you to cross borders."

In Subhi a-Zubeidi's *Light at the End of the Tunnel*, the opening of the space to the heights is achieved by the much-used, almost routine movement of the camera, passing from shots of interviewed prisoners, prison scenes, and demonstrations, upward – to the heads of the people, the balconies, the roofs and higher yet – to the sky. When that technique is applied across the heroic Socialist-Realist style of painting, it indicates that hope, which elevates the camera, tilting it upward, is related to the struggle. One of the female prisoners in the film, for example, recounts how the long years in prison have affected her. The camera passes from her face to a painting of a muscular man and slowly tilts up along his body, to his face and hands, while they are being released from the handcuffs that have bound them. From there, the camera ascends to a rainbow. The painting and the camera movement that scans it in rather worn-out and naive fashion evoke what has also been summoned forth in these films in other ways: the camera compensates for the blocking of space by controlling the air and the sky.

Palestinian cinema also uses its plots in order to overcome siege and borders and to create "open bridges" that link the different regions of the country, and the Diaspora. The structure of Abu Wa'el's film, *Waiting for Salah A-Ddin*, creates such bridges by using parallel plots, all of them dealing with similar distress and hardships, and also by depicting the exchange of messages broadcast from Palestinian relatives all over the world, who communicate by radio as they have no other means of contact. At the beginning of the film, we are presented with a parody of such fleeting messages that are meant to calm down the distant listener at the end of the line ("Our situation is wonderful, the *narghile's* coals are wonderful, the backgammon is great . . . the '67 war is over, and we were never better, the moon in our sky is still round and whole"). However, the film ends in a serious tone that is not at all parodic: "We lost all self-respect, the houses, the children, but we are still calling, Fatima sends her regards to her brother." Such a greeting bridges over the distances, turning the separate stories delineated by the film to a single story of one nation. This unity is created through the radio, through analogies between the different destinies in various episodes, through the tilt-up camera movement and its focus on the unifying symbol of the Al-Aqsa mosque that appears in shots between episodes and connects them. As will be elaborated on below, this symbol is what represents the lost wholeness, appropriating it from the pre-1948 historical time to which it originally belonged and turning it into an infinite object.

Unity, then, overcomes separation here, hope replaces distress, and the active movements of the camera compensate for the characters' passive and static stance. Unity, hope, and activism are constructed via cinematic means and are expressed more overtly in Mahmud Darwish's poem, quoted in the film: "The Jews penetrated our lives and our beds, but we are returning."

In May Masri's *Borders of Dreams and Fears* (2001), this unity is created through the plot that replaces the scarred landscape in which the refugees live, among the camps, away from their country, with an imaginary map, a new spatial cartography. The film follows the lives of children in two separate refugee camps: Shatila, in Lebanon, and Dheisha, in the West Bank. The map that the film charts is one of exile and separation, a map determined by the outcome of the 1948 war. Indeed, the film's opening shows arrows marking the route taken by refugees fleeing Palestine northward to Shatila, on the one hand, and eastward to the West Bank, on the other. The plot, which delineates the children's daily lives, tends to draw an alternative map that will create links and bridges over the distances imposed by the existing map, and thus resurrect an imaginary Palestinian community, in Benedict Anderson's terms (2000). The route taken by the letters and videotapes the children exchange between the two camps marks the first path charted on the map. It links their different stories. The two sites are then drawn closer geographically, as the children come to either side of the Israeli-Lebanese border to meet each other. Next, history leaves its imprint on this geographical chart as the child from Dheisha visits Saforie, from which the family of the girl from Shatila fled in 1948, and sends her a sachet of earth from the village. Eventually the children validate the map seen as the film begins, but this time with the arrows pointing in the opposite direction: from exile inward, into the lost country. This map operates on several symbolic planes for the film's protagonists. It frees them from the reality of the congested camps in which they live into the vast expanses of space, in particular that of their lost homeland, and also introduces a dynamic of movement into an otherwise stagnant existence. In addition it creates a harmonious, total homogeneity in the areas divided between different nations and between occupiers and occupied, as well as reassembling a puzzle that was taken apart, its various pieces scattered,[31] thus reconstructing the well-known lost paradise.

Ahmad Habash's film, *Moon Eclipse* (2001), merges overtly and explicitly the diverse personal stories into one collective narrative, clearly exemplifying how the parallel aspects of the different plots, occurring in different places, create national unity in a single broad collective space. This film is more student-like than seasoned and well formed. Yet, precisely because of that quality, it is easy to identify in it the components typical of the new cinema. *Moon Eclipse* is composed as a chain of linked individual stories. The plots include tales of two friends driving around the city in their car, a dentist pulling out a child's tooth, a couple trying to emigrate so that their son will be born in another country, a prisoner tortured in jail, and a young girl discovering that her parents plan to marry her off to an older man. Immaturely, perhaps, but certainly effectively, the film sums up some of the moves that have solidified in the new cinematic wave. It is concerned with private, everyday events, in the minute dramas taking place between one large-scale national drama and another, or entirely independently of them. It avoids presenting climactic events on screen (weddings, births, imprisonment, or death). Rather, it brings forth what has preceded those events (such as the preparations for the birth) or what follows (the already incarcerated man, the picture of a *shaheed* on the wall, which is a photo of one of the men riding in the car). More poignantly than had been seen in other films, the private anecdotes here are associated with the general national story. In certain cases, the allegorical link is pressed too transparently. That is the case in the scene of the madman, who approaches the stone sculptures in Ramallah, prompting them to rise up to action. Another is the episode of the child, who comes out to throw his uprooted tooth up against the glaring sun, a gesture that, according to popular belief, is meant to promise a future of hope. In other cases, the integration of all the separate individual stories into a single, collective national narrative is accomplished through obvious analogies. Distress and pain, for instance, are reflected by a series of similar, exaggerated facial expressions, and with one loud outcry that connects all episodes of suffering and pain, private and national. The aching cry, with which all the episodes are tainted, signifies the shared distress. Such a film accentuates what has found root in the new cinema: the use of analogies and recurring motifs that facilitate the move from the personal, private, everyday story to the national narrative that fills the one large space.

With the cinematic plots at their disposal, therefore, these films strive to overcome fragmentation and disintegration, to "steal the borders" and construct a unified national identity and territory. At times when the real territory is so fragmented, many films attempt to avoid contributing to that disintegration. They seek, on the contrary, wholeness, including the lost wholeness of the past.

Many Palestinian films, rather than "rebelling" against the continuous shrinking of space, choose to focus on small, isolated details and to turn them into symbols of wholeness and totality, a synecdochic substitute for the broad landscape of the past. In the face of a reality, in which the land is continuously being split by Jewish settlements, military forces, fences, and roadblocks, filmmakers find it difficult to depict it as wholeness. In order to describe the nonexistent completeness, they turn to the symbol. Anton Shammas (2002b: 114) articulates this notion as follows: "For A's grandmother, an old Lebanese refugee, Palestine means nothing more than the lemon tree in the backyard of the house she left in Jaffa, or Yafa, as she calls it."

Thus, instead of the land with the olive tree in its midst, which featured in Nassar and Khleifi's cinema, the films now concentrate on the olive tree itself, or even on a fig leaf or an individual lemon. When it is impossible to roam about the open expanses, the films concentrate on the street or the house. And even there, space is shrinking; rather than filming the structure in its entirety, the films pause on a curve, a stone wall, the ironwork of a window, a common dining table, and at times, a single plate. These details constitute the concrete, authentic, specific entity on to which the films cling, as a part of the whole, a detail representing the completeness. They indicate the need "to hold on to something tangible and present in an evasive world," in a disintegrated reality (McKean Parmenter, 1994: 74). When the entire complex becomes invisible, intangible,[32] they are transformed from a concrete entity to symbols denoting that which is gone[33] – the entire homeland, its vast expanses, its past and its future. Thus, the tranquility preceding the ruin is symbolized by a fig leaf[34] or a poppy field.[35] Hope is represented by flower buds with the sky as backdrop,[36] and resurrection is manifested by a flower on a tombstone.[37] The continuation, the memories, the dreams, the collective struggle, and private lives are now embodied by the children, who unite all these in their lives, and all these together with the wide expanses are now represented by the Al-Aqsa mosque.

In a situation in which the homeland becomes increasingly invisible, imagination and allegory are summoned forth "to conjure it up." The power of these allegories, furthermore, intensifies in the face of the threat of loss – the emblematic meaning of the olive tree, the mosque, a stone wall, or the living child is enhanced in view of the sights of uprooted olive trees, ruined houses, shattered stones, or dead children.[38] Death, uprootedness, and destruction are merged now in a slice of reality that revives the wholeness preceding them, a condition which would also triumph over those disintegrating states in the future.

That reduction, that focus on details, certainly suggests the young directors' need to find new means of expression, different from those that were established in Michel Khleifi's films. Yet, the "rebellion" against the cinematic fathers and the search for new means of expression that would suit the new reality have actually drawn New Cinema back to Palestinian poetry and literature, which are prone to using details such as "a shirt, a door or a key" (Darwish, 1978), "as symbols of identity, security and resistance" (McKean Parmenter, 1994: 74), as a replacement for the whole house or the entire space.

In Nada al Yassir's film, *Four Poems for Palestine* (2001), the threatened and ruined house is replaced by its parts: old tiles, ceiling paintings, cracked walls, windows, curved arches, ironwork, wooden and iron doors, clay pots.[39] This is a film about a woman who soundlessly does the housework. Outside, the *Intifada* rages, its echoes filtering in through the television set. Although the interior seems enclosed and protected from all of this, the outside terror infiltrates again and again, like in *The Milky Way* (1997), but this time only symbolically. The woman observes the ceiling and it is leaking, the walls are fractured, the window broken, she is nursing her infant while demonstrations can be seen on the television screen, people running with a stretcher, children throwing stones. She looks in the mirror, and in it sees demonstrations and graves. In the course of the film, the symbols of a wrecked and disintegrated reality are replaced by symbols of the wholeness of the past, the present, and the future. While the woman performs simple tasks, each one seems to flood the screen with a dense fluid: red fluid with the slicing of a tomato, black fluid after applying eye makeup, green after brewing tea, and white after nursing the baby. As in many other films, the details here represent the whole. Yet, this whole is not the reality from which these details have emanated, but an idyllic entirety that unifies the present, past and future, and it is manifested either in the white color indicating hope or in the tricolors of the Palestinian flag: the red, the black, and the green.

Just as the parts of the house are a synecdochic substitute for the house as a whole, the expanses are represented by the details in them. The olive tree, for instance, has long been emblematic of "rootedness, identity and resistance" (McKean Parmenter, 1994: 74), reappearing time and again in cinema, becoming an overworked image sold during the Second *Intifada* as a jewel, and cropping up again in its familiar roles in many films. Liana Badr's *Zaytounant* (2002) might serve as an example.

Badr uses the olive tree as a focal point around which four stories of home and exile revolve. One is the story of an artist who left the country as a young child and returns to paint its olive trees. In another, a woman who lives in a large stone house, surrounded by a garden where there are two olive trees, fears for the fate of her home, as well as for her own. The other stories are about simple villagers picking the olives from their trees, and who have to make do with the handful of trees left to them after some of their land has been expropriated; and, finally, the story of villagers whose trees have been uprooted by Israeli settlers. On the face of it, the different stories construct a heterogeneous stratified society, such as the one delineated in Khleifi's *Fertile Memories*, depicting the real, daily lives of at least some of the characters, whose subsistence is based on the produce of their land. However, the real point of the film is not this portrait of men and women of different classes, ages, and locales, but rather their collective story, which is signified by the olive tree. This tree is the symbol for the nation in its entirety – its soil, its rural heritage, and its future. And the stronger the threat to all of these becomes, so too does the potency of the symbol. There is great variety in the shots of olive trees, yet the manner in which the shots are cut or dissolved into one another integrates them all: a venerable gnarled olive tree; a newly planted olive shoot; an uprooted olive tree, vandalized by Israeli settlers; a painted olive tree, standing for the dream of the lost homeland; an olive tree as a postcard; and olive trees as the source of livelihood of those who live on the land. Like the curved arches and colored floor tiles that represent the typical Arab house, the olive tree is the single object that serves as a symbol for the lost but longed-for homeland, its past and future, its memories and reveries, its existence and its threatened fate. It exists as a symbol that no longer signifies an actual reality. It bridges over the distances and differences the film draws between its various protagonists and between various areas of life, and erases the differences between men and women, children and adults, rich and poor. They all become part of the national struggle embodied by the olive trees. The personal experience melts into the national experience when the one and only issue the interviewees are occupied with is the olive and its various symbolic meanings.[40]

As symbols became the main way of expressing Palestinian space in its entirety, many recent films use them as the axis of their plots. They start with cars breaking down, stopping, losing their way, or getting stuck in roadblocks,[41] but they end with kites, flags, birds or horses crossing borders and reaching distances and heights,[42] thus indicating that the power of imagination, dreams, and longing can reclaim the blocked national space.

The difference between notions of reality and space in Khleifi's films and in the films of the New Cinema can be traced to the use of these symbols. The child protagonist in Khleifi's *Tale of the Three Jewels* (1994) captures birds and takes care of them. The free-flying bird symbolizes a free, poetic world for which the child yearns. Its symbolic role, encompassing both the national and the universal story is, however, blurred by the realistic details of capturing and tending it. Similarly, a rogue mare that escapes to the fields in the middle of a wedding ceremony in *Wedding in Galilee* serves as a complex symbol of a feminine world, of national nostalgia, and of universal longings, as well as being part of a personal and familial story. The bird and the mare are burdened with multiple and conflicting meanings through which the reality of life, the identity and memory of the individual protagonists and of the Palestinian people, as also of those who do not belong to it, are brought to the screen.[43]

In general, even when focusing on allegorical details, Khleifi's camera wove them into the larger space of country, village, and home. Thus, his films constructed some spatial sequence containing both the present and the longed-for past, the divided fractured place and the missing wholeness.

The New Cinema grants special significance to the details representing the expanses, assigning them an unequivocal allegorical significance at the expense of their plain, realistic meanings. The galloping horse in *Light at the End of the Tunnel* or *Ticket to Jerusalem* and the bird in the sky in *Borders of Dreams and Fears* or *Fadwa* do not exist in any real contexts, nor do they represent a range of meanings. Their sole purpose is to epitomize national yearnings for liberty, the open expanses, freedom of movement, connection with the land – all of the components attributed to the glorious past, which is called forth to replace the flawed present.

Above and beyond all of the objects embodying the wholeness of the homeland, the house and the expanses, the Al-Aqsa mosque stands out as the focal point for the whole. This ubiquitous symbol, in its actual appearance, in pictures of it hanging on the wall, in the amplified sounds of prayer emanating from it and heard by the films' protagonists as they roam between heaps of debris and through the roadblock bypasses,[44] serves as a sacred icon (Naficy, 2001). Its existence as a geographical axis (the heart of the country) and cinematic focus (at the center of the frame), its lofty position (emphasized by the angle and the movements of the camera), and its dominance of the soundtrack (the *muezzin*'s call drowns out all other sounds) allow it to fulfill the function which the wide spaces encompassing house, fields, and trees had previously done. It serves as a substitute for everything that formerly symbolized the Palestinian people, evoking for its sake the past idyll of wholeness in the present. Though the mosque is a religious symbol, it has been appropriated by secular filmmakers, who have adopted the religious stance increasingly prevalent in Palestinian society.

Recent Palestinian cinema thus has been using specific, tangible details of daily life and landscape as preservers of the entire space, and within it, the memory of the fading past and the threatened present existence. All too often, however, the national-allegorical significance embedded in the detail comes at the expense of the reality it was meant to represent. Shehada (2003: 86) aptly describes this thus:

> I found myself looking at an olive tree, and as I was looking at it, it transformed itself, before my eyes, into a symbol . . . of our struggle, of our loss. And at that precise moment, I was robbed of the tree, and left in its stead with a hollow void into which rage and pain flow.[45]

Some of the emblems established in Palestinian culture were partially embraced by television networks around the world. Those were added to images of fighters, of stone-throwing children, and of destroyed houses, all of which served as symbols for Palestinian history and identity, while at the same time minimizing and obliterating them (Said and Mohr, [1986] 1999: 4).[46] Symbols formed within Palestinian society were linked to symbols of the Palestinian society created in the West, and together they contributed to the appropriation of the concreteness of Palestinian existence. This gradual process is explained by Sanbar thus: "In the beginning, you were required to burn our features into your gaze, so that you would not be able to forget our faces, or crease them, or whiten them out" (1997: 26). But, in fact, the face became an image and,

> once you grasp it, the face disappears. Soon the image of the *fedayeen* became an abstraction; concealing the image of the society behind him. After becoming a group of refugees, Palestinians were finally perceived by those who saw them as a group of armed fighters. But who is the one hiding beneath the *kaffiyeh* . . .? Those who could not banish

the Palestinians once more into the void, tried at least to imprison them in a new abstraction: that of the mask-wearing man, the terrorist with a rifle. (26–7)

As mentioned above, the Palestinians themselves also contributed to the creation of that abstraction.

The problem that has faced recent Palestinian cinema, therefore, was how to tell the stories of Palestinians when the sole available tools were a collection of images that defined Palestinian society for the West, and an assortment of symbols through which Palestinian society itself crystallizes its unity and narrative. Michel Khleifi (1997) describes this as an "automatic discourse," a "ready-made" language of images; or, to use the question Elia Suleiman poses in his film, *Arab Dream* (1998): "How can you make a film when all you have are two characters: the aggressor and the victim?"

Suleiman himself has proved in his movies that that mission can be accomplished. Yet, in order to succeed in the endeavor, he turned the question itself into a theme in his cinema. By exposing the distance created between symbol and referent, between signifier and signified, by estranging the details that have been exhausted, he renewed their significance.

Such estrangement is also created in other Palestinian films. Nizar Hassan's *Invasion* depicts the scenes of destruction in the Jenin refugee camp after its invasion by the Israeli army in April 2002. The scenes are cross-edited with what have become clichéd images of destruction in Palestinian cinema and the television networks: a red rose on a tombstone, a close-up shot of a fig leaf in front of a destroyed house, the fighter with the gun, children as emblems of hope, the dead *shaheed*, and so on. However, these tropes are embedded in the cinematic structures and contexts that concentrate on fragments of life, not necessarily on symbols. For example, in an interview with a woman whose fiancé was killed in the raid, the director ignores the symbols of death and the destruction of hope and insists on hearing the minute, meaningless details of the couple's daily life: the color of the settee or the kitchen design of their future apartment. Even when the camera pauses on sights and details that have become commonplace, such as the houses destroyed in the raid, it does so in a unique manner. They are first shown as televised images, being viewed by the director and the Israeli bulldozer driver he is interviewing. Thus, a certain distance is created between the very familiar dreadful sights of destruction, and the eye of the viewer, watching these scenes on fictitious screens and contemplating them through the mediation of two men holding different and opposing stances concerning what is viewed: the Palestinian director and the Israeli driver. Such a distance is also created when, in a graveyard shot, the tractor operator (in response to Hassan's enquiries) offers many lengthy explanations about the structure, strength, size, and abilities of the machine (which caused the death of those buried in the graves, seen on screen). The apparently minor, insignificant details once again infuse the worn-down images, thus renewing their power to astonish. The same scheme is further heightened in the film by its "detective structure" – only at the end of a sequence or chain of events are certain facts provided – the facts without which it cannot be understood: the fact that the woman's fiancé has been killed, that the ditches viewed by the bull-dozer driver are graves, that the child innocently strolling down the camp's street is an orphan. Hassan uses, in these cases and in others, symbols that have already been established in Palestinian cinema. However, these tropes are embedded in the cinematic structures and contexts that require a re-viewing of them, as problematic and painful details within an actual reality. This reality exists in all its complexity in the present. Yet, it serves as a kind of screen that simultaneously conceals and reveals the reality and the trauma of the past. In this way, continuity between realities is created, which enables a confrontation with the traumas of the past and the present and a chance of successfully coping with them.

Nabila Irshid's film, *Travel Agency* (2001), invigorates the overworked images in a different way. It is filmed with an old 8mm camera and seems, there-fore, an authentic documentation of the country in the past, and its particular characteristics: the threshold of a house, someone praying, children bathing in the Sahne lake. This documentation is accompanied by a narration in English, meant to "sell" the Holy Land to tourists, in the familiar orientalist manner, as an Eastern paradise, as the Holy Land for all religions. The irony toward this touristy text is prominent throughout, turning even more blatant toward the end, when the landscape goes up in smoke and the narrator concludes: "In our paradise, all rooms are vacant. Come and experience the adventure of a visit to a nonexistent land."

The bitter irony is aimed here not only at the orientalist images constructed by the West, and not merely at the obliteration of the Palestinian land, but also at the revival of this nonexistent land in the present, by the Palestinians them-selves, through the image. The revival occurring here is presented as impossi-ble, as (physically) worn-down film burdened by old clichés.

One of the means of exposing the distance between the symbol and what is supposed to be represented by it is the involvement of the spectator in the hesi-tations of the director, who is searching for his story. Such involvement, meant to expose the director's personal story and also to associate it with the authen-tic national narrative, is intended in these cases to present the attempt to tell both a personal and a national story as impossible. In Nizar Hassan's film, *Defiance* (2001), Hassan himself and his producer, in the roles of fictitious characters, attempt to cross borders, distances, and roadblocks to converge in Ramallah and make a movie about the child *shaheed*, Muhammad a-Durra.[47] This film was eventually not made since they could not include in it all the elements necessary for the story: time, space, and the character. They did succeed in conquering the space through traveling shots, using the same technique Khleifi had used. The director and the producer approached the meeting point in Ramallah from two different directions, the producer traveling the West Bank roads and the director arriving from the north of the country, the cross-editing linking different and distant areas of the country. Yet, as they neared each other and the roadblocks and border separated them, that link was broken. Like the expanses, the character of the boy whose story they had wished to tell also disappeared. It froze into the static a-Durra image that was distributed and duplicated in the media throughout the world. The boy's life story remained obscure, since the filmmakers could not interview his mother and relatives. Consequently, the film endeavors to revive the images by replacing the intended protagonist with another; the plan to shoot a film about Muhammad a-Durra is substituted with talk about portraying a different, living boy who is seen in a photograph throwing a stone at a tank. Yet, this hero too becomes a symbol of the uprising. Furthermore, it is revealed that he also was killed in the *Intifada*. Thus, the living and the dead children are frozen as symbols of a tenacious struggle in which death is embedded in life. The film reveals the reason for the transformation of characters into images when it captures conversations between the characters searching in their identity cards for their country of birth and not finding what they are looking for – Palestine. Palestine, the space of the past, is presented here as something absent, an entity that cannot be materialized into something currently present. That is why it is impossible to find the reality behind the symbols and images. The actuality that the filmmakers are striving to detect is gone. This absence also explains why the Palestinian film that they set out to make could not ultimately be produced.

Elia Suleiman offers the most exhaustive expression of the problematic aspects of the current Palestinian film, seeking a middle way between the personal and the national, between the flowing sequence and the traumatic fixated time of the past, between the actual blocked space and the allegories that represent it and open it up and, at the same time, also erase it. Suleiman is the filmmaker attempting to bring this third, open, heterogeneous space, constructed by Michel Khleifi, back to Palestinian cinema. Suleiman, therefore, will be the focus of the concluding chapter of this book.

NOTES

1. Not necessarily because they were created in the Third World, as Jameson (1986) says, but because they were created in a society striving to unite under a collective national consciousness and a shared struggle.
2. These films can be called "I movies."
3. See also Chapter 4, "Without Place, Without Time: The Films of Rashid Masharawi" on the protagonist's broken-down car in *Haifa* (1995) and in *Ticket to Jerusalem* (2002).

4. See the Introduction. See also the discussion of past memory in Chapter 4, "Without Place, Without Time: The Films of Rashid Masharawi." For an elaboration on the theme of remembrance in history, which is based on forgetting, see Elsaesser (2001).
5. See also Bresheeth (2001) and Avni (2001). Another example of an attempt to tell the story of 1948 from various angles is Muhammad Ibrahim Saadi's film, *Bleeding Dreams*, which reconstructs the Dir Yasin story.
6. See Shenhav and Hever (2002) on the possibility of writing history that is not subject to Western narratives.
7. Such as in the films of Khleifi, Masharawi, and Nassar.
8. Nizar Hassan's *Istiklal* (1994), offers a most interesting examination of the manner in which the Palestinian story was eliminated from the Israeli "cover story." The film observes the various ways in which the Palestinians emulated the Israelis in the early years of the state. These include the total identification of the Arab with the Jewish Israeli, and the partial imitations of those compelled to imitate Israelis, as well as the parodic mimicry of the boy who wears a skullcap to school. See Chapter 1, "A Chronicle of Palestinian Cinema." In all of these cases, the identities created by the imitations are flawed, being either too Israeli or not Israeli enough. This ill fit between the original and its replicas is the subversive basis of the film. See, on this theme, an elaboration of the term mimicry in Bhabha (1990) and Hever (1993). A similar phenomenon appears in several important Palestinian books, such as *The Pessoptimist* (Habibi, 1994) or *Dancing Arabs* (Kashua, 2002). Later, in *Arab Dream* (1998), Elia Suleiman will try to make a more conscious parodic imitation of the Israeli discourse. He disguises himself, for instance, as an Israeli soldier in a scene that seems completely documentary, when he pulls a Palestinian boy out of his home and takes him into detention, disregarding his mother's loud protests; or he has his picture taken while posing as a tourist climbing Israeli tanks. Another example is when his camera adopts the viewpoint of the Israeli who eliminates Arabs in a computer game. For a discussion of types of imitation, see Naficy (2001: 185).
9. In Rashid Masharawi's *Stress* (1998).
10. In Rashid Masharawi's *Ticket to Jerusalem* (2002), Subhi a-Zubeidi's *Crossing Kalandia (Roadblock)* (2002), and Elia Suleiman's *Divine Intervention* (2002).
11. The first film in the *Once Again (Marratan Okhra)* project, within the framework of which the Institute for Modern Media at Al-Quds University produced five documentary films (2002) on the subject of human rights in the Occupied Territories.
12. For example, Azza al-Hassan's film *News Time* (2001) and May Masri's *The Children of Shatila* (1998).
13. See Nizar Hassan's *Jasmine* (1996) and Subhi a-Zubeidi's *Women in the Sun* (1999). See also the condition of women in Rashid Masharawi's *Curfew* and *Haifa*. For an elaboration of this theme, see Chapter 1, "A Chronicle of Palestinian Cinema," and Chapter 3, "About Place and Time: The Films of Michel Khleifi."
14. In Subhi a-Zubeidi's film, *My Very Private Map*, for example.
15. In May 1972, members of the Black September organization kidnapped a Sabena aircraft on its way from Brussels to Tel Aviv. The plane was landed at Lod airport and the guerillas, two men and two women, demanded the release of guerillas arrested in Israel in exchange for the liberation of the captives on the plane. The release operation, during which one Israeli civilian and two of the attackers were killed, was highly successful and prompted a strong reaction throughout the world. The group's commander, killed during the release operation, was Ali Abu-Sneina (Taha), who had previously taken part in other hijacks (Shiff and Haber, 1976).
16. A theme that was suggested in Michel Khleifi's *Wedding in Galilee*.
17. Omar al Qwattan's documentary, *Dreams of Silence* (1991), is an example, a mini-analysis, of the way that woman is excluded from religious Palestinian male society

and the way that she is re-embraced by the same society as a consequence of the shared national disaster and dream of return to the past.

18. The girl in *Borders of Dreams and Fears* (Masri, 2001) dreams of becoming a doctor, the boy in *A Child Called Muhammad* (Najar, 2002, from the *Once Again* series) dreams of traveling to America to become a pilot and to live in a villa, the child in *The Children of Shatila* (Masri, 1998) dreams of having money, and another child in the same movie dreams of owning a cellular phone. The child in *The Green Bird* (Badr, 2002) wants to become a soccer player and others wish to become engineers, veterinarians, astronauts, blacksmiths or farmers, for example.

19. It is the children who continue to dream naive dreams of the idyllic past. Through their guileless eyes, it is possible to continue the presentation of these dreams as reliable. The memory of drawing water from a village well may seem like an idyllic beatification of a reality that was perhaps not so idyllic at the time. But when it is heard from the mouth of the eponymous boy, for example, in Najwa Najar's film *A Child Called Muhammad*, such a description seems more natural and feasible. In a large part of Palestinian cinema, as early as the 1970s; and later, in the films of Khleifi, Masharawi, and Nassar, children embody not just the past but hope for the future as well. Therefore, these films end with a close-up of the children's faces. Their role as the personification of hope and the future further intensified with the First *Intifada* as a result of the roles that they played in reality, in the stone-throwing war against the Israeli army.

20. Thus, they fill here the same roles as they did in third period cinema, during the 1970s, and in several later films, such as *The Milky Way* (1997), *In the Ninth Month* (2002), *Curfew* (1993), *Haifa* (1995) and *Invasion* (2003). These are also roles that other marginal characters, like women, play in Palestinian society.

21. The boy Muhammad a-Durra was killed at the Netzarim Junction on 30 September 2000, probably by an Israeli sniper's bullet. The images of a-Durra and his father seeking shelter from the shooting, the moment he was shot, and his death in the arms of his father were all filmed by a French television crew and were broadcast around the world. The Israeli army was severely criticized for the incident. Later investigations could not positively determine whether a-Durra had indeed been shot by an Israeli soldier or by the Palestinians themselves. The incident became a symbol of the occupation and the harm it does to the Palestinian people.

22. This shared fate dominates other films, as well. It is clear that in the given national reality, personal dreams cannot come true. "What do we study for?" asks the girl in *Borders of Dreams and Fears*. "We have no future. We grow up, our dreams grow, but how can we realize our dreams when we are refugees without any rights? These are dreams of young dead people." In *The Children of Shatila*, the mother responds to her daughter's plan to become a doctor thus: "I don't like to spoil things for them by telling them the truth. And then I think to myself, wondering what kind of a future awaits us." The nonexistent tranquil future is substituted by a future of struggle; death, in which this struggle sometimes culminates, becomes the symbol of a harmonious future that would be realized through it, either here or in another world, a restoration of a harmonious past from which one cannot disconnect. See, for instance, the cut in Liana Badr's *The Green Bird* from the dead children's paintings to the events surrounding their death. See also the child who, through his name, Amal, embodies hope, in Ali Nassar's *In the Ninth Month*, as does the child who observes Rana's rage and despair in *Rana's Wedding* (2003).

23. See Chapter 2, "From Bleeding Memories to Fertile Memories."

24. See Chapter 4, "Without Place, Without Time: The Films of Rashid Masharawi."

25. See Chapter 3, "About Place and Time: The Films of Michel Khleifi."

26. In Kimmerling's terms (1989), these borders are defined as frontiers, rather than boundaries.
27. For the role of journeys in cinema, their significance and their components, see Naficy (2001).
28. See, for instance, Antonioni's *Red Desert* (1964), or Bergman's *Wild Strawberries* (1957).
29. In one part of the house, Jews live; in another, Arabs.
30. The technical reason for this occurrence is that, this way, cars traveling in the opposite direction do not block the sea view. Yet, beyond the technical reason, this indicates the director's complicated relationship with the landscape. Al-Hassan herself clarifies this (in a private interview, Ramallah, 2003):

> My relationship with Haifa is problematic. Perhaps because the presence of the Other is very tangible there. I had not noticed that the drive was in the opposite direction, but generally, my feelings about the Palestinian place are ambivalent, because it does not resemble the Palestine in my memory. That is why my frames are narrow and my camera static.

31. For the function of mapping, see Rogoff (2000). Also, see Zanger (forthcoming) on the gap between geography and cartography.
32. As a part of a disintegrating world, well perceived in all the films. See, for instance, *Debris* (2001), *The New Apartment* (2002), *Waiting for Salah A-Ddin*, and *Zero* (2002).
33. As substitutes, fetishes, or synecdoches, as Naficy defines it (2001: 27). On the use of the icons of homeland, see Bresheeth (2002a, 2002b).
34. See Nizar Hassan's film, *Invasion*.
35. See Liana Badr's *Siege, a Writer's Diary* (2003).
36. See Liana Badr's *Fadwa*. See also the above discussion of other symbols in this film.
37. See Nizar Hassan's *Invasion*.
38. See Liana Badr's films, *Zaytounat* and *Fadwa*, Tawfik Abu Wa'el's *Waiting for Salah a-Ddin*, and Subhi a-Zubeidi's *Crossing Kalandia (Roadblock)*.
39. Also, see Yasser Abed Rabbu's visit to his Jaffa home in *1948* (1998); the granddaughter's visit to her grandmother's house in Azza al-Hassan's *Place*, or *Outside of Paradise* (2000); the old woman's visit to her Dir Yasin house in *Bleeding Memories*; Liana Badr's films, *Fadwa* and *Zaytounant*; and Azza al-Hassan's *Three Centimeters Less*, where the daughter takes the door of her father's house as a memento, and so on.
40. The cinematic technique for turning the olive tree into a symbol is by stopping the moving image, repeating that same image, slowing the speed down in a floating or jumpy style, or taking it out of context. All of these grant the olive tree "an abstract state, allowing it to become a fetish" that restores the lost wholeness. See Naficy (1993: 100); on this theme his discussion is particularly interesting, pointing to the way in which cinematic movement in time breaks the static fixation of the image.
41. See Masharawi's films, *Haifa* and *Ticket to Jerusalem*, a-Zubeidi's *Crossing Kalandia (Roadblock)*, Elia Suleiman's *Chronicle of a Disappearance* and so on.
42. In Liana Badr's *Fadwa* and *The Green Bird*, and in Subhi a-Zubeidi's *Crossing Kalandia (Roadblock)*, for instance.
43. On the possibility of creating a "dense," information-packed image, as opposed to a single image symbolizing the entire collective, see Elsaesser (1997).
44. For example in Rashid Masharawi's *Ticket to Jerusalem*.
45. Representation, as such, has become impossible in a place where details strive to represent the absent, lost object that cannot be represented, rather than what is

currently present yet seems unworthy of representation. For the traumatic background to this paradox, see Elsaesser (1997; 2001; 2004).

46. These joined a collection of images which represent history today through the media, while concealing it, in fact, behind the picture – the shots of the attack on the Twin Towers, photographs of swollen-bellied African children, snapshots of tortured Iraqis. As Elsaesser argues, in these cases and others, the single image has obtained power, strength, and a halo that were once bestowed on art alone.

47. See footnote 21.

7. BETWEEN EXILE AND HOMELAND: THE FILMS OF ELIA SULEIMAN

A comparison of Suleiman's two feature films, *Chronicle of a Disappearance* (1996) and *Divine Intervention* (2002), lends itself to a comprehensive review of what had transpired in Palestinian society in general and in its cinema in particular during the period between the signing of the Oslo peace accords and the Second *Intifada*, from "the calm before the storm," as Suleiman calls it, to "total devastation and disintegration" (Erickson, 2003). The two films revolve around similar episodes. In both, some of the scenes take place in the home of Suleiman's parents in Nazareth and others in Jerusalem; in both the director adopts a comical stance toward the ordinary day-to-day friction between the Arabs of Nazareth and toward the Jewish-Israeli violence in Jerusalem; and both culminate in a fantasy of revenge against the Israelis.

The differences between ostensibly similar films highlight the historical, ideological, and cinematic developments that took place in the short time that elapsed between the making of the first film and the production of the second. In the earlier film, we encounter diverse locations: the house of Suleiman's parents in Nazareth, the director's home in Jerusalem, and the width and breadth of the various vistas unfolding in the course of his journeys across the country. Although these spaces are crowded and threatened, it seems possible to remain in them and to conduct one's daily life, albeit one charged with violence. The second film, however, realizes what in the first film was only suggested indirectly. Here, there are no open spaces, and the house in Nazareth is reduced to the kitchen. Its living room is displayed only once, while its contents are impounded by the income tax authorities. Rather than Jerusalem, the film features the nearby A-Ram roadblock separating Jerusalem and Ramallah, and daily life has turned into a stagnant routine encumbered by hate, anger, and arguments. The contrast between the spaces in the different films is denoted by discrepancies between the structure of the plots and the images. In the first film, as in all his other work, Suleiman examines images that relate to reality; he deconstructs them, sets them up as parodies, and reconstructs them as complex poetical intersections fraught with multiple meanings.[1] In these junctions, the Palestinian story appears as one among many, as a narrative that cannot be told yet is recounted nevertheless. This story both exists and does not exist in the minutiae of everyday life, independent of images, symbols, and clichés, and yet beyond it lies, veiled yet apparent, a broader meaning – the Palestinian meaning. In the second of these films, *Divine Intervention*, as in many other Palestinian movies of the period, the episodes and the plot, as well as the details of the landscape and of daily life, delineate first and foremost the Palestinian situation; thus they lose their independent existence and become instead the symbolic representation of the Palestinian condition. That condition, which dominates all the layers of the film, creates a coherent plot – more linear than its earlier manifestations – of conquest and struggle, and Suleiman mobilizes the details of daily life to do this.

> I don't want to tell the story of Palestine [he explains in an interview with Anne Bourlond]. My right as a Palestinian lost its meaning as a point of departure for my work, at least politically speaking. Of course I am aware of people's need to share a common language, way of life, safety and democracy. But I will always doubt this collective institution called nation. The concept root is meaningless for me. In my case, land is not the element creating passion. (Bourlond, [1999] 2000: 96–7)

In the same interview, Suleiman defines the rift between cinema and nationalism: "Cinema is not meant to reinforce the national image or its opposite: the negative image of the other" (99). He also clarifies his outlook on the cinema he wishes to create: "I want to open the way to multiple spaces that lend themselves to different readings . . . I am trying to create an image that transcends the ideological definition of what it means to be a Palestinian, an image far from any stereotype" (98). That is to say, he is attempting to create a "democratization of the image" (Erikson, 2003).

The film *Divine Intervention* testifies to the difficulty of creating this kind of multiplicity of spaces during a time of national threat. As Suleiman explains:

> I didn't really change . . . When I filmed *Arab Dream* (*Al-Holmo-l-'Arabi*, 1998), I seriously felt how fascism was growing and strengthening in Israel. Since that time, because this fascism has filled up the whole space

and has penetrated into the soul, the space for the poetic has diminished (Joyard, 2002).

In spite of this, *Divine Intervention* also testifies to the possibility of overcoming this diminishment of "poetic space" and for creating – through parody, fantasy, and humor – a rich range of meanings, a "third space" that exists between languages, identities, nationalities, and cultures.[2] This "third space" can be found in all of Suleiman's films, even those aspiring toward a single national significance.

THE HOME – THE PRIVATE SPACE

The New Palestinian Cinema characteristically delineates a fragmented and blocked geography in which the home is cut off from the land and both are diminished and divided by borders and barricades. Therefore, there is an inherent difficulty in the endeavor of this cinema to form a whole imaginary map. It attempts to capture limited places, to elevate the camera in order to encompass open expanses, or to highlight a specific detail and turn it into a symbol of wholeness. Suleiman reflects, with particular strength and accomplishment, the obstacles that Palestinian cinema faces: the process of reduction as well as some possible ways to overcome it.[3] This process is what differentiates his two full-length films from one another; while in the first there are still homes and spaces, by the second these elements have disappeared.

In *Chronicle of a Disappearance*, the private home, that of the director's parents in Nazareth, is not an integral part of the public space, as it is in Khleifi's films, and does not represent the public space, as it does in the late Palestinian cinema. Yet the public domain lies beyond it, as another layer, a palimpsest. The film follows the minute details of what is going on inside the home, the life of a middle-class Christian family that could be taking place anywhere in the world. Yet the director, in an interview with Jason Wood, connects it with the Palestinian condition:

> Nazareth is a ghetto and my humor emanates from dealing with a population living in a claustrophobic state of stasis, an impotent inability to change the face of their reality. Unable to dislocate or shake free of the dominant power ruling them, they eventually unleash their frustrations against each other. (Wood, 2003)

This statement somewhat simplifies what actually occurs in the film, which depicts a small society occupied with its own affairs, with its inner life, and with various conflicts – between neighboring cities,[4] different families,[5] and within the individual family itself.[6] The recurring scene of two people getting out of a car, striking each other, and then returning to the car to continue their journey satirically reflects these inner conflicts.

And yet, in the end, all sides are reconciled and life calmly resumes without frustration or violence. If anything is demonstrated in this film about the Palestinian experience, about life in the ghetto, it is done inadvertently, coincidentally, and indistinctly, and as part of a spectrum of many diverse meanings.

The first part of the film, which takes place in Nazareth, focuses on the director's family and friends and appears unrelated to the national political plot, occurring in Jerusalem. Ostensibly, it seems that the bridge constructed by Khleifi between the home and the homeland has been cracked and that this rupture divides the film's space in two. Yet although Suleiman's family home in Nazareth does not necessarily represent the public space, it is linked to it, if only as one more image concealing a deeper reality. This becomes particularly apparent at the end of the film, when the opening scene showing the director's parents dozing in front of the television set is repeated. This time the Israeli flag flutters on the television screen, accompanied by the national anthem *Hatikva*, which marks the end of each day's public television broadcast. It is accompanied by the caption: "My family, my only homeland" (*'A'ilati, watani al waheed*). The homeland, represented in so many Palestinian films by the home, does not exist here. It is embodied in the image of the dozing parents,[7] who represent only themselves, as the captions indicate. Neither is the homeland present in the image of the Israeli flag which invalidates it. And yet this absence constitutes the strongest presence in the scene, the presence of what is missing.[8] It could be argued that, compared to films which dissolve the individual into the collective, or to Khleifi's work, which fuses both domains into a unity only to be deconstructed and reconstructed as disparities, Suleiman's cinema focuses from the outset on the domestic domain alone. The homeland seems absent from the film. However, here, absence itself bears meaning. The absent homeland is what the director seeks but does not find within the home and the family.[9]

The film's second episode, "Political Diary," takes place in Jerusalem. "If the Israelis, and the Israeli army, are missing from the Palestinian city of Nazareth, Jerusalem is a space reverberating with the occupation and its iniquities" (Bresheeth, 2002b). In this part, the national significance of the home, veiled in the first half of the film, becomes clearer. Jerusalem, as Bresheeth (2002b) claims, "expresses a world of difference. It is the locus of Israeli-Palestinian conflict." Suleiman's home in Jerusalem is a cramped and dark apartment, repeatedly obscured as a claustrophobic prison through whose barred windows the director gazes at the outside world. In this respect, it is perhaps no different from his home in Nazareth, but here the claustrophobic experience is associated with the occupation. This connection becomes obvious when we see the Israeli police break into the apartment in a way that is reminiscent of the many break-ins that did actually happen and of their depiction in numerous

Palestinian films.[10] Here, as in the films of Ali Nassar and Rashid Masharawi, the trauma of the occupation and the trauma of the loss of one's private home, as well as of the national homeland, are brought to the fore.[11] This trauma casts a different light upon the film's first episode, which initially appears untouched by trauma. In retrospect, we detect the undercurrent flowing beneath the image of a comparatively peaceful Nazarene reality. The second part of the film, therefore, elucidates why the homeland appears as a missing presence in the first part.

The home of Suleiman's parents in Nazareth, where family life takes place in *Chronicle of a Disappearance*, also appears in *Divine Intervention*. In the latter film, however, there is neither family life nor any other kind of life. The camera is set up in the kitchen and captures the father, over and over again in recurring episodes, as he sits at the table with a cup of coffee, a plate, and a hard-boiled egg in an egg-cup before him and sorts through a pile of letters, with the annoyingly monotonous sound of birds chirping outside. The static monotony that was present in *Chronicle of a Disappearance* dominates the scenes here and all that goes on in them. The house is narrowed, reduced now only to the kitchen; the mother is gone, friends do not come. Toward the end of the episode focusing on Nazareth, the house is appropriated by the income tax officials, who arrive on the scene, take an inventory of all the furniture, and seize it. This episode ends with the father's collapse, hospitalization, and subsequent death. Thus, while the first film ends with the caption: "My family – my only homeland," at the end of the second film there is no home and no family and the caption is: "In memory of my father." What is described by the director as the Israeli occupation that has turned the city into a ghetto, is responsible for annihilating the home within the private sphere, and, as in many other films, its erasure leaves a void that is filled by contents with a national significance.

THE OUTSIDE – THE NATIONAL SPACE

In *Chronicle of a Disappearance*, the external space, like the interior of the house, has a double existence both as connected to and separate from the national domain. The outside is usually hidden from the director. Sitting in the house, his view is obstructed by the laundry hanging out to dry, by the head of the observer, or by a closed window. It is divided, disjointed, apprehended only bit by bit – a minaret, a tree, a plot of land – and then cut up even further by the editing. That outside is in many cases dark, filmed through the grille of the window, from a boat rocking on the waves, through flickering light that challenges the existential certainty as to what is seen, reminiscent of *film noir*.

Nevertheless, in three different scenes the director abandons his limited point of view, from which the landscape seems fragmented and dim, and shoots the scenery in its entirety. He does so while traveling, in long takes without cuts, and accompanied by a singing voice. These are the director's private journeys, touring his homeland.

Yet, like many journeys in Palestinian cinema, they also draw a blurred image of the map of the land in its length and breadth, thus conveying the organic connection with the landscape and control over it.

One journey takes place in the northern part of the country and ends in a monastery on the Mount of Beatitudes (also called "Mount Happiness"), overlooking the Sea of Galilee. Another takes place in the eastern side of Jerusalem, approaching the city from the direction of the Mount of Olives, and concluding in front of the Old City wall and the Al-Aqsa mosque. The third journey is in the south, in the desert, and ends in Jericho. If we add to these Suleiman's stroll along the promenade at the Tel Aviv seashore, and the fishing expedition to the coast at Acre that his father and friends undertake, we can chart a map of the land from north to south, and from east to west. The Arab songs of which the soundtrack to parts of these journeys is composed charge the filmed spaces with national meaning, turning them into "Arabic-speaking" spaces. Nevertheless, the map drawn by these journeys is the map of an absent land, owned by others.[12]

In the film's second episode, which takes place in Jerusalem, the national significance of space is also strengthened. During both episodes the fictitious director – the film's protagonist – constitutes an absent presence. He does not utter a word, move or act; he only looks and does not always see because the sights in front of him are usually blocked. In the second part of the film, this absent presence is embodied by the Palestinian Arab, from whom the Israelis took his home, his space, his voice, his identity. As suggested by Haim Bresheeth (2002b), the disappearance of the director becomes a symbol of the disappearance of the Palestinian: "Through the speechless Suleiman, his father, cousin, and friends, a certain feature of Palestinian reality, a reality of being throttled, of being silenced, is being spoken here by passages of expressive silence."

Thus, the elements that had seemed in the first part of the film unrelated to the conflict are linked to it in the second part; the loss of voice, the loss of identity, the loss of home and land, and the disappearance of the director are revealed in Jerusalem to have been the result of Israeli action.

The film's second half begins at a clubhouse, where Suleiman is to give a lecture about "peace" as the theme of his latest film. However, he is unable to do so as the sound system does not work. Instead of his voice, which we cannot hear, the hall is filled with the clutter of conversations, babies crying, and the ringing of cellular phones. The scene, which is a satirical portrayal of cultural life in Nazareth, is reminiscent of a similar scene from Suleiman's earlier film, *Homage by Assassination* (1991), in which the host of a radio program tries to interview Suleiman about a film (the same one we are watching) and is unsuccessful because of a faulty phone line. The silence, the absence of a voice, the impossibility of telling any story let alone that of the film he is making, then, are repeated in Suleiman's films in different contexts – and in all instances there remains a doubt as to whether the speaker is, indeed, mute or perhaps it is his audience who are deaf (as suggested by the translation of an Arab song into sign language, in the film *Arab Dream*). In the second part of *Chronicle of a Disappearance*, muteness and disappearance are set in the context of the Israeli-Palestinian conflict. When asked about the meaning of the scene described above, Suleiman says: "I felt that 'talking about peace' is simply a title. Real peace does not exist" (Kaufman, 2003). However, silence in the present case becomes part of the broader Palestinian story. As mentioned above, in the first scene the director loses his voice. In another scene he loses his home and his identity when police officers burst into his apartment and conduct a search, all the while totally ignoring his presence as if he were just one more object among the other objects in the house. At the next stage, Eden, Suleiman's girlfriend, rebels. She uses a two-way army radio that the Israeli police have left behind in order to voice absurd commands, first sending the Israeli army scurrying back and forth all over Jerusalem and the surrounding area and then ordering them to evacuate the city. The voice that betrayed her in the earlier scene and thwarted her chances of obtaining a place to live, wins the entire space for her. Everything that was taken away from the director – his voice, his identity, his space – is restored by his girlfriend; through her voice she controls the Israeli army and sends them all over the place, thus replacing the director's passivity with (fantastic) actions and exploits. The filming supports this; the camera captures her from a low angle, as she orchestrates the chaos of military vehicles zipping aimlessly beneath her.[13] One can thus summarize and say, in the words of Elsaesser (1997), that the abstract malaise, in the first half, finds its "concrete wound" in the second half: the wound of the Israeli occupation.

Just as in the first part of the film the homeland is both present and absent, so too its past is simultaneously apparent and concealed. The obstructed spaces or open expanses are not steeped in the Palestinian past, as they were in Michel Khleifi's cinema. Neither does Suleiman attempt to excavate and seek historical relics, as some of the new films have done. In an interview with Prokhoris and Wavelet (1999), Suleiman explains: "For me, there is no homeland. The only homeland is memory and memory is first and foremost in the body." Yet, once again, what is missing from the film permeates it by virtue of its absence: personal memory, the parents' home, the music of the 1950s, longing for the Sea of Galilee prior to the founding of the State of Israel (in the monk's monologue), or even the move from Nazareth to Jerusalem which is, according to the director (ibid.), the transition from the Palestine of 1948 to the Palestine of 1967; all these revive in the film that which is not depicted, that which is inaccessible and out of reach, a clouded memory of something that is vanishing into oblivion. This memory drives the second half of the film and affects its every detail. The homeland, its past and its vistas, which are conceived as present though absent in the first half of the film, are transformed in the second half into a sort of a cover story for the "present absentees" of the past – the refugees who did not voluntarily leave the land in 1948, who were in fact exiled from their villages against their will because they were not at home on the first day of the war.[14]

While in *Chronicle of a Disappearance* landscapes still existed and one could travel through them from one place to another, in the later films, such as *Arab Dream* or *Cyber Palestine* (2000), as in a considerable number of other Palestinian films of this period, this landscape gradually disappears and trips across the country no longer reveal it. In *Cyber Palestine*, the journeys completely lack direction. The route from the refugee camp in Gaza to Bethlehem goes around in circles and keeps returning to the refugee camp until it reaches the Israeli Erez roadblock at the northern end of the Gaza Strip. In *Arab Dream*, bushes form hedgerows that block the landscape, and darkness or rapid movements of the camera prevent it from being seen. In *Divine Intervention*, even those subdued landscapes have vanished. The first part of the film is reduced to the narrow and enclosed streets of Nazareth, shown as a place choked by courtyards crowding each other, occupied parking spots, neighbors who violently infringe on each other's territory. The second part of the film is reduced to the border – the roadblock. Seemingly, from the gloomy and static atmosphere of the hospital where the father is treated, the film shifts sharply to the dynamic movements of a vehicle driven by the son. However, this dynamic is imaginary, and it is immediately cut off by the roadblock. In a similar manner, *Arab Dream* cuts abruptly from a map of the entire world on the computer screen to a map of Israel, and Jerusalem and on to a search for the Palestine website, which does not appear on the Web, or from the film's theme song, which recounts the dream of a united Arab world, to a blocked house with a sign posted in front of it that reads "Forbidden Zone." These transitions, in fact, tell the story of the vast, universal or national pan-Arabic space that has shrunk and is now severed by a border that tears down and encloses private and public places alike, that intrudes on the home and tears apart the Palestinian identity that can no longer define itself by movement, space, or the gaze, and is defined only by the border that bisects it. This process of the reduction of space is manifested not only in the film itself, but also in the difference between it and the earlier *Chronicle of a Disappearance*, in which home and space were still evident.

As mentioned before, in order to accomplish what is impossible in reality, and to break down the stifling blocked borders, Palestinian cinema turned to the dream and to film, to love and to fantasy. All those were meant to reunite the fractured space and to rejoin the divided identity. Such integration also occurs in Suleiman's second film, *Divine Intervention*.

Suleiman, the protagonist (referred to as E. S.),[15] meets his lover at the border between Ramallah and Jerusalem, from where they observe the Israeli road-block at A-Ram and all that transpires there. The bond between the two is a physical one – they silently hold hands. Thus the film demonstrates the possibility of breaking through the roadblock and transforming it from a place which fragments the Palestinian identity into a place of connection and love.[16] Suleiman – the director – attempts to overcome this border, not through love alone but also by way of the camerawork. The static camera that was dominant in the first part of the film is now replaced with a more "dynamic" one that charts the breadth, the depth, and the height of the place (via tracking and crane shots). The love between the two protagonists not only allows the merging of the split Palestinian identity into a single whole, including the man and the woman, it also leads the Palestinian to action. The woman gives material form to the fantasies and desires of the passive man as she passes through the roadblock, paralyzing the soldiers and causing the watchtower to collapse behind her, or as she wipes out a unit of Israeli marksmen in scenes taken directly from the Ninja warrior films and from the virtual world of *The Matrix*.[17]

In *Chronicle of a Disappearance*, too, it is the woman who, by controlling space through the use of a two-way radio, personifies male yearnings. In the present film, where there is no space to control, she crosses the border and "destroys the enemy." In the former film, an absurd and humorous scene was used instead of physical violence, and was open to many interpretations; in the latter film physical violence is portrayed vividly and realistically, and it most clearly relates to the Palestinian resistance, although only as a fantasy.

After directing his first film, Suleiman was asked why he ignored the violence that pervades the reality around him and he answered:

> First of all, I think that all presentation of violence promotes violence, and secondly, how does one measure a man's suffering, how can we take responsibility for defining sorrow or suffering? Let's say that I show a Palestinian being beaten; when I put this on the screen I limit his pain. (Kapra, 1998)

Following his second film, Suleiman was asked the opposite question: why he expressed the violence. To this he answered:

> Instead of criticizing these individual separate scenes,[18] perhaps it would have been more useful to think of me as a test case. The film is meant to raise questions – how is it that an artist like myself, who doesn't even live here, who neither he nor his family have ever been harmed by Israeli forces, creates such violent scenes? (Pinto, 2003)

He also explains: "This film can be considered an example of how a violent environment affects the consciousness of a person like me" (Kelly, 2002).

Palestinian viewers living in the Occupied Territories who saw *Chronicle of a Disappearance* reacted angrily to the scene showing Suleiman sitting passively with his cousin at the entrance of the Holyland store, and wondered why these people did not take up arms (Bourlond, [1999] 2000). In *Divine Intervention* their demand/query was answered.

The difference between the two films, *Chronicle of a Disappearance* and *Divine Intervention*, is most apparent in their use of well-known and sometimes well-worn Palestinian symbols. If in *Chronicle of a Disappearance* Suleiman endeavors to free himself of these symbols through a loving insistence on depicting the smallest of details of the actual reality in Nazareth and Jerusalem, in *Divine Intervention* space disappears and time shrinks, leaving the hero with no real existence. This may explain why in the latter film, as in so many other Palestinian films made during this period, the image again dominates the reality and the specific detail that has ceased to be part of what "is there" is transformed into a symbol of what is absent.

Divine Intervention employs virtually the entire inventory of symbols used by Palestinian culture in general and Palestinian cinema[19] in particular: the black-and-white checkered *kaffiyeh*, the rifle, Kalashnikov and hand grenade, the Muslim symbol of star and crescent, the map of Palestine, a stuck car, a blocked road, the Dome of the Rock in Jerusalem, pictures of Arafat, kites and birds in the sky – almost all of the many symbols that typify recent Palestinian cinema and literature appear in this film. However, although Suleiman exposes, here as in other films, the fictitious status of these symbols through the use of parody, absurdity, and humor, he also searches for the truth behind them and renews their lost significance. The balloon that Suleiman sends up to soar over the roadblock and over Jerusalem, sporting Arafat's wrinkled face grinning widely, is an example of the symbols' double status in these films. Arafat's portrait is indeed perceived here as a caricature, yet it floats above the roadblock, leaving the soldiers there stunned and helpless, and then crosses the border, hovers over the Jerusalem skyline, over churches and synagogues, and finally lands on the Al-Aqsa mosque. The music that accompanies this flight merges Eastern and Western motifs, thus introducing a dream-like atmosphere of beauty and a dimension of cultural openness. All that is signified in Palestinian cinema by kites, flags, high-flying birds, is symbolized by this flight upward and away, crossing borders, thus liberating the imagination, hope, and the dream. In its flight, it captures the city of Jerusalem and the mosque, which as mentioned already, today symbolizes Palestinian unity – its present, its past, and its future – more than any other image. The highly political and almost didactic episode of the balloon can thus be read in different ways, any one of which can both cancel out the others and, conversely, strengthen them. Through this, the symbol of Arafat is ridiculed and rejuvenated simultaneously.

While the floating balloon portrays the Palestinian dream, then the "Ninja" scene signifies the Palestinian struggle, with all the prerequisite symbols: the woman's face hidden by a *kaffiyeh*, the gun in her hand, hand grenades, a map of Palestine serving as her shield, the star and crescent projected like a spear, stones flying from her slingshot, and a halo of bullets surrounding her head which introduces a religious element. This scene was universally understood as a symbol of the Palestinian resistance and won the appreciation of the Arab critics and audience, who had disapproved of the director's first film. When this was shown at the Carthage Festival in 1997, loud objections were inside and outside the theater, some calling Suleiman a traitor and collaborator.[20] "The land is burning," wrote Samir Farid (no date), "but according to Suleiman it looks like Switzerland in the middle of World War II." The scene in which the heroine makes fools of the Israeli soldiers, ordering them to leave Jerusalem, was perceived by Farid as an unconvincing joke that did not portray any kind of Palestinian struggle. In contrast, the balloon and "Ninja" scenes evoked excitement and pride. One of the journalists at the press conference in Ramallah, in 2002, said of them: "[They] rescued me from despair and led me to optimism and pride; they reminded me of the heroic resistance that I witnessed yesterday in the street."

Indeed, the "Ninja" scene, like the balloon episode, is more political than its parallel in *Chronicle of a Disappearance*. Yet, it too projects two opposing messages both summarizing the symbols of the struggle, hope, and, Palestinian resistance and ridiculing them by presenting them as if they are taken from a computer program and video games rather than from the real world.

This oscillation between a "straight" representation of the Palestinian narrative and a parody of it is the new language through which Suleiman revives the discourse of contemporary Palestinian cinema.

The Postmodern Language

Suleiman's unique cinematic language, which always juxtaposes two versions of reality – one present and the other absent, each concealing yet exposing the other[21] – is revealed as *Chronicle of a Disappearance*'s second language. On the one hand, the plot of the film and its sequences are cut into separate episodes, the frame is divided into its components, and the harmony between sound and picture, between picture and context, and between the event and its pace are severed. On the other hand, all these fragmentations that also shatter human identity are integrated at the end through the gaze of the director, who is aware of the impossibility of healing them.

The film opens, for example, with an extreme close-up of a shape, so blurred that it is difficult to identify. Only when the camera moves away does it become clear that this is a face, more particularly the nose of a sleeping man who is, as is revealed later, the director's father. The director's parents are filmed in a similar manner throughout the film; body parts are seen through doors, reflected in mirrors, or displayed as "real" pictures. The off-screen soundtrack is sometimes disconnected from the picture and suggests action that will never be seen. The music and choreography are related to one context, while the action is taking place in another; for example, the car check in a garage takes place to the rhythm and sound of dance music. The dissonance between these three components – music, movement, and event[22] – creates a surrealistic comic atmosphere that clashes with the hyper-realistic style of other scenes in the film. In addition, the object of the gaze, disconnected from the watching eye,[23] is revealed to the viewers as a chaotic conglomeration of details, frames, doors, windows, furniture, which are filmed in deep focus with a wide-angle lens, lacking a unifying focal point. The split space – Suleiman's parents' home, the coffee house where he is sitting, his girlfriend, Eden's, apartment, and so on – is also divided between different virtual levels: between the cinematic reality, the television screen, and the computer monitor. In many cases the materiality of the human figure itself is cast in doubt within the deconstructed spaces. It is unclear whether a figure in the director's girlfriend's apartment is a living human being or a sculpture of a human being, whether the Syrian choir that is singing a love song to Palestine[24] exists in the reality of the film or is merely seen on a television screen within the film, if the director is looking out of a window or is illuminated by the computer screen. As Bresheeth (2002b) puts it: Reality is seen here not as the order of things, but the device undermining reason and logic." The characters are blurred in long shots or are seen with their backs to the camera, as in the film of Godard films and, later, Jim Jarmusch, and as painted by Magritte – artists who deconstruct the illusion of a coherent reality with the human being at its center. From these angles, *Chronicle of a Disappearance* could be defined according to the criteria of postmodernism, as outlined by Jameson (1991), Hutcheon (1988), Ophir (2002), and others. Indeed, all of Suleiman's early films could be defined as such. *Cyber Palestine* opens with a man sitting in front of a computer screen. The light from the monitor illuminates his face while opposite him, on the monitor, appears an Internet site called "Palestine." The man presses the Search key and then the Home key. The camera focuses on a tourist poster hanging on the wall that says: "Visit Palestine."

This is an example of Elia Suleiman's virtual world, the world of simulacrum. The man sitting in front of the computer is Joseph, and the pregnant woman standing at his side is his wife, Mary. In the background are the sounds of Bach's Art of the Fugue. The sounds of the pipe organ change into electronic sounds, and Bach's music becomes the tune of a cellular phone ringing. On the phone's monitor the sender's name, Gabriel, appears, along with the message: "Joseph, take your wife to Bethlehem. There she will give birth to her son." The father and the mother stand by the window. A great light shines on them and the electronic Bach switches back to the powerful sound of the pipe organ. But Mary and Joseph cannot get to Bethlehem because they are stuck at the Erez roadblock, the Israeli checkpoint at the border of the Gaza Strip.

In all of Elia Suleiman's early films, the words, even the most charged ones, do not represent their plain meaning. Behind Suleiman's signifiers, we find unpredictable objects and concepts. In *Cyber Palestine* and in *Arab Dream*, the name Palestine is a website, and in *Homage by Assassination* the computer "Home" and "Return" keys are meant to represent the place and the right of return. In both films the computer's monitor (the frame) is used as a "writing tablet."[25] It is loaded with texts from different sources that clash with and contradict one another, in both their original tongues and in the translations. In *Introduction to the End of an Argument* (1990), bygone landscapes of an Arab town, perhaps from the 1920s, which are captured by the camera, turn out to be an advertisement for Kodak. In *Cyber Palestine*, footage of the peace accords and entertainment programs are interspersed with images of Palestinian fighters and a refugee camp.

Introduction to an End of an Argument attacks the images of the East in Western civilization, but like other films, it exposes not only the East but rather the whole world as a simulacrum.[26] As a reality whose only existence is a televised,[27] cybernetic, or cinematic one, this is a world of texts without referents. It is a world that "can no longer set out to represent the historical past; it can only 'represent' our ideas and stereotypes about that past" (Jameson, 1991) – disconnected fragments, with no unifying focal point.[28]

In *Homage by Assassination*, a young woman stands in an empty street next to a car, waiting. The director-protagonist (E. S.) observes her from afar. A car approaches. A young man emerges from the car. They speak, maybe argue, the young man returns to the car, starts it up, and drives away. The young woman is still standing. She smokes a cigarette. Maybe she is excited, maybe not. It is impossible to know. Neither the viewers nor the director know the whole story: who the protagonists are, what has happened to them up to this moment, and what will happen to them in the next moment. That is how *Homage by Assassination* and most of Suleiman's other films are structured. In a world where there is no connection between image and reality, there is also a gap between events and their contexts and between the events themselves. For instance, while in New York, the director hears the wailing of an alarm emanating from a car parked on his street; the alarm is transformed into an air raid siren and the caption reads, "At this moment my mother in Nazareth is putting on her gas mask."

In this fragmented world, it appears that Palestine itself has turned into an additional representation, one among many, and as such its story perhaps cannot really be told. Hence, the journeys embarked upon by Suleiman in the first part of *Chronicle of a Disappearance* not only connect the traveler to the landscape or trace its map, but also cast doubt on these landscapes when they end in tourist sites: the bustling tourism at the Sea of Galilee, the camel on which tourists take a very brief ride in Jerusalem, and a brand-new but empty hotel in Jericho, built for the hordes of tourists expected to arrive in the wake of the Peace Accords. The director leaves his home for the landscape and instead he finds an illusion – a constant static picture postcard – something to look at and enjoy from afar but not a tangible place in which to live. In another version, the land is presented through endless meetings between the director and his cousin at the entrance to the "Holyland." Although this place is a real souvenir shop in Nazareth, where Suleiman used to sit for hours and hours during his visits home, it is still connected to the fictitious homeland; its name has replaced the actual Holy Land that it represented, and the picture postcards on a revolving stand have replaced the real landscape.

Although space is deconstructed in this film, the subject is fragmented and reality is divided, the director's view of this reality is not a postmodern perspective split between infinite possibilities and angles, lacking clear focus. It is, rather, the view of the exile, the placeless émigré who longs for a clear yet unattainable foothold. Thus, it is true that the camera is always at a distance, in some inconvenient observation point from where one cannot see all the details in full, and from where the picture seems fractured and incomplete. However, this kind of view[29] is not only alienated and distant; it is also the view of one who clings to all of the details – the sensuous, the concrete, the minute – of the reality he is describing. This is the view of one who can no longer enter his filmed image and therefore remains outside of it as a voyeur. However, the image is dear to him, and so he continues to observe it, attentively, taking in all the details long after the event is over.[30]

The director's double vision in *Chronicle of a Disappearance* reflects the duality characteristic of the entire film. Everything that fragmented and deconstructed the picture and cast doubt on the filmed reality, on the observing eye, and on the possibility of reassembling the puzzle of the old home as a total existence in time and space, is also an attempt to do the opposite. It is an endeavor to examine the pieces of the puzzle and to let the eye rest on the tiniest and most casual and incidental details that appear in the cinematic frame or in the story itself: women's conversation in the house, the preparation of fish, the father who goes off with his friends to fish, feeding his pet bird, playing with his two hound dogs or playing backgammon on the computer, the man who hangs a note on a pole, and another man who passes by and looks at it. These marginal details of ordinary living that have no place in the heroic national narrative are included in this film not because they "mean" something, but simply because "they were there." This is also true of the details of the picture: parts of a bed, sections of a balcony, and women in the kitchen seen from the back. The director tries to reconstruct all that he has lost, to no avail. Everything remains fragmented, broken. As a result, everything about the filmed images that alienates the viewers is simultaneously meant to compel them to participate actively in their construction.[31]

In that endeavor, too, the private yet universal experience of loss, embedded in human existence itself,[32] represents the Palestinian story in a new way: through the struggle to preserve all that is threatened and is in danger of disappearing. The details of reality and daily life do not represent anything other than themselves alone. And yet it is precisely in this disconnected way that the particulars are tied to the passive Palestinian struggle of *sumud*,[33] clasping on to the land or, in Shehada's words: "to bow one's head until the storm has passed," "to remain human despite existing conditions" (Shehada, 1982; Bresheeth, 2002a). In this way they undermine the narratives that have erased Palestinian reality and have hidden it beyond its various representations.

In the first part of *Chronicle of a Disappearance*, the weaving together of unrelated contexts creates a surrealistic, absurd world with neither hierarchy nor meaning. In the second part, this cinematic technique transforms the Israelis into ridiculous puppets; they are the ones who violated order and hierarchy, and they are punished for this through humor. For example, they get out of the car to urinate and do so in rhythmic steps, or they burst into the director's apartment in a comical Chaplinesque choreography, to the music of a tango. They also find the director's girlfriend, Eden, and drive her out of her apartment to the rhythm, music, and words of Leonard Cohen's song, "First We Take Manhattan, Then We Take Berlin," but fail to notice when she suddenly disappears and is replaced by a doll. What could well have been perceived as a pastiche in the film's first part, as an imitation without an original, according to Jameson (1991), is directed here toward a clearly identified source, which it ridicules and mocks. Life as an absurdity, within the twentieth-century context of trauma, is revealed here as a picture obscuring a different trauma behind it, the trauma of occupation.

Similarly, the fiction that has disguised reality is part of the estrangement and alienation of the exilic cinema in particular and contemporary film in general. In this respect, too, a general phenomenon whose national significance only reverberated indirectly beyond it, in the second part of the film, takes on a clear and overt national meaning. In this case, the objectification of the landscape, its transformation into a touristic commodity, into an empty representation, is explained by suggesting that the Israelis have turned it into a tourist site and the real land into the Promised Land or, as the film's captions indicate, the Missed Land.

Hamid Naficy asks whether a postmodern play of meanings is possible in films that "place the homeland as a stable referent" and his answer is no. He describes what he calls "accented cinema,"[34] filmmaking of exile, as cinema that at its core is not postmodern despite the fact that it employs postmodern poetics. It is a cinema that seeks for the origin beyond the imitations and attempts to reveal the truth behind the images and the manipulations of language (Naficy, 2001).

Naficy's definition partially applies to Suleiman's early films. In these films, neither the homeland nor its history provides a stable referent. In this respect, the films are essentially postmodern. The attempt to tell a tale of struggle and solidarity and to construct unity instead of disintegration, creating a sense "of home, of a people, of tradition" (Said, 1990: 359) rather than exile and alienation, is represented in them as fiction alone. And yet, the absent referent is overpoweringly present, thus affiliating them with modern poetics, with its endeavors to "create matter and meaning where there is perhaps no content" (Alter, 1975: 142). Unity, therefore, has not disappeared in Suleiman's first films, and neither has the homeland or the Palestinian story. Nevertheless they are now contained within the search itself or in the fantasy that creates them. As a director in exile, who is both inside and outside his country, Suleiman manifests an ambivalent stance, oscillating between the modern and the postmodern.[35] Possibly, this perspective is what enables Suleiman's films to overcome the worn-out version of the Palestinian story, to estrange it and so, as other directors did – both precursors and contempories – to renew it.

The Palestinian narrative that is delineated only indirectly in the earlier film, *Chronicle of a Disappearance*, is presented more clearly and in a more precise and coherent manner in the later *Divine Intervention*. As in Suleiman's other films, in this one too the lack of a framework that organizes the picture according to the hierarchy of center versus periphery goes hand in hand with the lack of plot that gives coherence to the different episodes. However, because a major proportion of the episodes in this later film concentrate on acts of violence, the violence itself becomes the common denominator that provides cohesion or explanation for the disconnected parts. Thus, someone throwing a bomb into a collaborator's home, someone spraying it with bullets, people beating a snake violently with clubs and then shooting it, children chasing after Santa Claus and murdering him are all a part of the big picture. A man filmed from afar as he washes his dentures at a water tap in a gas station does not fit into the plot of *Chronicle of a Disappearance* in any way, while the people throwing the bomb, spraying the bullets, or beating the snake in *Divine Intervention* do fit into the general atmosphere of violence. The fact that, at least in the first few moments, it is difficult, because of the distance from which they are filmed, to discern who the people are beating, what the target of the bomb is, or who is chasing Santa Claus, intensifies the general atmosphere of inexplicable violence and evil – a violence which, while apparently devoid of any specific tangible motive, is nevertheless – in Suleiman's words – an aspect of the "loss of innocence, in a decaying city" (Kipp, 2003).

The film's entire plot, like its individual episodes, revolves around a common theme, which imparts a more coherent structure. Israeli culpability dominates the first part of the film; it clarifies the reciprocal acts of violence in the streets of Nazareth and indirectly leads to the death of the father.[36] Only after the collapse of the father does his son, Elia Suleiman (E. S.), enter the picture. The second part, in which Suleiman focuses on what is happening at the A-Ram roadblock, now deepens the Israeli guilt and establishes it as the reason for what has occurred in the first part. The result is a plot culminating in a fantasy of revenge against the Israelis. Thus the causal links in the plot, which generally outline *Chronicle of a Disappearance* as well, became clearer and the fundamental element driving it, affecting its every minute detail – the Israeli occupation – is directly referred to.

Compared to the situation in the earlier film, the Israeli occupation in the second completely transforms daily life in Nazareth. Life there seems to have turned into a violent system of vicious cycles, Sisyphean acts: a man repeatedly tossing bags of garbage into his neighbor's yard and the woman next door repeatedly cleaning the yard and gathering the filth into one pile; someone constructing the edges of a path and someone else destroying them; a man waiting for the bus and someone who keeps coming out to tell him that the bus is not coming; a boy playing ball and a man ripping it apart, and so on. The narrowed-down place, the reciprocal violence, and the futile repetition of the same acts and the same events are all connected, and they find their comic parallels in the multiple and split characters: two people dressed identically walking down a hospital corridor and smoking cigarettes in the same exact rhythm; a man talking to his friends repeating the number six dozens of time; three Palestinians standing with their arms raised against a wall while three Israeli soldiers clean their shoes in unison as if to he rhythm of a dance, and so on. A kind of parallel is created between repetitions of the same acts and of the multiplicity of characters, which is reflected once again in the traffic encircling the A-Ram roadblock, by cars that do not move and never arrive, and by the stultified daily life. In his film *Arab Dream* Suleiman defines this as "not daily life but daily death." In both films, the daily time frame ceases to be the time of the Palestinian *sumud*, as it was in *Chronicle of a Disappearance*, and becomes the static time of the ghetto.

The coherent plot of *Divine Intervention*, which leads from suffering to violent military action, the Palestinian narrative that clearly emerges from the images and from disconnected details of everyday life, and the escape from a fragmented space and an absent past towards the retrieval of the whole homeland, are all hallmarks of the New Palestinian Cinema that has endeavored to establish a stable and durable Palestinian narrative. While Elia Suleiman deconstructs this story in his early films, he reconstructs it in his latest movie. Yet, in all of his works, he still expresses the inability to hold on and to shape it.

NOTES

1. Or "poetic image," as he himself calls it in an interview with Anne Bourlond ([1999] 2000).
2. For an explanation of this term, see the Introduction.
3. In the words of Bresheeth (2002b), it deals "with the liminality of loss and disappearance of country, of the people, of the self."
4. The people of Nazareth consider themselves superior to the people of Sh'faram, and the population of Sh'faram considers itself superior to Tamra.
5. All of the families are bad, except for the speaker's family. This is what comes up in a conversation between two people during a fishing trip.
6. As described in the aunt's account, as she sits facing the camera at the beginning of the film and recounts a long story about family squabbles.
7. The event is not a national allegory in the sense attributed to it by Jameson (1986). See footnote 16 in the Introduction.
8. Haim Bresheeth defines this existence thus: "The anthem of the oppressor . . . is used by the oppressed. This cinematic device offers great power, and derives this power from the very act of transgressing, of breaking boundary lines, of stepping into Hebrew, into the national anthem of Israel, of Zion" (Bresheeth, 2002b: 76).
9. In this sense, the film completely fulfills the type of confrontation with trauma identified by Elsaesser (forthcoming) as parapraxis. See also footnote 8 in the Introduction.
10. See, among others, Ali Nassar's film *The Milky Way* (1997), Rashid Masharawi's *Curfew* (1993), Azza al-Hassan's *Three Centimeters Less* (2002), and Nizar Hassan's *Invasion* (2003).
11. The absence of home is also experienced by the director's girlfriend, Eden, who is unsuccessful in finding an apartment to rent in Jerusalem. The Jewish landlords immediately recognize her accent and identify her as Arab. In the end the police take her from her apartment. Consequently, home in the film is a sealed place, a breached place, or a non-existent place.
12. This idea is illustrated by the monologue of the monk living above the Sea of Galilee, who mourns the vistas conquered by local tourism and commercial development.
13. This interpretation is based upon a lecture delivered by Ala Alryes at Yale, in 2001.
14. See Bresheeth (2001).
15. See Chapter 1, "A Chronicle of Palestinian Cinema."
16. According to Laura Marks (1994), the energy which was blocked by the roadblock turns into sexual energy.
17. See *The Matrix* (Wachowski Brothers, 1999).
18. Referring here to the Ninja scene and to another where Suleiman pelts a tank with an apricot pit and the tank explodes.
19. Including Suleiman's own films.
20. Also, see Chapter 1, "A Chronicle of Palestinian Cinema."
21. As noted, this description is based on the definitions of parapraxis according to Elsaesser (forthcoming). See also footnote 7 in the Introduction.
22. This is also revealed in other places: for example, in a fountain at the Tel Aviv beach that sways to the sound of music, similar to the fountains in Jacques Tati's film, *Mon Oncle* (1958).
23. Which receives parts of dissected images, lacking any context.

24. "The hidden tears to console us cannot be found."
25. One of the characteristics of "accented cinema," according to Naficy (2001). See footnote 2 in Chapter 3, "About Place and Time: The Films of Michel Khleifi."
26. "Models of a real without origin or reality: a hyperreal" (Baudrillard, 1981), or, in Jameson's words: "the identical copy for which no original has ever existed" (1991).
27. Such as the Gulf War, which was only a televised spectacle, according to Baudrillard, whom Suleiman quotes in his film. See also Baudrillard (1981).
28. On this subject see Anne Bourlond's interview with Suleiman ([1999] 2000).
29. Always tainted by the subjective consciousness of the director-as-hero even when, in fact, it is not him who views the sights.
30. For more on the character of the director, see Chapter 1, "A Chronicle of Palestinian Cinema."
31. See also Haim Bresheeth (2002b), who explains the director's position as a melancholy stance in relation to the lost object.
32. Adorno, paraphrased by Said (1990: 366).
33. For a definition of the *sumud*, see footnote 11 in Chapter 3, "About Place and Time: The Films of Michel Khliefi."
34. See also footnote 2, in Chapter 3, "About Place and Time: The Films of Michel Khleifi."
35. This stance, which would be defined as parapractic by Elsaesser (2004), contains both the absent and the present as images that exist beyond each other, in a layered structure.
36. After the repossession of his home, his workshop, and his car. No explanation is given for these scenes of repossession and they may not be understood by the viewer. Therefore, like many scenes in earlier films, they seem unrelated to the main plot. However, once the viewer comprehends what they actually convey, the connection between them becomes clear.

CONCLUSION

In this book we have examined the place of the Palestinian people in history and the place of history in the Palestinian narrative. We have explored the connection between Palestinian history and Palestinian cinema, analyzing the manner in which cinema has constructed Palestinian memory and space, representing the places that once existed and those that are now gone. Also contemplated is the cinematic documentation of the lives of Palestinian men, women, and children, both within Israel and outside it, in the family, the village, and the refugee camp. We have traced the cinematic expression of the hardships of exile together with longing for the lost past and its return.

Palestinian cinema is a national cinema. Throughout its history, it has given form to a militant Palestinian nationalism, recounted Palestinian history, and sought the place and daily lives of ordinary Palestinians within that history. This delicate fabric of intertwined personal narrative and national history has been closely related to the national traumas.

In the early cinema, created in the 1970s under the auspices of the Palestinian organizations, the individual represented the national collective, its struggles, and its fate, which was perceived as stagnant and unchanging. The portrayal of the present, moreover, merely amounted to a reconstruction of the past – a restoration of the fixed structure of profound tranquility that had been disturbed by the sudden violence of 1948 and which is continuously reflected in each and every present event depicted. Thus, rather than being experienced as a living reality, life in the refugee camps was perceived not only in its own right but also as a repetition or an echo of another experience from an earlier era.

Since the present time was considered dead, hollow, and non-existent, it was deemed suitable for reviving the past. Such preservation of the 1948 trauma and what had preceded it served as a focal point of identification and consolidation for the entire Palestinian people.

During the 1980s, particularly with Michel Khleifi's films, past and present became distinct, the individual was set apart from the collective, and two time sequences were formed. The first is traumatic time that restores the past in the present; the second is diverse and richly detailed current everyday life. Time, in these movies, flows simultaneously in two different veins, alternately concealing and revealing each other. Thus a gap was created that allowed a working-through of the trauma while reflecting the diverse facets of Palestinian society: on the one hand, the various strata, genders, and regions that typify it, and on the other, the unity that consolidates it into a unified force, with one goal and a single memory.

A generation of directors, who began their creative endeavors in the late 1980s and during the 1990s, have attempted to follow in Michel Khleifi's footsteps and focus on everyday, mundane Palestinian life, forming through it a personal memory based on testimonies, individual histories, and interviews. The attempt to construct the nation's unity through recognition of the heterogeneity of Palestinian society and to shape the flowing time of memory instead of historical time was disrupted to a large extent by the two *Intifadas*. In the late 1980s and especially during the 1990s, the present that turned into a series of disasters and defeats was again perceived as a vacant time. Once more, cinema considered it in relation to the glorious time of the past and the trauma that severed it. Palestinian cinema created during those years has oscillated between the option of describing the diversity of Palestinian life and articulating various Palestinian experiences and memories, and the need to unify this variety and delineate the collective traumatic memory.

Palestinian cinema has coped, in various ways, with the history that "urged" the individual toward the collective and directed present life toward past traumas. One of the most interesting modes of coping with this aspect is the choice in films to present Palestinian unity, people, past, and history paradoxically as absentees whose presence is more strongly felt than those of other, actual, current realities.

Elia Suleiman's *Chronicle of a Disappearance* is an example of a film structured according to this model. It focuses on the individual's life and family, refusing to present beyond them Palestinian society and its past. Yet, that which is left untold in the film still reverberates in it. Suleiman thus represents the unrepresentable, indicating a possibility of spinning national unity and memory out of a lack of such unity and history. It evokes the forgotten, even if only as a distant impression lurking beyond the image of the present, and with the distance between the two in mind lures us into observing it.

Chronicle of a Disappearance typifies the way Palestinian cinema confronts the difficulties in narrating Palestinian history and documenting the national and personal life of the Palestinian people. Palestinian cinema offers an abundance of other examples of various – similar as well as different – ways of coping with the same task. This book has attempted to recount the chronicle of this cinema, which is intertwined with the history of the Palestinian people.

EPILOGUE

The writing of this book was completed in 2003. While it was being prepared for publication, several important events took place in Palestinian cinema and some of its best films were produced. We can only refer to these films in brief, hoping that additional books written in due course will fill the gap.

The first Palestinian film to transcend the local scene and reach an international audience was released in 2005. It won the European Film Academy Award for best script, the 2006 best foreign film award at the Golden Globes, and was also nominated for the best foreign film award at the Oscars. That film was *Paradise Now*.

Paradise Now was financed as a German, Dutch, and French co-production, but presented at the Oscars as a "Palestinian film." From the onset, the film was highly controversial in Israel, since it was the first Palestinian feature film to deal directly with the issue of the suicide attacks. Director Hani Abu-Assad and producer Amir Harel applied in 2003 for a public grant from the Israeli Film Fund. Several fund members denied their request and one, the writer Irit Linor, harshly criticized the film, which she called "a moving and high-brow Nazi film" (Linor, Ynet, 2006. *Anti-Semitism Now* (7 February)). After it won the Golden Globe award no Israeli distributor agreed to take on the film and show it in Israel. Consequently, it was only screened at the cinematheque, enjoying little success.

Some of the debate concerning the film was in fact partly unnecessary, for the real topic of *Paradise Now* is not the "Paradise" but the "Now." It does not necessarily deal with the eternal life promised to the suicide bombers, but rather with the present time in which they are living. It is the time of Palestinian life within the West Bank and Gaza Strip, described by the best Palestinian cinema discussed in this book. We have encountered it in *Waiting for Salah A-Ddin*, *Chronicle of a Disappearance, Curfew, Stress,* and many others. It is the time of two people sitting at the entrance of a coffee house doing nothing, it is the time of cars that do not move, it is the time of people sitting in their house during curfew, waiting in line, at roadblocks. That slow, empty time permeates the first part of *Paradise Now*'s, depicted via means that are familiar from Palestinian cinema, and sometimes calling on the same images and symbols (a stationary car, standing at roadblocks, smoking a narghile and so on). It is a time threatening to burst, explode, burn, or overflow in all of the films. Yet, while in the other films the camera or symbolic and even surrealistic absurd images enact the blast, in *Paradise Now* the detonation is an actual suicide attack.

In this respect, it is possible to understand the plot of the film as an attempt to replace the time of desperation with two other types of time: on the one hand, the time of eternity in heaven after the suicide act, and on the other hand, the Hollywood time of action and pursuit. Thus, the first part of the film is constructed as a long anticipation of and preparation for the suicide act, and its second part is set up as a Hollywood chase after the protagonist who did not perform his role, who hesitated at the last minute and escaped. This structure is probably what was responsible for the success of the film, where better, more important films failed.

Among the most important of the films made during this period is Juliano Mer's debut as a director, *Arna's Children* (2004). The film tells the story of the lives and deaths of children participating in the theater founded by Arna Mer-Khamis, the director's mother. *Arna's Children* focuses in particular on Yussef and his three friends – Ashraf, Alaa, and Nidal. Yussef carried out a suicide attack in Hadera in 2001, Ashraf was killed by the Israeli army during the battle at the Jenin refugee camp, and Alaa led the Al-Aqsa Martyr Brigades until he was killed in November 2002.

Yussef, Ashraf, and Alaa were actors at the Stone Theater, which was part of the alternative education system that Arna Mer founded during the First *Intifada* at the Jenin refugee camp, after the collapse of the official education system under the Israeli occupation. She won the alternative Nobel Peace Prize (the Right Living Award) for that project, and invested the prize money of $50,000 in building a children's theater in the camp. Arna's son, Juliano, joined his mother in working with the camp children as the theater director. During his time at the camp his camera documented his mother and the theater children.

The film was produced in several stages. Mer's original plan was to shoot a documentary film about his mother, who had fallen ill with cancer. On the day that the New Foundation for Cinema and Television informed him that it had approved the film's budget, the doctors told his mother that she had one year to live. Mer began filming, and as the film progressed so did Arna's disease. Thus the film gradually became more concerned with the illness and less with Jenin. But Arna was not interested in such a film, as Juliano Mer tells Uri Klein in an interview:

> She begged that if I was determined to do a film about her, then her character should be used to facilitate a discussion of a broader array of issues. She did not want the film to only be about her and her illness, which were naturally the subjects that I connected to most directly and urgently. And indeed, several days before her death I stopped filming. The last time I shot her was during her final visit to Jenin, and this visit is documented in *Arna's Children*. (Klein, 2004)

After her death in February 1995 Mer shelved the movie,

> and then one day I sat in my house in front of the television set and saw the face of Yussef, one of the children appearing in Arna's theater, on the screen. He was killed in a suicide attack he had committed in Hadera. I called Osnat, the producer, and told her "Yussef has committed a suicide attack. I am going to Jenin to check how and why. Can you buy a camera?" (Klein, 2004)

The film is one of the few in Palestinian cinema that both observes Jews and Arabs separately and examines their relationship when they are together. Another important film employing a similar perspective is Michel Khleifi and Eyal Sivan's film *Road 181* (2004), which documents the lives of Jews and Arabs along the armistice line in 1948.[1]

Yet other aspects make *Arna's Children* unique. At first it seems like any other film focusing on children, delineating their distress and dreams, using them as an allegory of the Palestinians' suffering and dead-end situation, and personifying the hope spurring the Palestinians on toward the future. The film's basic structure, which commences and concludes with images of children, accentuates the cyclical repetition that operates in other films. However, Mer infuses this structure with a series of time reversals, shifts back and forth expressed in flashbacks and flashes forward, which shock the spectator, immersing the gloomy future in the present and the wondrous past in the future.[2]

Into the opening scenes which focus on Arna's final visit to the camp before her death are injected rehearsals for a show a few years earlier, at a time when Arna was still healthy; in the scenes of rehearsal and other glimpses of the young children at play and at work, the news of their deaths, in battle and in suicide attacks several years later on, is revealed. Thus their deaths are intertwined with Arna's own approaching death. In this way, the future does not appear to counter hopes and dreams, as it does in other films. Rather, it is already there at the heart of the present. Thus, the dead warriors and the living children, the camp in its heyday and the devastated camp after the invasion, the lively theater and the ruined building, all of these, like the tanks roaming the dark town before and after it, its destruction, become a single image that counters all hopes and dreams and yet does not allow us to forget them or forsake them.

Juliano Mer's mother, Arna, was the daughter of a medical professor, born in Rosh Pina, who enlisted in the *Palmach*, the Israeli defence force, when she was young. There she wore the *kaffiyeh* (Muslim headwear) for the first time, and this became her trademark until her final days. After the war she joined the Communist Party and married a Palestinian party activist, Saliba Khamis. They had three boys – Juliano, Spartkus, and Abir. Mer has defined himself on different occasions as a "Hebrew-speaking Palestinian with Communist views." He is married to a Jewish woman and has acted in many Israeli films, including *Rage and Glory* (1984), *Bar 51* (1986), *Tel Aviv Stories* (1992), *Under the Domim Tree* (1992) and more. In Amos Gitai's *Day After Day* (1998) and *Kippur* (2000), as in Michel Khleifi's *Wedding in Galilee*, he played the role of an Israeli army officer.

Arna's Children premiered in March 2004, and screened in Israel at the cinematheques in Tel Aviv, Jerusalem, and Haifa, in addition to special screenings in front of various audiences. Concurrently, it was also shown in Nazareth, Ramallah, and Beit Sahur, and won fourth place in the audience choice competition at Idfa, the most important international documentary film festival. In 2004, it also won first prize in the best film category at Another World in the Czech Republic, a festival dedicated to documentary films dealing with human rights issues. In that same year it also won best documentary film at the Tribeca Festival in New York.

Hana Elias's *Olive Harvest* (2003) is more closely linked to the structure and content of films preceding it. Elias was born in the Upper Galilee village of Al-Gish, studied film at Los Angeles University in California, and in 1991 wrote and directed a short film called *The Mountain* that won the best short film award at the Paris Arab Film Biennale in 1992.

Olive Harvest has a melodramatic winding plot about the battle between two brothers for the heart of a woman they both love. One of the brothers is a fighter who has just been released from prison, while the other is a political activist in the Palestinian Authority. This love story is interlaced with a tale recounting the battle over land through the figure of the girl's dying father, who struggles to preserve his land and olive groves, intending to give his daughter to the man who will also guard the land.

The film's subject matter is familiar – a generations-old fight over land, which is also the conflict between rural legacy and urban culture. The film is heavily layered with allegorical overtones. The brothers' brawl, for instance, is reminiscent of the clash between Cain and Abel, and the woman is identified with the land, while the Jewish settlements are described as a cancer spreading over the country. In this respect, the movie is not particularly innovative. Nevertheless it revives Michel Khleifi's early cinema in the construction of the landscape and the camera movements, in the links it weaves between the home, the yard, the village and the olive groves – in the delineation of a complete map of the Palestinian place. At the same time the film also indicates a new tendency to focus on conflicts and tensions within Palestinian society, leaving the Israeli-Palestinian conflict in the background. This tendency is prevalent in several new short films such as *Going for a Ride* (Nahad Awad, 2004), *Maybe Life will be Good* (Ra'id al Hilo, 2004), and most prominently in Tawfik Abu Wa'el's *Thirst* (*Atash*) (2004).

Tawfik Abu Wa'el belongs to the younger generation of Palestinian filmmakers. He graduated in film studies at Tel Aviv University and worked from 1996 until 1998 at the university archive. From 1997 till 1999 Tawfik taught drama at the Hassan Arafa School in Jaffa. He has directed several short films, including *Waiting for Salah A-Ddin* (2001). In 2004 his first feature film, *Thirst*, was released.

Thirst describes the Abu Shukri family, who settled somewhere in an abandoned valley, far from their own village. The family members live in complete isolation from the world, cutting down trees without the permission of the authorities and making charcoal for a living. Although the valley landscape is empty and open, it seems as if it is trapped between deserted hills, dotted with several sheds that give the impression of a prison within a prison. The family lives in the shadow of Abu Shukri, an authoritative and violent father, who rules his family with a rod of iron, forbidding any contact with civilization, shutting his daughters home in the house, and stopping his son from going to school. Life here is a life of oppression, imprisonment, and isolation.

The film is constructed as a disrupted sequence – image after image that seems to assemble according to the shapelessness of time flowing from day to night, from night to misty morning and again into night. However, there is no dynamic plot flow. There is no action except for dominating acts of oppression and eventually the son's rebellion against his father. The disrupted time corresponds with the disrupted music and disrupted images showing family members wandering around the empty yard, through the rooms, looking at the walls which seem like a prison and at the other family members who move around, enclosed within themselves, seen through the lens and the building's unfinished structure.

The Israelis are quite clearly and conspicuously absent from the film. The distress, the waste, the time that stood still, the obstructed space – all the characteristics of Palestinian cinema in recent years – which the Israeli occupation was blamed for, are presented here as an existential condition, explained by various reasons and by no single definite one.

Ostensibly, the main reason for the family's distress is the father's stubborn refusal to return to a more usual place of residence; he uses the funds intended to secure his children's future to connect a pipe to transfer stolen water to the yard and house, and refuses his family's wish to enjoy civilization in the form of television, radio, or books. However, the film leaves too many issues open and ambiguous for everything to be exclusively blamed on the father. It is not clear, for example, what happened to one of the daughters. Was she involved in a forbidden affair? Was she raped? Why did the family leave the village? What exactly is the relationship between father and daughter? Is it violence, perhaps, or erotic attraction? What kind of passion does the fire indicate and what exactly does the water symbolize? What do they, as well as the soil and the smoke, symbolize? Freedom? Desire? Liberation from family constraints? From the Israeli occupier?

The reasons, the sources, and the significance that remain open leave us with poetic, amazingly beautiful images of despair and waste disconnected from any context and yet thus perhaps linked to all contexts at once: the family's condition in a Palestinian village, the state of the women and children in it, the occupation (the land the family lives on is expropriated and the father who dominates his family is terrified of the Israelis), and above all – the human condition.

At the end of the film, in a demonic scene, the son kills his father, but instead of liberating himself and his family members from the constraints of the patriarchal occupier, the son adopts his father's apparel, appearance, mannerisms, and values, himself becoming the new tyrant of the family. In an interview the director has said,

> For my character, there is no option or choice here beside to knock his head against the wall. My character has no power or support to fight back; therefore I do not think that he really could change his situation. My view is not pessimistic, it includes a call for freedom and liberation, and the only problem that can occur here is embedded in the nature of man rather than in my point of view. I really don't believe that man can realize himself.

Thirst won the International Critics Award at the Cannes Festival in 2004, the Judges' Award at the Arab Film Biennale in 2004, and two Israeli awards – Wolgin at the 2004 Jerusalem Festival and the Ophic best cinematographer award from the Israeli Film Academy. Now, with the completion of this book, we might consider the film alongside Juliano Mer's *Arna's Children*, as testimony to the possibility for Palestinian cinema to cross over the barriers that fixated it within a historical and geographical trauma, within the distress caused by the "dead-end" occupation, within unity that can only tell a single story with two protagonists, us and them. The two films discussed here use a cinematic language that breaks down walls and barriers and evokes the possibility of a new story and a new cinema.

NOTES

1. In this film, both sides travel in time. The Arabs remember the moment of expulsion from the homeland, and the Jews remember their version of the same traumatic event. Despite or perhaps because of the fact that one of the directors is an Israeli, this film was harshly criticized by educated European Jews, and provoked a heated debate in France, where the filmmakers were accused of anti-Semitism.
2. See an analysis of the film and its structure in Friedman (2005).

BIBLIOGRAPHY

Abdel Malek, Kamal and David Jacobson, 1999a. *Israeli and Palestinian Identities in History and Literature*, New York: St Martin.
—, 1999b. "Living on Borderline: War and Exile in Selected Works by Ghassan Kanafani, Fawaz Turki, and Mahmud Darwish," in: Kamal Abdel Malek and David Jacobson (eds), *Israeli and Palestinian Identities in History and Literature*, New York: St Martin.
Abu Amr, Ziad, 1990. "The Politics of the Intifada," in: Michael Hudson (ed.), *The Palestinians: New Directions*, Washington: Center for Contemporary Arab Studies, Georgetown University. pp. 3–24.
Abu Gh'nima, Hassan, 1981. *Palestine and the Cinematic Eye (Filistin Wal Ayno-s-sinemaeya)*, Damascus: United Arab Writers' Press. [Arabic]
Abu Shawer, Rashad, 1970. "The Return of the Stranger," *Zickra Al Ayyam Almadiyaa*, Beirut: All Aadab. pp. 24–31. [Arabic]
Adams, Ann Jensen, 1994. "Competing Communities in the 'Great Bog of Europe': Identity and Seventeenth-Century Dutch Landscape Painting," in: W. J. T. Mitchell (ed.), *Landscape and Power*, Chicago: University of Chicago Press. pp. 35–101.
Ahmad, Aijaz, 1992. *In Theory*, London: Verso.
Ailebuni, Mary, 1987. "The French Prefer Him Bad" ("Al Faranciyoon Yofaddiloonaho Kareehan"), *Pilistin A-Thaura* (May). [Arabic]
Al Aris, Ibrahim, 1997. "No Surprises: Carthage Film Festival Fails to Recognize Remarkable Chronicle," *Al Jadid*, 17. pp. 14–15.
Al Batrawi, Muhammad, 2002. "The Pre-Naqba Theatre," *Azzawia Quarterly*, Ramallah (Summer). [Arabic]
Alexsaan, Jean, 1999. *The Arab Novel: From the Book to the Screen*, Damascus: Ministry of Culture/General Film Institute. [Arabic]
Al-Hout, Shafiq, 1998. "Reflections on Al Nakba," *Journal of Palestinian Studies*, xxviii (Autumn), 1. pp. 23–7.
—, 1967. "The Fiddaee" ("Al Fidaee"), *Al Adeeb* (December). pp. 24–7. [Arabic]

—, 1968. "The Escape from Tul Karem" ("Arraheed Min Tulkarm)", *Al Adeeb* (January). pp. 10–13.

Al Kaisy, Jalal, 1969. "Zulika, the Distance is Getting Near ("Al Bo'do Yaktareb")," *Muakef*, Vol. 4 (May–June). pp. 113–20. [Arabic]

Al Khalidi, Rashid, 1997. *Palestinian Identity*, New York: Columbia University Press.

—, [2001] 2002. "The Palestinian and 1948: the Underlying Causes of Failure," in: Eugene L. Rogan and Avi Shlaim (eds), *The War for Palestine: Rewriting the History of 1948*, Cambridge: Cambridge University Press. pp. 12–36.

Al Mallah, Yasser, 2002. *Folded Pages from the History of the Palestinian Theatre (Safahat Matwiyya min Tareech al Masrah-el-Filistini)*, Hebron: Al Ankaa Association. [Arabic]

Al Irany, Mahmud Saifi-deen, 1933. "The Bread Loaf," *Awwalo-Sh-Shawt*, Jaffa: Al-Fajr.

—, 1932. "A Scary Man," *Awwalo-Sh-Shawt*, Jaffa: Al-Fajr.

Alter, Robert, 1975. *Partial Magic*, Berkeley: University of California Press.

Al Udath, Hussein, 1989. *Cinema and the Palestinian Issue (A-s-sinema Wal Kadiyyato-l-Filistiniyya)* (second edition), Acre: Dar Al-Aswar. [Arabic]

Amar, 1957. "Father, Put Me Down ("Nazzilni Ya Abi")," *Al Jadid for Literature, Science and Art*, Vol. 10 (October). pp. 15–18. [Arabic]

Anderson, Benedict, 2000. *Imagined Communities: Reflection on the Origin and Spread of Nationalism*, Tel Aviv: Open University Press. [Hebrew]

A-Rais, Allaa, 2001. "Elia Suleiman's Cinema," Research Paper: Yale University.

Armes, Roy, 1987. *Third World Film Making and the West*, Berkeley: University of California Press.

Ashrawi-Mikhail, Hanan, 1990. "The Politics of Cultural Revival," in: Michael Hudson (ed.), *The Palestinians: New Directions*, Washington: Center for Contemporary Arab Studies, Georgetown University. pp. 77–87.

Avishar, Ilan, 1998. "National Anxieties, Personal Nightmares: The Holocaust Complex in Israeli Cinema," in: Nurith Gertz, Orly Lubin and Judd Ne'eman (eds), *Fictive Looks: On Israeli Cinema*, Tel Aviv: Open University Press. [Hebrew]

Avni, Carmit, 2001. *Representation of Trauma in Palestinian Cinema*, Seminar Paper: Department of Cinema and Television, Tel Aviv University.

Azzam, Samira, [1961] 1970. "The Clock and the Man" ("A-s-Sa'a Wal Insan"), Beirut: Dar Al Awda. [Arabic]

—, 1982a. "Another Year," in: *The Great Shadow*, a collection of short stories, Beirut: Dar Al Awda. [Arabic]

—, 1982b. "Because He Loves Them," in: *The Clock and the Man*, Beirut: Dar Al Awda. [Arabic]

—, 1982c. "For the Time Being," in: *The Great Shadow*, Beirut: Dar Al Awda. p. 67. [Arabic]

Badarshi, Yael, "Cyber Palestine: A Site in Construction," *42 Degrees*, Vol. 7 (April–May). pp. 60–4. [Hebrew]

Baidas, Riad, 1987. "The Visit" ("A-z-Ziyara"), in: *A-r-Reeh (The Wind)*, a collection of short stories, Nikosya: Dar-s-Somoodi-l-'Arabi. pp. 67–86. [Arabic]

Balas, Shimon, 1978. *The Arab Literature in View of the War*, Tel Aviv: Ofakim, Am Oved. [Hebrew]

Bannura, Jamal, 1976a. "The Return," *Al Awda*, Jerusalem: Salah A-Ddin Press. [Arabic]

—, 1976b. "The Victory," *Al Awda*, Jerusalem: Salah A-Ddin Press.

—, 1990. "The Lantern that did not Extinguish," *Al Jadeed*, 11–12.

Baudrillard, Jean, 1981. *Simulacres et Simulation*, Paris: Galilée.

Becker, Avihai, 1999. "Memories from Plot # 9" (Interview with Ali Nassar), *Ha'aretz* (5 February). pp. 55–8. [Hebrew]

Benedict, Sebastien, 2002. "Nazareth Ninja," in: *Cahiers du Cinéma* (October), Vol. 18, 19.

Ben Nun, Ran, 1995. "Who Is A Palestinian?" (Interview with Elia Suleiman), *Iton Tel Aviv* (10 February). [Hebrew]

Ben-Shaul, Nitzan, 1997. *Mythical Expressions of Siege in Israeli Films*, Lewiston: Edwin Mellen.

Bhabha, Homi K., 1990. "Dissemination: Time, Narrative and the Margins of the Modern Nation," in: Homi K. Bhabha (ed.), *Nation and Narration*, London: Routledge. pp. 291–323.

Biale, David, 1992. *Eros and the Jews*, New York: Basic.

Bordo, Jonathan, 2000. "Picture and Witness at the Site of the Wilderness," *Critical Inquiry*, Vol. 26, 2. pp. 224–47.

Bourlond, Anne, [1999] 2000. "A Cinema of Nowhere: Interview with Elia Suleiman," *Journal of Palestine Studies*, xxix, No. 2 (Winter). pp. 95–101.

Boyarin, Daniel, 1997. *Unheroic Conduct: The Rise of Heterosexuality and the Invention of the Jewish Man*, Berkeley: University of California Press.

Bresheeth, Haim, 2001. "The Boundaries of the Palestinian Memory: Home and Exile, Identity and Disappearance in the New Palestinian Cinema," *Theory and Criticism*, Vol. 18 (Spring). pp. 77–102. [Hebrew]

—, 2002a. "Telling the Stories of Heim and Heimat, Home and Exile: Recent Palestinian Films and the Iconic Parable of the Invisible Palestine," *Intellect*, 1, 1. pp. 24–39.

—, 2002b. "A Symphony of Absence: Borders and Liminality in Elia Suleiman's *Chronicle of a Disappearance*," *Framework*, 43, 2 (Fall). pp. 71–84.

Bronfen, Elisabeth, 1992. *Over her Dead Body: Death, Femininity and the Aesthetic*, New York: Routledge.

Brooks, Xan, 2003. "When We Started Shooting, So Did They" (Interview with Elia Suleiman), *Guardian*, (13 January).

Camus, Albert, 1943. *L'Étranger*, Paris: Gallimard.

—, [1942] 1978. *The Myth of Sisyphus*, Paris: Gallimard.

—, 1947. *La Peste*, New York: Alfred A. Knopf.

Caruth, Cathy, 1991. "Unclaimed Experience: Trauma and the Possibility of History," *Yale French Studies, No. 79: Literature and the Ethical Question*. pp. 181–92.

— (ed.), 1995. *Trauma: Explorations in Memory*, Baltimore: Johns Hopkins University Press.

—, 1996. *Unclaimed Experience: Trauma, Narrative and History*, Baltimore: John Hopkins University Press.

Dahoud, Siham, 1979. "Ashoddo-l-Horoofa Ila Shafati," *Al I'lamo-l-Mowahhad* (United Information), Beirut: PLO. p. 161.

Darwish, Mahmud, 1978. *Diwan Mahmud Darwish*, Beirut: Dar Al Awda. [Arabic]

Deleuze, Gilles and Felix Guattari, 1990. "What is Minor Literature?," in: Russell Ferguson, Martha Gever, Trinh Minh-ha and Cornel West (eds), *Out There: Marginalization and Culture*, New York: New York Museum of Contemporary Art. pp. 59–71.

Elad, Ami (ed.), 1993. *Writer, Culture, Text: Studies in Modern Arabic Literature*, Fredricton: York.

Elias, Juri's and Ella Shohat, 1995. "Anomalies of the National: Representing Israel/Palestine," in: Jonathan Friedlander (ed.), *UCLA Near-East Center Colloquium Series*, Los Angeles: University of California at Los Angeles.

Elmessiri, Abdelwahab M., 1982. *The Palestinian Wedding*, Washington: Three Continent.

Elsaesser, Thomas, 1997. " 'One Train May Be Hiding Another': Private History, Memory and National Identity," in: Josef Delau et al. (eds), *The Low Countries: Arts and society in Flanders and the Netherlands – A Yearbook, 1996–1997*, Rekkem: Flemish–Nederlands Foundation/Stichting Ons Erfdeel.

—, 2001. "Trauma, Memory, History," *Screen*, 42, 2. pp. 193–5.

—, 2004. *Melodrama and Trauma: Modes of Cultural Memory in the American Cinema*, New York: Routledge.

— forthcoming. "Absence as Presence, Presence as Parapraxis," *Assaf Kolnoa*, 3.

Erickson, Steve, 2003. "A Breakdown of Communication: Elia Suleiman Talks About *Divine Intervention*," www.indiewire.com (30 March).

Even-Zohar, Itamar, 1990. *Polysystem Studies/Poetics Today* (Spring), 11, 1.

Farid, Samir, no date. *Palestinian Cinema in the Occupied Land (As-s-Sinema-l-Filistiniyya Fi-l-Ardi-l-Mohtalla)*, Cairo: Film Collection/Public Authority for Cultural Institutions. [Arabic]

Fayyad, Tawfik, 1968. "The Bristled Up Dog" ("Al Kalb Sammoor"), *A Shari'-l-Asfar (The Yellow Street)*, a collection of short stories, Nazareth: Al Hakeem. pp. 108–20. [Arabic]

Ferguson, Russell, Martha Gever, Trinh Minh-ha and Cornel West (eds) 1990. *Out There: Marginalization and Culture*, New York: New York Museum of Contemporary Art.

Ferro, Marc, 1976. *Cinéma et Histoire*, Paris: Denoël.

Fishbein, Einat, 2003. "Hani Abu-Assad: A Man with a Load," *Yediot Aharonot* (7 November). pp. 55–76. [Hebrew]

Freud, Sigmund, [1901] 1951. *Psychopathology of Everyday Life*, New York: Mentor.

—, [1909] 1974a. "Remembering, Repeating and Working Through," *Standard Edition of the Complete Psychological Works*, Vol. 12, London: Hogarth Press and Institute of Psychoanalysis. pp. 147–56.

—, [1917] 1991. "Mourning and Melancholia," *On Metapsychology*, Vol. 11, London: Penguin. pp. 245–68.

—, [1939] 1955. *Moses and Monotheism* (trans. Katherine Jones), New York: Vintage.

—, [1949] 1969. *An Outline of Psychoanalysis*, New York: Norton.

—, [1953] 1974b. "Mourning and Melancholia," *Standard Edition of the Complete Psychological Works*, Vol. 12, London: Hogarth Press and Institute of Psychoanalysis. pp. 243–58.

Friedlander, Saul, 1992. *Probing the Limits of Representation*, Cambridge, MA: Harvard University Press.

—, 1994. "Trauma, Memory, and Transference," in: Geoffrey H. Hartman (ed.), *Holocaust Remembrance: The Shapes of Memory*, Oxford: Blackwell. pp. 252–63.

Friedman, Regine-Mihal, 2002. "The Double Legacy of Arbeit Macht Frei," *Prooftext*, 23: pp. 199–202.

—, 2005. "Orphans of the Storm: Children, the Intifada and the Documentary Cinema." Lecture given on 9 April at the "Together Today" conference, Paris.

Funckenstein, Amos, 1991. "Social Memory and Historical Consciousness," in: *The Image of History and Consciousness in Judaism and its Cultural Milieu*, Tel Aviv: Am Oved. [Hebrew]

Fynero, Edna, 2002. "Late Marriage, the Moslem Version" (Interview with Hani Abu-Assad), *Ha'ir* (23 May). pp. 50–1. [Hebrew]

Gabriel, Teshome, 1989a. "Third Cinema as Guardian of Popular Memory: Towards a Third Aesthetics," in: Jim Pines and Paul Willemen (eds), *Questions of Third Cinema*, London: British Film Institute. pp. 30–53.

—, 1989b. "Toward a Critical Theory of Third World Films," in: Jim Pines and Paul Willemen (eds), *Questions of Third Cinema*, London: British Film Institute. pp. 1–30.

Genocchio, Benjamin, 1996. "Discourse, Discontinuity, Difference: The Question of 'Other' Spaces," in: Sophie Watson and Katherine Gibson (eds), *Postmodern Cities and Spaces*, Oxford: Blackwell.

Gertz, Nurith, 2000. *Myths in Israeli Culture*, London: Vallentine-Mitchell (Parkers-Wiener Series).

—, 2001. "Gender and Geography in the New Israeli Cinema," in: Nurith Gertz, Orly Lubin, Judd Ne'eman and Mihal Friedman (eds), *Assaph Kolnoa*, 2. pp. 227–47.

—, 2002. "Space and Gender in the New Israeli and Palestinian Cinema," *Prooftexts*, Special issue: The Cinema of Jewish Experience (Winter/Spring), 22, 1–2. pp. 157–85.

Ghanayem, Muhammad Hamza, 2000. "Before Birth, After Death," *Gagg*, Vol. 3 (Winter). pp. 12–17. [Hebrew]

Givony, Yossef (ed.), 1986. *A Place on Earth: Arab Stories*, Jerusalem: Van Leer Institute Press. [Hebrew]

Gloria, Anzaldua, 1987. *Borderlands/La Frontera: The New Mestiza*, San Francisco: Aunt Lute.

Gocek, Fatma Muge and Shiva Balaghi, 1994. *Reconstructing Gender in the Middle East*, New York: Columbia University Press.

Greenberg, Gershon, 1988. "Orthodox Jewish Theology, 1945–1948: Responses to the Holocaust," in: *Remembering for the Future*, Oxford: Pergamon.

Greenberg, Judith, 1998. "The Echo of the Trauma and the Trauma of Echo," *American Imago*, 55, 3. pp. 319–47.

Gross, Natan and Yaacov Gross, 1991. *The Hebrew Film: Chapters in the History of the Cinema in Israel*, Jerusalem: limited edition, self-published. [Hebrew]

Grossman, David, 1987. *The Yellow Wind*, Tel Aviv: Siman Kriaa/Hakibutz Hameuhad.

Gurevitz, Zali and Gideon Aran, 1991. "About the Place (Israeli Anthropology)," *Alpayim*, Vol. 4. pp. 9–45. [Hebrew]

Habibi, Emile, 1968a. *The Six Day Sextet (Sodasyyato-l-Ayyami-s-Sitta)*, Haifa: Dar Alitihad. [Arabic]

—, 1968b. "At Last the Almond Tree Blossomed" ("Wa'akheeran Nawwara-l-Lawz"), *The Six Day Sextet*, Haifa: Dar Alitihad. [Arabic]

—, 1968c. "Robabikia," *The Six Day Sextet*, Haifa: Dar Alitihad. [Arabic]

—, 1974. *The Pessoptimist (Al Wakai'-l-Ghareeba Fi-Khtifaa Said Abi-n-Nahsi-l-Motasha'il)*, Haifa: Dar Alitihad. [Arabic]

Halbreich-Euvrard, Janine, 2003. *D'ailleurs et d'ici: Israeliens-Palestiniens, Que peut le Cinéma?*, Paris: Ministère de la culture.

Hall, Stuart, 1990. "Cultural Identity and Diaspora," in: Jonathan Rutherford (ed.), *Identity, Community, and Cultural Difference*, London: Lawrence and Wishart. pp. 222–38.

Haluzin-Dovrat, Limor, 1999. "The Memory of the Things of Laughter and Tears," *Cinematheque* (January–February). pp. 4–7. [Hebrew]

Hamami, Rima and Salim Tamari, 2001. "Anatomy of Another Uprising," in Adi Ophir (ed.), *Real Time: The El-Aqsa Intifada and the Israeli Left*, Jerusalem: Keter. [Hebrew]

Haniya, Akram, [1979] 1989. "That Village, that Morning" ("Tilka-l-Karya, Thalika-s-Sabah"), *As Safina-l-Akheera, Al Mina'o-l-Akheer (The Last Ship, The Last Harbor)*, a collection of short stories, Jerusalem: Salaheddin. pp. 33–43. [Arabic]

Harkabi, Yehoshafat, 1975. "The Palestinians in the Fifties and their Awakening as Reflected in Their Literature," in: Moshe Ma'oz (ed.), *Palestininian Arab Politics*, Jerusalem: Jerusalem Academic Press.

Harshav, Benjamin, 1990. *The Meaning of Yiddish*, Berkeley: University of California Press.

Hassan, Manar, 2000. "Gender and Memory in the Palestinian City," Proposal for Dissertation: Department of Sociology and Anthropology, Tel Aviv University. [Hebrew]

Hassassian, Manuel, 2002. "Historical Dynamics Shaping Palestinian National Identity," *Palestine–Israel Journal*, Vol. 8/9, 4/1. pp. 50–60.

Hennebelle, Guy and Khemais Khayati, 1977. *La Palestine et le cinéma*, Paris: E. 100.

Herman, Judith, 1992. *Trauma and Recovery*, Tel Aviv: Am Oved. [Hebrew]

Heung, Marina, 1997. "The Family Romance of Orientalism: From *Madame Butterfly* to *Indochina*," in: Matthew Bernstein and Gaylyn Studlar (eds), *Visions of the East: Orientalism in the Film*, New Brunswick: Rutgers University Press.

Hever, Hanan, 1993. "No Refuge for the Refugees: Emile Habibi and the Hebrew Literature Canon," in: M. Yaacov Landaw (ed.) and Elad Ami (guest ed.), *The New East: The Israeli Oriental Society Periodical* (Special issue about the literature of Israeli Arabs), Vol. 35. pp. 102–14. [Hebrew]

—, 2000. "We did not Arrive from the Sea: Sketches of the Geography of Oriental Literature," *Theory and Criticism*, Vol. 16 (Spring). pp. 181–97. [Hebrew]

Hirsch, Marianne, 1996. "Past Lives, Postmemories in Exile," *Poetics Today* (Winter), 17, 4. pp. 659–87.

Hobsbawm, Eric and Terence Ranger (eds), 1983. *The Invention of Tradition*, Cambridge: Cambridge University Press.

Hoffman, Ann Golomb, 1997. "Bodies and Borders: The Politics of Gender in Contemporary Israeli Novelists," in: Alan Mintz (ed.), *The Boom in Contemporary Israeli Fiction*, Hanover: Brandeis University Press. pp. 35–70.

Hopkins, Jeff, 1994. "Mapping of Cinematic Places: Icons, Ideology, and the Power of (Mis)representation," in: C. Aitken Stuart and Leo E. Zonn, *Place, Power, Situation and Spectacle: A Geography of Film*, Lanham: Rowman and Littlefield. pp. 47–65.

Hudson, Leila, 1994. "Coming of Age in Occupied Palestine: Engendering the Intifada," in: Fatma Muge Gocek and Shiva Balaghi, *Reconstructing Gender in the Middle East*, New York: Columbia University Press. pp. 123–39.

Hutcheon, Linda, 1988. *A Poetics of Postmodernism*, New York: Routledge.

Ibrahim, Bashar, 2000. *A Look at Palestinian Cinema in the Twentieth Century* (*Nathra 'Ala-s-Snema-l-Filistinyya Fi-l-Karni-l-'Ishreen*), Damascus: A Tarek Press for Research. [Arabic]

Ibrahim, Hanna, 1972. "Holiday Eve" ("Laylato 'Eid"), *Azharon Barriyya* (*Wild Flowers*), a collection of short stories, Hifa: Al Ittihad. [Arabic]

Idris, Suhil, 1971. "The Crossing" ("Al 'Oboor"), *Al Adaab* (August). pp. 2–4. [Arabic]

Jabra, Jabra Ibrahim, 1986. "The Other Rooms" *A-r-Ridfo-l-Okhra* (*The other Hip*), Beirut. [Arabic]

Jacobs, M. Jane, 1996. *Edge of Empire: Postcolonialism and the City*, London: Routledge.

Jadanov, A. A., 1949. *About Culture and Society*, Merhavia: Sifriat Hapoalim and Hakibutz Ha'arzi. [Hebrew]

Jahshan, Shakeeb, 1997. "The Immigrant" ("Al Muhajir"), *Al Jadeed*, Haifa. [Arabic]

Jameson, Fredric, 1981. *The Political Unconscious*, Methuen: London.

—, 1986. "Third World Literature in the Era of Multinational Capitalism," *Social Text* (Fall), 15. pp. 65–88.

—, 1990. "Postmodernism or the Cultural Logic of Late Capitalism," *Kav*, Vol. 10 (July). pp. 101–20. [Hebrew]

—, 1991. *Postmodernism or the Cultural Logic of Late Capitalism*, Durham, NC: Duke University Press.

Jawwad, Islah Abdul, 1990. "The Evolution of the Political Role of the Palestinian Women's Movement in the Uprising," in: Michael Hudson (ed.), *The Palestinians: New Directions*, Washington: Center for Contemporary Arab Studies, Georgetown University. pp. 63–77.

Jayyusi, Salma Al Khadra, 1992. *Anthology of Modern Palestinian Literature*, New York: Columbia University Press.

Jayyusi, Salma Al khadra, 1999. "Palestinian Identity in Literature," in: Kamel Abdel Malek and David Jacobson (eds), *Israeli and Palestinian Identities in History and Literature*, New York: St Martin Press.

Jibril, Awad, 1985. "Cinema at the Popular Front for the Liberation of Palestine," *Alhadaf* (23 December). [Arabic].

John, D. and Dowing, H. (eds), 1987. *Film and Politics in the Third World*, New York: Autinomedia.

Joyard, Olivier, 2002. "Palestine, Intervention Divine," *Cahiers du Cinéma* (October). pp. 13–15.

Kabha, Mustafa, 2007. *The Palestinian Press as a Shaper of Public Opinion 1929–1939: Writing up a Story*, London: Valentine Mitchel.

Kaes, Anton, 1992. "Holocaust and the End of History: Postmodern Historiography in Cinema," in: Saul Friedlander (ed.), *Probing the Limits of Representation*, Cambridge, MA: Harvard University Press.

—, 1998. "Cinema and Migration," *Assaf Kolnoa*, 1. Tel-Aviv University. pp. 101–16.

—, forthcoming. "The Return of the Undead," *Assaf Kolnoa*, 3. Tel-Aviv University.

Kamp, Adrianna, 2000. "The Border as Yanus's Face: Space and National Consciousness in Israel," *Theory and Criticism*, Vol. 16 (Spring). pp. 13–45. [Hebrew]

Kanafani, Ghassan, 1963. "The Horizon Behind the Gate" ("Al Ofk Wara'al Bawwaba"), *Ardo-l-Bortolcali-l-Hazeen*, Beirut: Al Fajro-l-Jadeed.

—, 2000. *Palestine's Children: Returning to Haifa and Other Stories*, Colorado: Lynne Rienner. pp. 149–96.

Kapra, Michal, 1998. "I Saw an Amusing Palestinian" (Interview with Elia Suleiman), *Maariv* (November). [Hebrew]

Karni, Yuval, 2003. "High Hopes" (Interview with Ali Nassar), *Yediot Aharonot* (24 April). [Hebrew]

Karpel, Dalia, 1986. "A Palestinian Tragedy," *Ha'ir* (6 June). [Hebrew]

Kashua, Sayed, 2004. *Dancing Arabs*, New York: Grove.

Kaufman, Anthony, 2003. "Seven Questions to Elia Suleiman, Director of *Chronicle of a Disappearance*," www.indiewire.com (19 March).

Keith, Michael and Steve Pile, 1993a. "Conclusion: Towards New Radical Geographies," in: Michael Keith and Steve Pile (eds), *Place and the Politics of Identity*, New York: Routledge. pp. 220–6.

Keith, Michael and Steve Pile, 1993b. "Introduction Part 1: The Politics of Place," in: Michael Keith and Steve Pile (eds), *Place and the Politics of Identity*, New York: Routledge. pp. 1–21.

Kelly, Richard, 2002. *"Divine Intervention,"* *Sight and Sound*, 17, 1.

Kenan, Amos, 1975. *Holocaust II*, Tel Aviv: A. L. special edition. [Hebrew]

Kennedy, Christina B., 1994. "The Myth of Heroism: Man and Desert in *Lawrence of Arabia*," in: Stuart C. Aitken and Leo E. Zonn, *Place, Power, Situation and Spectacle: A Geography of Film*, Lanham: Rowman and Littlefield. pp. 161–79.

Khalifa, Sahar, [1976] 1978. *A Sabbar (The Cactus Tree)*, Jerusalem: Galileo. [Hebrew]

Khater, Akram F., 1993. "Emile Habibi: The Mirror of Irony in Palestinian Literature," *Journal of Arabic Literature*, xxiv (March), Part 1. pp. 75–94.

Khleifi, George, 2001. "A Chronicle of Palestinian Cinema," *Theory and Criticism*, Vol. 18 (Spring). pp. 177–93. [Hebrew]

Khleifi, Michel, 1987. "La Force du Faible" (Entretien avec Michel Khleifi), *Cahiers du Cinéma*, 87, 3 (November).

—, 1997. "From Reality to Fiction, From Poverty to Expression," *El País* (February).

Khouri, Elias, 1998. *Bab A Shams*, Beirut: Al Aadab.

—, 2001. "The Homeland is a Refugee Camp, the Homeland is Exile," *Palestinian Studies*, Vol. 41. pp. 137–42. [Hebrew]

Khouri, Issam, 1982. "Farhud's Ideal," *Oghniato-l-mawassimi-l-Atiya (The Song of the Coming Seasons)*, Akre: Al Borj.

Kimmerling, Baruch (ed.), 1989. *The Israeli State and Society: Boundaries and Frontiers*, Albany: State University of New York Press.

Kimmerling, Baruch and Joel Migdal, 1993. *Palestinians: The Making of a People*, Cambridge, MA: Harvard University Press.

Kipp, Jeremiah, 2003. "Silence Before the Storm," www.filmmakermagazine.com (3 March).

Kivorkian-Shalhoub, Nadira, 1999. "Female Victims in the Palestinian Society," in: Adel Manaa (ed.), *The Palestinians in the Twentieth Century: An Inside Look*, Tel Aviv: Center for Research of the Arab Society in Israel. [Hebrew]

Kiwan, Soheil, 1997. "Worry," Akre: Al Aswar. [Arabic]

Klein, Uri, 2003a. "The Same Garbage Bag, Again and Again," *Ha'aretz* (5 February). [Hebrew]

—, 2003b. "A Caressing Close-up on the Microphone," *Ha'aretz* (22 June). [Hebrew]

—, 2004. "We Are the Children of Spring 2002," *Ha'aretz* (10 September). [Hebrew]

Kristeva, Julia, 1974. *La Révolution du langage poétique: l'avant-garde à la fin du XIXème siecle, Lautréamont et Mallarmé*, Paris: Du Seuil.

—, 1984. *Revolution in Poetic Language*, New York: Columbia University Press.

—, 1986. "About Chinese Women," in: Toril Moi, *The Kristeva Reader*, New York: Columbia University Press. pp. 138–60.

Lacan, Jacques, 1977. *Écrits: A Selection*, New York: Norton.

LaCapra, Dominick, 1997. "Revisiting the Historians' Debate," *History and Memory* (Fall), Vol. 9, No. 1/2. pp. 80–113.

—, 1998. *History and Memory after Auschwitz*, Ithaca, NY: Cornell University Press.

Langer, Lawrence L., 1991. *Holocaust Testimonies: The Ruins of Memory*, New Haven: Yale University Press.

Levi, Hagai, 1991. "We Got Carried Away" (Interview with Rashid Masharawi), *Hadashot* (21 June). pp. 46–7. [Hebrew]

Litvak, Meir, 1994. "A Palestinian Past: National Construction and Reconstruction," *History and Memory* (Fall/Winter), 6. pp. 24–56.

Livni, Orny, 1996. "A City of Empty and Dark Streets" (Interview with Elia Suleiman), *Kol Ha'ir* (December). pp. 58–60. [Hebrew]

Lonni, Ada, 2002. "Parallel Tragedies in Israeli and Palestinian Experience," *Palestine–Israel Journal*, 8.4/9.1. pp. 71–83.

Lotan, Urri, 1993. "Between Shati and Sheinkin" (Interview with Rashid Masharawi), *Hadashot* (11 June). [Hebrew]

Lubin, Orly, 1998. "The Woman in Israeli Cinema," in: Nurith Gertz, Orly Lubin and Judd Ne'eman (eds), *Fictive Looks: On Israeli Cinema*, Tel Aviv: Open University Press. [Hebrew]

—, 2000. "Shehur," *Fifty to Forty Eight* (special issue of *Theory and Criticism*). pp. 423–8. [Hebrew]

Lustic, Ian, 1985. *Arabs in the Jewish State*, Tel Aviv: Mipras. [Hebrew]

Macdonald, Gerald M., 1994. "Third Cinema and the Third World," in: Stuart C. Aitken and Leo E. Zonn, *Place, Power, Situation and Spectacle: A Geography of Film*, Lanham: Rowman and Littlefield. pp. 27–45.

McKean Parmenter, Barbara, 1994. *Giving Voice to Stones: Place and Identity in Palestinian Literature*, Austin: University of Texas Press.

M. C., 1981. "Peace in *Wedding in Galilee* and the War in Lebanon," *Alhasanaa (Magazine)* (9–16 October). [Arabic]

Manaa, Adel (ed.), 1999a. *The Palestinians in the Twentieth Century: An Inside Look*, Tel Aviv: Center for Research of the Arab Society in Israel. [Hebrew]

Manaa, Adel (ed.), 1999b. "Introduction: The Palestinians in the Twentieth Century," in Adel Manaa (ed.), *The Palestinians in the Twentieth Century: An Inside Look*, Tel Aviv: Center for Research of the Arab Society in Israel. [Hebrew]

Marks, Laura, 1992. "The Language of Terrorism," *Framework*, 38/39. pp. 64–73.

Marks, Laura, 1994. "A Deleuzian Politics of Hybrid Cinema," *Screen* (Autumn) 35:3. pp. 244–64.

Massey, Doreen, 1993. "Politics and Space/Time," in: Michael Keith and Steve Pile, *Place and the Politics of Identity*, New York: Routledge. pp. 141–61.

Mdanat, Adnan, 1993. *History of the Speaking Arab Film*, Cairo: United Arab Artists/Cairo Film Festival. [Arabic]

—, 1990. *The Palestinian Encyclopedia*, research volumes, Vol. 4. [Arabic]

Mitchell, W. J. T., 1994. "Imperial Landscape," in: W. J. T. Mitchell (ed.), *Landscape and Power*, Chicago: University of Chicago Press. pp. 5–34.

—, 2000. "Holy Landscape: Israel, Palestine, and the American Wilderness," *Critical Inquiry* (Winter), 26, 2. pp. 193–224.

Moi, Toril, 1985. *Sexual/Textual Politics: Feminist Literary Theory*, London: Routledge.

—, 1986. *The Kristeva Reader*, New York: Columbia University Press.

Morley, David, 1999. "Bounded Realms: Household, Family, Community, and Nation," in: Hamid Naficy (ed.), *Home, Exile, Homeland: Film, Media, and the Politics of Place*, New York: Routledge. pp. 18–41.

Morley, David and Kevin Robins, 1995. *Spaces of Identity*, London: Routledge.

Müge, Fatma Gocek and Shiva Balaghi (eds), 1994. *Reconstructing Gender in the Middle East: Tradition, Identity and Power*, New York: Columbia University Press.

Murkus, Nimer, 1956. "Abd-el-jabbar," *Al Jadid for Literature, Science and Art*, Vol. 4. pp. 34–5. [Arabic]

Nafaa, Muhammad, 1989. "The Camel" ("Al Jamal"), *Kushan and Other Stories*, Cairo: Daro-th-Thakafati-l-Jadeeda/Department of Culture, PLO. p. 57.

Naficy, Hamid, 1993. "Exile Discourse and Televisual Fetishization," in: Hamid Naficy and Teshome H. Gabriel, *Otherness and the Media*, New York: Harwood Academic. pp. 85–117.

— (ed.), 1999. *Home, Exile, Homeland: Film, Media, and the Politics of Place*, New York: Routledge.

—, 2001. *An Accented Cinema*, Princeton: Princeton University Press.

Nahoi, Adiv, 1970. "Palestinian Wedding," *Al-Aadav* (June). pp. 62, 66–77. [Arabic]

Nasrallah, Ibrahim, 1999. "The Fever Prairies" ("*Barari-l-Humma*"), Beirut: Mo'assasato-d-Dirasati-l-'Arabiyya Manasher. [Arabic]

Nassar, Issam, 2002. "Reflections on Writing the History of Palestinian Identity," *Palestine-Israel Journal*, Vol. 8/9, 4/1. pp. 24–37.

Natour, Salman, 1978. "Bashir Mosallam Aljabaii," *A-sh-Shajarato-l-Lati Tamoddo Jorhaha Ila Sadri* (*The Tree whose Roots Come up to my Chest*), a collection of short stories, Akre: Al Aswar. p. 57. [Arabic]

Ne'eman, Judd, 1991. "Soft Porn and Israeli War Movies," *Maariv* (26 July). [Hebrew]

—, 1998a. "The Modernists: The Genealogy of the New Sensitivity," in: Nurith Gertz, Orly Lubin and Judd Ne'eman (eds), *Fictive Looks: On Israeli Cinema*, Tel Aviv: Open University Press. [Hebrew]

—, 1998b. "The Jug, the Blade and the Holy Grail: The Jewish-Arab Conflict Movies and the Romance," in: Nurith Gertz, Orly Lubin and Judd Ne'eman (eds), *Fictive Looks: On Israeli Cinema*, Tel Aviv: Open University Press. [Hebrew]

Ophir, Adi, 2002. "Nine Principles of a Postmodern Stance," in: Elazar Weinrib (ed.), *Postmodernism and History*, Tel Aviv: Open University Press. [Hebrew]

'Oun, Iman, 2000. "The Woman in the Palestinian Theatre," *Al-Kalima: The Palestinian Writers' Quarterly*, Vol. 6 (Fall). [Arabic]

Pertz, Don, 1990. *Intifada – The Palestinian Uprising*, London: Westview.

Peters, John Durham, 1999. "Exile, Nomadism, and Diaspora: the Stakes of Mobility in the Western Canon," in: Hamid Naficy (ed.), *Home, Exile, Homeland: Film, Media, and the Politics of Place*, New York: Routledge. pp. 18–41.

Pines, Jim and Paul Willemen (eds), 1989. *Questions of Third Cinema*, London: British Film Institute.

Pinhasi, Maya, 1999. "The 'Other's' 'Other': About the Representation of the Israeli in the Cinema of Masharawi and Khleifi," Seminar paper: Department of Film and Television, Tel Aviv University. [Hebrew]

Pinto, Goel, 2003. "Ninja from Nazareth," *Ha'aretz* (7 February). [Hebrew]

Prokhoris, Sabine and Christophe Wavelet, 1999. Entretien avec Elia Suleiman, www.vacarme.eu.org (May).

Rabinovitz, Dani and Ha'oula Abu Backr, 2002. *The Upright Generation*, Jerusalem: Keter. [Hebrew]

Rogoff, Irit, 2000. *Terra Infirma: Geography's Visual Culture*, New York: Routledge.

Rose, Gillian, 1993. *Feminism and Geography: The Limit of Geographical Knowledge*, Minneapolis: University of Minnesota Press.

Rosenstone, Robert A., 1995. *Visions of the Past: The Challenge of Film to Our Idea of History*, Cambridge, MA: Harvard University Press.

Said, Edward, 1990. "Reflections on Exile," in: Russell Ferguson, Martha Gever, Trinh Minh-ha and Cornel West (eds), *Out There: Marginalization and Culture*, New York: New York Museum of Contemporary Art. pp. 357–67.

—, 1991. "Reflections on Twenty Years of Palestinian History," *Journal of Palestinian Studies*, Vol. 20, 4. pp. 5–22.

—, 2000. "Invention, Memory and Place," *Critical Inquiry* (Winter), Vol. 26, 2. pp. 175–92.

—, [2001] 2002. "Afterword: The Consequences of 1948," in: Eugene L. Rogan and Avi Shlaim (eds), *The War for Palestine: Rewriting the History of 1948*, Cambridge: Cambridge University Press. pp. 206–19.

Said, Edward and Jean Mohr, [1986] 1999. *After the Last Sky: Palestinian Lives*, New York: Columbia University Press.

Sanbar, Elias, 1997. "De l'Identité Culturelle des Palestiniens," in: Elias Sanbar, Subhi Hadidi and Jean Claude Pons, *Palestine: l'enjeu culturel*, Paris: Circe/Institut du Monde Arabe.

Sand, Shlomo, 2002. *Film as History: Imagining and Screening the Twentieth Century*, Tel Aviv: Am Oved/Open University of Israel. [Hebrew]

Sayigh, Yazid, 1998. "Reflections on Al Nakba," *Journal of Palestinian Studies* (Autumn), xxviii, 1. pp. 19–23.

Senins, George, 1978. "Looking for Popular Cinema," *The Palestinian Picture*, Vol. 1 (November). [Arabic]

Sever, Osnat, 1986. "Blowup Wedding," *Lahiton* (9 July). [Hebrew]

Shaaban, Awad, [1962] 1970. "The Jew and the Spirit Jar," in: Shimon Balas (ed. and trans.), *Palestinian Stories*, Tel Aviv: Akad.

Shafik, Viola, 1998. *Arab Cinema: History and Cultural Identity*, Cairo: American University in Cairo Press.

—, 2001. "Cinema in Palestine," in: Oliver Leaman (ed.), *Middle Eastern and North African Film*, New York: Routledge. pp. 509–32.

Shammas, Anton, 1986. *Arabesque*, Tel Aviv: Am Oved. [Hebrew]

—, 2002a. "Introduction to Khouri, Elias," *Bab A-Shams* (trans. Moshe Haham), Tel Aviv: Andelos. [Hebrew]

Shafik, Viola, 2002b. "Autocartography: The Case of Palestine, Michigan," *Palestine–Israel Journal*, Vol. 9, 2. pp. 111–19.

Shamush, Tuvia (trans.), 1972–9. "Arab Stories," in: Zaki Darwish, *The Grapevine will not Die Alone*, Tel Aviv: Sifriat Tarmil. [Hebrew]

Shehada, Raja, 1982. *The Third Way*, London: Quartet.

—, 2003. *When the Bulbul Stopped Singing: A Diary of Ramallah Under Siege*, London: Profile.

Shenhav, Yehuda and Hanan Hever, 2002. "The Postcolonialist Look," *Theory and Criticism*, Vol. 20 (Spring). pp. 9–23. [Hebrew]

Shiff, Zeev and Eitan Haber, 1976. *Lexicon of the Security of Israel*, Jerusalem: Zemora, Bitan, Modan. [Hebrew]

Shimoni, Yaacov, 1988. *A Political Lexicon of the Arab World*, Jerusalem: Keter. [Hebrew]

Shohat, Ella, 1988. "Wedding in Galilee," *Middle-East Report* (September–October). pp. 44–73.

—, 1989. *Israeli Cinema: East/West and the Politics of Representation*, Austin: University of Texas Press.

—, 1995. "Anomalies of the National: Representing Israel/Palestine," in: Jonathan Friedlander (ed.), *UCLA Near East Center Colloquium Series*, Los Angeles: University of California at Los Angeles.

Shohat, Ella and Robert Stam, 1994. *Unthinking Eurocentrism: Multiculturalism and the Media*, New York: Routledge.

Shoshan, Boaz, 2000. *Discourse on Gender: Gendered Discourse in the Middle East*, Connecticut: Praeger.

Siddiq, Muhammad, 1984. *Man is a Cause: Political Consciousness and the Fiction of Ghassan Kanafani*, Seattle: Dept of Near Eastern Languages and Civilization, University of Washington, distributed by University of Washington Press.

Sidky, Najaty, 1970. "The Sad Sisters," in: Shimon Balas (ed. and trans.), *Palestinian Stories*, Tel Aviv: Akad. [Hebrew]

Silverman, Kaja, 1996. *The Threshold of the Visible World*, London: Routledge.

Soja, Edward, 1996. *Thirdspace: Journeys to Los Angeles and Other Real and Imagined Places*, Oxford: Blackwell.

Soja, Edward and Barbara Hooper, 1993. "The Spaces that Difference Makes: Some Notes on the Geographical Margins of the New Cultural Politics," in: Michael Keith & Steve Pile (eds), *Place and the Politics of Identity*, New York: Routledge. pp. 183–205.

Solzhenitsyn, Alexander, [1962] 1963. *A Day in the Life of Ivan Denisovich*, Tel Aviv: Sifriat Hapoalim. [Hebrew]

Somech, Sasson, 1995. "Inbar Lulu: Palestinian Love Stories," in: Samira Azam (ed.) and Moshe Haham (trans.), *The Great Shadow*, Tel Aviv: Akad-Gevanim. [Hebrew]

Sorlin, Pierre, 1997. *Mass Media*, London: Routledge.

Suleiman, Elia, 2000. "Lettre d'un Cinéaste Palestinien," *Cahiers du Cinéma* (November). pp. 24–5.

Suleiman, Yasir, 1991. "Palestine and the Palestinians in the Short Stories of Samira Azzam," *Journal of Arabic Literature* (September), xxii, Part 2. pp. 154–65.

Taha, Muhammad Ali, 1965. "Spain" ("Esbanya"), *Al Jadeed*, Haifa, Vol. 4. pp. 34–5. [Arabic]

—, [1974] 1997. "The Planted in the Land," *Jisron 'Ala-n-Nahri-l-Hazeen* (*A Bridge on a Sad River*), a collection of short stories, Nablus: Arabesque. [Arabic]

Talmon, Miri, 2001. *Israeli Graffiti*, Tel Aviv: Open University Press. [Hebrew]

Tamari, Salim, 1999a. "The Palestinian Society: Continuation and Change," in: Adel Manaa (ed.), *The Palestinians in the Twentieth Century: An Inside Look*, Tel Aviv: Center for Research of the Arab Society in Israel. [Hebrew]

—, 1999b. "The Local and the National in Palestinian Identity," in: Kamal Abdel Malek and David Jacobson, *Israeli and Palestinian Identities in History and Literature*, New York: St Martin. pp. 3–9.

Taussig, Michael, 2000. "The Beach (A Fantasy)," *Critical Inquiry*, Vol. 26, 2. pp. 248–78.

Timen, Mickey, 1999. "So They Will Look Us in the Eye," *Maariv* (3 February). [Hebrew]

Turim, Maureen, 1989. *Flashback in Film: Memory and History*, New York: Routledge.

Tzimerman, Moshe, 2001. *Signs of Cinema: The History of the Israeli Film Between 1896 and 1948*, Tel Aviv: Dyunon/Tel Aviv University. [Hebrew]

—, 2002. *Don't Touch My Holocaust: The Effect of the Holocaust on the Cinema and Society in Israel*, Haifa/Lod: Haifa University/Zemora Bitan.

Tzoreff, Mira, 2000. "Fadwa Tuqan's Autobiography: Reconstructing a Personal History into the Palestinian National Narrative," in: Boaz Shoshan, *Discourse on Gender: Gendered Discourse in the Middle East*, Connecticut: Praeger. pp. 57–79.

Waked, Ali, 1993. "A Director in a Realist Path" (Interview with Rashid Masharawi), *Hadashot* (1 June). [Hebrew]

Wood, Jason, 2003. "A Quick Chat with Elia Suleiman," www.kamera.co.uk (19 March).

Yehoshua, A. B., 1990. *Mr. Mani*, Tel Aviv: Hakibutz Hameuhad. [Hebrew]

—, 1997. *A Journey to the End of the Millennium*, Tel Aviv: Hakibutz Hameuhad. [Hebrew]

—, 2002. *The Liberating Bride*, Tel Aviv: Keter. [Hebrew]

Yerushalmi, Yosef Hayim, 1982. *Zakhor: Jewish History and Jewish Memory*, Washington: University of Washington Press.

Yizhar, S., 1949. *Khirbit Khiz'aa* [*The Captive*], Merhavia: Sifriat Hapoalim. [Hebrew]

Young, Robert, 1995. *Colonial Desire: Hybridity in Theory, Culture and Race*, New York: Routledge.

Yudlevich, Meirav, 2003. "Where is the Border?" www.ynet.co.il (14 September). [Hebrew]

Yuval-Davis, Nira, 1997. "Ethnicity Relations and Multiculturalism," in: Pnina Werbner and Tariq Modood (eds), *Debating Cultural Hybridity*, London: Zed.

Zanger, Anat, forthcoming. "Landscapes and Maps in *Mezizim* and in *Te'alat Blaumlich*," in: Miri Talmon and Moshe Tzimerman (eds), *Peeing Toms, Cocks and Other Israelis*, Tel Aviv: Keter/Open University Press. [Hebrew]

Zerubavel, Yael, 1995. *Recovered Roots: Collective Memory and the Making of Israeli National Tradition*, Chicago: Chicago University Press.

Zureik, Elia T., 1979. *The Palestinians in Israel: A Study in Internal Colonialism*, London: Routledge and Kegan Paul.

FILMOGRAPHY

Abu-Ali, Khadija, 1981: *Children But . . . (Atfal Walakin . . .)*
Abu-Ali, Khadija, 1982: *Women for Palestine (Nisaa'on Min Filistine)*
Abu-Ali, Mustafa, 1971: *With Blood and Spirit (Bir-Rouh Bid-Dam)*
Abu-Ali, Mustafa, 1972: *Al 'Arkoub*
Abu-Ali, Mustafa, 1973: *Scenes from the Occupation in Gaza (Mashahed Minal Ih'tilal Fi Ghazza)*
Abu-Ali, Mustafa, 1973: *Zionist Aggression ('Odwan Sahyouni)*
Abu-Ali, Mustafa, 1974: *On the Road to Victory ('Ala Tarikin Nasr)*
Abu-Ali, Mustafa, 1974: *They do not Exist (Laysa Lahom Wojood)*
Abu-Ali, Mustafa, 1977: *Palestine in the Eye (Filistine Fil 'Ayn)*
Abu-Ali, Mustafa, Jean Sham'oun and Pino Adriano, 1977: *Tel a-Za'tar*
Abu-Ali, Mustafa and others, 1968: *Say No to the Peaceful Solution (La Lil Hallissilmi)*
Abu-Assad, Hani, 2000: *Nazareth 2000 (An-Nassira 2000)*
Abu-Assad, Hani, 2003: *Rana's Wedding (Ors Rana)*
Abu-Assad, Hani, 2002: *Ford Transit (Ford Transit)*
Abu-Assad, Hani, 2005: *Paradise Now (Al Jannato-l-An)*
Abu Wa'el, Tawfik, 2001: *Waiting for Salah A-Ddin (Fintithar Salah-Eddin)*
Abu Wa'el, Tawfik, 2002: *The Fourteen (A-Rabe' 'Ashar)* (from the *Once Again* series)
Abu Wa'el, Tawfik, 2004: *Thirst (Atash)*
A-Dawud, Hikmat, 1983: *Forever in Memory (Abadan Fith-Thakira)*
A-Zubeidi, Kaise, 1977: *A Voice from Jerusalem (Sawton Mina-l-Quds)*
A-Zubeidi, Kaise, 1978: *An Opposite Siege (Hisar Modadd)*
A-Zubeidi, Kaise, 1982: *Barbed-Wire Homeland (Watano-l-Aslaki-Sha'eka)*
A-Zubeidi, Kaise, 1984: *A Slaughter File (Malaffo Majzara)*
A-Zubeidi, Kaise, 1984: *Palestine: the Chronicle of a People (Filistine: Sijillo Sha'ab)*
A-Zubeidi, Subhi, 1998: *My Very Private Map (Kharitati-l-Khassa Jiddan)*
A-Zubeidi, Subhi, 1999: *Ali and his Friends ('Ali Wa-Asdika'oho)*
A-Zubeidi, Subhi, 1999: *Women in the Sun (Nisa' Fish-Shams)*
A-Zubeidi, Subhi, 2000: *Light at the End of the Tunnel (Ad Daw' Fi Nihayatin-Nafak)*

A-Zubeidi, Subhi, 2001: *Looking Away* (*'Hawal*)
A-Zubeidi, Subhi, 2002: *Crossing Kalandia (Roadblock)* (*An Ta'bor Qualandia*)
Alhabbash, Isma'il, 2002: *New Apartment, The* (*Ash-Shakkato-l-Jadeeda*) (from the *Once Again* series)
Al-Hajar, Rafik, 1973: *The Road* (*At-Tareek*)
Al-Hajar, Rafik, 1974: *United Guns* (*Al Banadik Mottahida*)
Al-Hajar, Rafik, 1974: *May of the Palestinians* (*Ayyaro-L-Filistiniyeen*)
Al-Hajar, Rafik, 1975: *Born in Palestine* (*Mawloodon Fi Filistine*)
Al-Hajar, Rafik, 1975: *The Intifada* (*Al Intifada*)
Al-Hassan, Azza, 1996: *Women Talking* (*Arabiat Tatakallamna*)
Al-Hassan, Azza, 1998: *Kushan Musa* (*Kushan Musa*)
Al-Hassan, Azza, 1999: *She, the Sindibad* (*Hya-S-Sindibad*)
Al-Hassan, Azza, 2000: *Place, or Outside of Paradise or Out of Eden* (*Makan aw Kharija-l-janna*)
Al-Hassan, Azza, 2001: *News Time* (*Zamano-l-Akhbar*)
Al-Hassan, Azza, 2002: *Three Centimeters Less* (*Thalathato Centimeteratin Akall*)
Al-Hassan, Azza, 2004: *Forgotten Images* (*Sowar Mansiyah*)
Al Quattan, Omar, 1991: *Dreams of Silence* (*Ahlam Fi Faragh*)
Al Yassir, Nada, 2001: *Four Poems for Palestine* (*Arbaa'to Aghanin Li Filistine*)
Al Yassir, Nada, 2002: *Naim – Paradise* (*Naim Paradise*) (from the *Once Again* series)
Andoni, Sa'ed, 2002: *Last Frontiers* (*Al H'odoudo-l-Akhira*)
Andoni, Sa'ed, 2002: *Zero* (*'Alas-s-sifir*)
Asaf, Roger and others, 1973: *Sirhan and the Pipe* (*Sirhan Wal-Masoura*)
Awad, Jibril, 1982: *Berlin, the Trap* (*Berline, Al Masyada*)
Awad, Jibril, 1983: *Good Morning Beirut* (*Sabaho-L-Khayri Ya Beyrout*)
Badr, Liali, 1984: *Road to Palestine, The* (*Attareeko Ila Filistine*)
Badr, Liana, 1999: *Fadwa* (*Fadwa*)
Badr, Liana, 2002: *Green Bird, The* (*At ta'iro-l-Akhdar*)
Badr, Liana, 2002: *Zaytounat* (*Zaytounat*)
Badr, Liana, 2003: *Siege, a Writer's Diary* (*Hisar, Mothakkarato Katibah*)
Bakri, Muhammad, 1998: *1948*
Bakri, Muhammad, 2002: *Jenin, Jenin* (*Jenin, Jenin*)
Elias, Hana, 1991: *The Mountain* (*Al Jabal*)
Elias, Hana, 2003: *Olive Harvest* (*Mawsimo-z-zaytoon*)
Habash, Ahmad, 2001: *Moon Eclipse* (*Khosoufo-l-Kamar*)
Halil, Mahmud, 1984: *Tayseer* (*Tayseer*)
Hassan, Nizar, 1994: *Independence* (*Istiklal*)
Hassan, Nizar, 1996: *Jasmine* (*Yasmin*)
Hassan, Nizar, 1998: *Myth* (*Ostura*)
Hassan, Nizar, 2000: *Cut*
Hassan, Nizar, 2001: *Defiance* (*Tahaddi*)
Hassan, Nizar, 2003: *Invasion* (*Ijtiah*)
Hawal, Kassem, 1971: *Al Bared River* (*An Naharo-L-Bared*)
Hawal, Kassem, 1973: *Ghassan . . . The Word/The Gun* (*Ghassan . . . Al Kalimato-L-Bondokiya*)
Hawal, Kassem, 1974: *Why We Plant Flowers, Why We Carry Weapons* (*limatha Nazra'o-l-ward, limatha Nahmilo-s-Silah*)
Hawal, Kassem, 1976: *New Life* (*Hayaton Jadeeda*)
Hawal, Kassem, 1978: *Tel A-Za'atar* (*Tel-A-Za'atar*)
Hawal, Kassem, 1982: *The Return to Haifa* (*'A'idon Ila 'Haifa*)
Irshid, Nabila, 2001: *Travel Agency* (In English: *Travel Agency*)
Khleifi, Michel, 1980: *Fertile Memories* (*Safa'haton Min Mothakkaratin Khasba*)

Khleifi, Michel, 1984: *Ma'aloul Celebrates its Destruction* (*Ma'aloul Tah'tafel Bidamariha*)
Khleifi, Michel, 1987: *Wedding in Galilee* ('*Orso-l-Jaleel*)
Khleifi, Michel, 1989: *Canticle of the Stones* (*Nashido-l-Hajar*)
Khleifi, Michel, 1994: *Tale of the Three Jewels* (*Hikayatol Jawahiri-th-Thalath*)
Khleifi, Michel, 1996: *Forbidden Marriage in the Holy Land* (*Az-zawajo-l-Mamnou' Fi-l Aradi-l-Mokaddasa*)
Lutfi, Nabiha, 1977: *Because Roots Don't Die* (*Li 'Anna-l-Jothoora La Tamout*)
Malas, Muhammad, 1987: *Dream, The* (*Al Manam*)
Masharawi, Rashid, 1981: *Partners*
Masharawi, Rashid, 1986: *Passport* (*Jawazo Safar*)
Masharawi, Rashid, 1989: *The Shelter* (*Al-Malja'*)
Masharawi, Rashid, 1991: *House-Houses* (*Daro-w-Dour*)
Masharawi, Rashid, 1991: *Long Days in Gaza* (*Ayyamon Tawilaton Fi Ghazza*)
Masharawi, Rashid, 1992: *The Magician* (*As-Sahir*)
Masharawi, Rashid, 1993: *Curfew* (*Hatta Ish'aarin Aakhar*)
Masharawi, Rashid, 1995: *Haifa* ('*Haifa*)
Masharawi, Rashid, 1997: *Rabab* (*Rabab*)
Masharawi, Rashid, 1998: *Stress* (*Tawattor*)
Masharawi, Rashid, 2001–2: *Here is the Voice of Palestine* (*Hona Sawto Filistin*)
Masharawi, Rashid, 2002: *Ticket to Jerusalem* (*Tathkaraton Ila-l-Quds*)
Masharawi, Rashid, 2002: *Upside-Down* (*Maklouba*)
Masri, May, 1982: *Beneath the Ruins* (*Tahatal Ankad*)
Masri, May, 1990: *Children of the Mountain Of Fire* (*Atfalo Jabal-in-Nar*)
Masri, May, 1998: *Children of Shatila, The* (*Atafalo Shatila*)
Masri, May, 2001: *Borders of Dreams and Fears* (*Hodoido-l-Holmi Wal-Khawf*)
Mdanat, Adnan, 1976: *A Report from Tel a-Za'tar* (*Khabaron Min Tel A-Za'tar*)
Mdanat, Adnan, 1977: *Palestinian Visions* (*Rou'an Filistiniya*)
Mer, Juliano, 2004: *Arna's Children* (*Atfal Arna*)
Najar, Najwa, 1999: *Wadi'a and Na'im* (*Wadi'a Wa-na'im*)
Najar, Najwa, 2001: *A Forgetfulness Ointment* (*Jawharo-s-Silwan*)
Najar, Najwa, 2002: *A Child called Muhammad* (from the *Once Again* series)
Nassar, Ali, 1983: *Story of a Coastal Town, The* (*Hikayato Madinatin 'ala-sh-Shati'*)
Nassar, Ali, 1994: *The Wet Nurse* (*Al Mourdi'aa*)
Nassar, Ali, 1997: *The Milky Way* (*Darbo-t-Tabbanat*)
Nassar, Ali, 2002: *In the Ninth Month* (*Fish-Shahri-t-Tassee'*)
Nimer, Samir, 1973: *The Four-Day War* (*Harbo-L-Ayyami-L-arba'a*)
Nimer, Samir, 1973: *Palestinian Night* (*Laylaton Filistiniya*)
Nimer, Samir, 1973: *Zionist Terrorism* (*Irhabon Sayouni*)
Nimer, Samir, 1974: *The New Yemen* (*Al Yamano-l-Jadeed*)
Nimer, Samir, 1974: *The Winds of Liberation* (*Ryaho-t-Tahreer*)
Nimer, Samir, 1974: *Whose Revolution is This?* (*Limani-th-Thawrra?*)
Nimer, Samir, 1975: *Kafr Shuba* (*Kafr Shuba*)
Nimer, Samir, 1977: *War in Lebanon* (*Al Harbo Fi Loubnan*)
Nimer, Samir, 1984: *Roots* (*Al Jouthoor*)
Phauzi, Ali, 1980: *Youth from Palestine* (*Shabeebaton Min Filistin*)
Sa'adi, Muhmud Ibrahim: *Bleeding Memories* (*Thikrayaton Damiya*)
Salame, Marwan, 1984: '*Aida* ('*Aayda*)
Salame, Marwan, 1986: *The Olive Tree* (*Shjarato-z-Zaytoun*)
Saleh, Tawfik, 1972: *The Dupes* (*Al Makhdo 'oun*)
Sha'ath, Ghaleb, 1976: *The Key* (*Al Miftah*)
Sha'ath, Ghaleb, 1978: *Earth Day* (*Yawmo-L-A'harar*)

Sha'ath, Ghaleb, 1980: *Don't Drop the Green Leaf* (*La Toskiti-L-Ghosna-L-Akhdar*)
Shahhal, Randa, 1977: *Step by Step* (*Khotwatan Khotwa*)
Shammut, Isma'il, 1972: *Youth Camp* (*Mo'askarato-sh-Shabab*)
Shammut, Isma'il, 1973: *Memories and Fire* (*Thikrayaton Wanar*)
Shammut, Isma'il, 1973: *Stubborn Call* (*An Nidao-L-Molih*)
Shammut, Isma'il, 1974: *The Road to Palestine* (*'Ala Tareeki Filistine*)
Shamoun, Jean, 1980: *Song of Freedom, The* (*Ounshoudato-L-A'harar*)
Shehada, Abed A-Salam, 1995: *Women's Rights, Human Rights* (*Hukuko-l-Mara'a Hukuko-l-Insan*)
Shehada, Abed A-Salam, 1996: *Small Hands* (*Al-Aydi-s-Saghrira*)
Shehada, Abed A-Salam, 1997: *Close to Death* (*Karibon Min-Al-Mawt*)
Shehada, Abed A-Salam, 2000: *The Cane* (*Al-'Okkaz*)
Shehada, Abed A-Salam, 2000: *The Shadow* (*A-Thell*)
Shehada, Abed A-Salam, 2001: *Debris* (*Radm*) (from the *Once Again* series)
Shehada, Abed A-Salam, Nazih Darwaza and Soheir Isma'il, 1991: *Palestinian Diaries* (*Yaumayat Filistinya*)
Suleiman, Elia, 1990: *Introduction to the End of an Argument* (*Mokaddimaton Linihayaati Jidal*)
Suleiman, Elia, 1991: *Homage by Assassination* (*Takreemon Bil Katl*)
Suleiman, Elia, 1996: *Chronicle of a Disappearance* (*Waka'eo Siljill Ikhtifaa'*)
Suleiman, Elia, 1998: *Arab Dream* (*Al Holmo-l-'Arabi*)
Suleiman, Elia, 2000: *Cyber Palestine*
Suleiman, Elia, 2002: *Divine Intervention* (*Yadon Elahiyya*)
Tawfik, Muhammad, 1981: *Surrender Process, The* (*Masirato-l-Istislam*)
Tawfik, Muhammad, 1983: *Um Ali* (*Um Ali*)
Unknown director, 1969: *The Fedayeen Diary* (*Yawmiyat Fida'i*)
Unknown director, 1970: *With the Pioneers* (*Ma'a-t-Tala'ii'*)
Unknown director, 1974: *The Filmed Record*, Vol. 1 (*Al Jareeda-L-Mousawara*)
Unknown director, 1974: *The Filmed Record*, Vol. 2 (*Al Jareeda-L-Mousawara*)
Unknown director, 1974: *The Filmed Record*, Four Volumes (*Al Jareeda-L-Mousawara*)
Unknown director, 1974: *Training Camp* (*Mo'askaro-t-Tadreeb*)
Unknown director, 1974: *Al Khalisa Operation* (*'Amaliato-L-Khalisa*)
Unknown director, 1974: *Fedayeen Operation* (*'Amaliyaton Fida'iya*)
Zantoot, Fou'ad, 1971: *The Way of the Palestinian Revolution* (*'Ala Tareeeki Thawrati-L-Filistiniya*)
Zantoot, Fou'ad, 1979: *Black Leaves* (*Awrakon Sawdaa*)
Zantoot, Fou'ad, 1980: *The Betrayal* (*Al Khiyana*)

INDEX